Mighty to Save

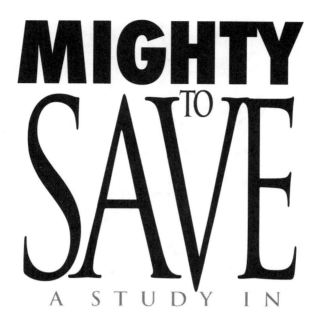

MIGHTY TO SAVE

A STUDY IN

OLD TESTAMENT SOTERIOLOGY

T. V. FARRIS

BROADMAN PRESS
NASHVILLE, TENNESSEE

© 1993 • Broadman Press.
All rights reserved.

4260-22

ISBN: 0-8054-6022-5

Dewey Deciaml Classification: 234
Subject Heading: SALVATION
Library of Congress Catalog Card Number: 92-37014
Printed in the United States of America.

Unless otherwise indicated, Scripture quotations are from the Holy Bible, *New International Version*, copyright © 1973, 1978, 1984 by International Bible Society. Quotations marked (KJV) are from the *King James Version of the Bible*, and those marked (ASV) are from the *American Standard Version.*

Library of Congress Cataloging-in-Publication Data

Farris, T. V., 1927-
    Mighty to save / T.V. Farris.
        p. cm.
    ISBN 0-8054-6022-5 :
    1. Bible. O.T.—Theology. 2. Salvation—Biblical teaching.
3. God—Biblical teaching. I. Title.
BS680.S25F37 1993
234—dc20
                                            92-37014
                                             CIP

To the memory of

RICHARD C. HENDERSON

preacher, missionary,
scholar, exegete,
teacher, colleague,
and dear friend.

Preface

This book represents an attempt to evaluate selected Old Testament passages and terminology that represent the core salvation message contained in the "Old Covenant." My survey of such material is by no means extensive or exhaustive. The book is a study in Old Testament soteriology. It is certainly not a complete, fully structured soteriology. Still, in the light of surprisingly limited information currently available on the subject, I hope that this effort will at least introduce the theme and call attention to the exciting "Gospel in the Old Testament."

In the development of the project, I have attempted to keep the busy pastor, overworked student, and inquisitive layperson in mind. Some evaluations are rather general in nature and self-evident in any good English translation. In some instances, however, I have found it necessary to deal with rather technical aspects of the biblical text, including grammar, semantics, and syntax of the Hebrew language. I have tried to explain such matters without unduly complicating the exegetical process. But for the benefit of the more serious student, I have inserted pertinent linguistic data into the main body of the discussion. I hope that this approach does not seriously encumber the reading and understanding of the material.

Without apology, though, I encourage the reader to persevere and, with Bible in hand (Hebrew or English), patiently examine the evidence of the text. Our task is not to uncover a theological "lost ark." Instead, we search for an eternal message and dig through linguistic and theological debris to discover the treasure of His truth. A worthy task indeed!

I want to express sincere appreciation for those who helped and encouraged me during the research and writing process. The patience of my wife, Sue, during my long "absences" at the word processor was a source of inspiration and motivation. I am grateful to friend and student Charles (Chuck) Henderson, whose preliminary research confirmed the paucity of material related to Old Testament soteriology. I am indebted to Jennifer Crawford, who patiently read early drafts and whose positive response inspired persistence in the task. I owe a special word of thanks to my friend and colleague David Skinner for his kind and helpful suggestions about form, style, and content.

I am especially indebted to B. Gray Allison and the faculty and staff of Mid-America Baptist Theological Seminary, whose patience, support, and understanding made it possible for me to complete the writing project. In particular, Mr. Terrence Brown, seminary librarian, provided optimistic and cheerful assistance in locating pertinent source materials. Paula Rast, my secretary, organized and logged bibliographic data that were essential to the total process. Finally, I am grateful to my students, who, across the years, have challenged my mind and heart to persevere in the quest for truth and excellence.

Contents

Introduction

Who is this coming from Edom,
  from Bozrah, with his garments, stained crimson?
Who is this, robed in splendor,
  striding forward in the greatness of his strength?

"It is I, speaking in righteousness,
  mighty to save."

Why are your garments red,
  like those of one treading the winepress?

"I have trodden the winepress alone;
  from the nations no one was with me.
I trampled them in my anger
  and trod them down in my wrath;
their blood spattered my garments,
  and I stained all my clothing.
For the day of vengeance was in my heart,
  and the year of my redemption has come."

Isaiah 63:1–4

A crimson-spattered apparition loomed unexpectedly on the screen of Isaiah's[1] prophetic vision! The appearance of the red-stained warrior advancing rapidly from Edom[2] prompted the seer to call out in alarm, "Who is this?" The figure identified himself as "one speaking in righteousness ... mighty to save." Since the ability to speak righteousness and the power to save are exclusive rights of the Lord alone (Ps. 3:8; Isa. 45:8), the mysterious "crusader" must have been some visual, tangible disclosure of the Lord appearing to the prophet—a theophany.[3] The prophet himself clearly understood the manifestation to be a revelation of Israel's covenant God.

That recognition, in turn, prompted a second question: "Why is your clothing sprinkled with red, like one who has been treading in a winepress?" (Isa. 63:2, paraphrased). The ominous response (v. 3) revealed God's active involvement in a process of judgment and retribution.

Issues

The response to the prophet's questions about the figure's identity and appearance contains an intriguing paradox. The implicit tension between "righteousness" and "mighty to save" in verse 1 corresponds to the contrast of "vengeance" and "redemption" in verse 4. How can the "righteousness-vengeance" factor be reconciled to the "mighty to save-redemption" factor, much less be intimately related as the context implies? In the light of this apparent contradiction, at least two matters require consideration.

First, what is the God of the Old Testament really like? Is He a God of uncontrollable rage, anger, and vindictiveness, as this passage might seem to indicate? If so, how are the apparently contradictory affirmations about His love and compassion to be construed? Is God, after all, some transcendent being with a dual personality?

Second, what kind of salvation is actually described in the Old Testament? What is its character and its basis? What are its benefits? How does it relate to the demands of divine holiness and judgment?

In addition, consideration of the nature of salvation as taught in the Old Testament raises the question of the theological relationship of the two Testaments. It involves the issues of unity versus disunity, priority, authority, and hermeneutics. Fortunately, these matters have been addressed in print. While unanimity has not been achieved, at least some of the critical factors have been examined.[4] Strangely enough, the theme of Old Testament soteriology has been largely ignored.

John S. Feinberg noted:

> What does the Bible teach about salvation? Ask this question of most people, and they will respond with their understanding of the New Testament's teaching on salvation. One

> can search for hours and find little written about salvation in the Old Testament. Biblical theologians tend to discuss it more often than systematic theologians, but neither group devotes much attention to it. Moreover, if one were to peruse course outlines for most classes taught in seminaries or Bible colleges in soteriology, he would find that the question of salvation in the Old Testament receives little or no treatment whatsoever.
>
> If it is difficult to find discussions on the Old Testament's approach to the broad theme of salvation, it is even harder to find treatments of the Old Testament's perspective on the specific matter of salvation of the individual. Although there are studies of such topics as corporate election and national salvation . . . it seems that theologians and exegetes have tended to shy away from a consideration of the Old Testament teaching about how an individual was to acquire spiritual salvation.[5]

In the search for what the Old Testament teaches about salvation, particularly personal salvation, Paul D. Feinberg's list of possible approaches to the meaning of an Old Testament text is of significance. They include the attempt to determine the "intention of the author," the "understanding of the author," the "understanding of the readers in the prophet's day," and the "significance of the text."[6]

The determination of the intent or understanding of another is a highly subjective matter, however. Evaluations must be tentative, then, regardless of the identification of author or readers. The only real, tangible clue to the intent of the author is the evident meaning of the text itself. The text of the Old Testament, accordingly, must first be carefully examined for its apparent meaning before one dare speculate about the intent of the author or what the ancient readers might have understood. To do otherwise is to reject exegesis and engage in eisegesis.[7]

Moreover, while we recognize the superiority of the New Testament revelation over the Old, we are persuaded that the Old Testament contained specific meaning and purpose in its own structure. So the goal of this investigation is to attempt to determine the approximate meaning of selected Old Testament texts that relate to the matter of salvation. More specifically, an effort will be made to determine what the Old Testament had to say about salvation to the recipients of the Old Testament message(s). If this can be accomplished, as I believe it can, then we can move with some confidence in the attempt to understand how the Old Testament teaching about salvation relates to that of the New.

What difference does it make? John Bright answered that question forcefully:

> The Old Testament must be retained in the Christian's Bible precisely because it is impossible to be true to the New Testament faith itself while getting rid of it. If there is one point upon which the New Testament is unanimous, it is that Jesus came, lived, died, and rose again "according to the scriptures."[8]

Although the one essential factor in the grand redemptive design for humanity was the Calvary event, God's saving activity surely did not begin in the first century A.D.[9] The salvation record is only partially complete, then, without the Old Testament account.

Bright concluded:

> The Old Testament holds the gospel to history. It is its surest bulwark against assimilation with alien philosophies and ideologies, against a flight into a sentimental and purely otherworldly piety, and against that disintegrating individualism that so easily besets it.[10]

Approach

This study evaluates selected key passages that reflect Old Testament instruction and/or illustration concerning its total message of salvation. Materials contained in the law and the Prophets are examined in that order (with one study based on Job),[11] with a secondary reference to chronological sequence. Pertinent exegetical information is presented, followed by an interpretation of the meaning of the passage. The reader may not always agree with the conclusions as to meaning, but the evidence is available for examination.

The perspective of the investigation is admittedly Christian. This in no way compromises the legitimacy of the study. As Childs contended, "Old Testament theology is essentially a Christian discipline."[12] Indeed, I would have little or no interest in the history or religious instruction of the Old Testament were it not for a personal, profound, and life-changing encounter with the Messiah described in the Old Testament. A Christian orientation, however, does not condone a haphazard treatment of the text. Drane warned that the Christian exegete cannot "avoid the important historical and literary questions posed by the Old Testament literature."[13] Integrity in exegesis may not be waived or ignored.

A careful distinction must be preserved between the perceived teaching of the Old Testament and the apparent understanding of its message by its original recipients. At times, the people of Judah and Israel obviously failed to comprehend the purposes of their covenant God, the meaning of the Torah, and the preaching of their prophets. Even today, popular opinion about the content of biblical truth may be radically contradictory to what the Bible does, in fact, teach. The accuracy of theological interpretation does not depend on the results of surveys and polls.

In like fashion, a distinction must be maintained between the instruction of the Old Testament and the personal piety and religious performance of its ancient devotees. Even when biblical truth is known and understood correctly, individual conduct may deviate from the revealed truth.[14] So the teaching of the Old Testament about personal salvation must be distinguished from possible misapprehension or misapplication by the original Old Testament audience.

Finally, the item of bias or presupposition must be considered candidly. Bright addressed this issue in a straightforward manner:

> If by presuppositionless exegesis one means that the exegete must divest himself to his predilections, his inherited beliefs, and personal convictions—all those factors in his background and training that have made him what he is—and come to the text as a newborn babe, then no such thing is possible. The exegete cannot be expected to be neutral toward the text, or to approach it with complete unconcern. On the contrary, his Christian commitment (or want of it), his professional training and interest, his personal needs and concerns, will inevitably condition his approach to the text and, to a large degree, determine the questions he will ask of it and the use he will make of it. In this sense of the word presuppositionless exegesis is not possible—nor is it really desirable. But this must not be taken as meaning, as some seem to have done, that the possibility of *objective* exegesis has been impeached.[15]

One presupposition of the writer is that the written revelation of God should make sense and its parts be consistent and compatible with the whole. Truth is neither
fragmentary (though our perception may be only partial)
nor contradictory. In the light of the remarkable rational
symmetry and predictable consistency of the physical universe, to assume that the Supreme Creator has communicated His redemptive message to persons in an irrational
or irresponsible manner is a highly questionable premise.
Some may search for inconsistency, contradiction, and error in the biblical record and believe that their search has
been fruitful. If, on the other hand, one carefully and rev-
erently sifts the biblical data, looking for cogency and com-
patibility, I am convinced that abundant evidence for the
integrity of the text and the authenticity of its message
will appear.

So is the God of the Old Testament a righteous God or
One "mighty to save"? Is he preoccupied with vengeance or
redemption? Is it "all of the above" or "none of the above"?
Only a careful scrutiny of the text itself will provide the
answer.

Notes

[1]Despite the wide acceptance of theories of multiple authorship for
the Book of Isaiah, I remain dubious about the evidence for the "phantom" Isaiah(s). Moreover, the intricate rhetorical, theological, and hom-
iletical structure of the material strongly suggests compositional unity.
For a discussion of divergent theories, compare James Muilenburg,
"The Book of Isaiah," in *The Interpreter's Bible*, vol. 5, ed. George
Arthur Buttrick (Nashville: Abingdon Press, 1982), 381–418 and Edward J. Young, *The Book of Isaiah* (Grand Rapids: William B. Eerdmans Publishing Company, 1978), 3:538–49.

[2]Note the play on Edom (אֱדוֹם) and "red" (אָדֹם).

[3]See Richard N. Soulen, *Handbook of Biblical Criticism* (Atlanta:
John Knox, 1978), 164. In light of the content of the manifestation (and
the writer's admittedly Christian perspective), however, the phenomenon could be described as a "Christological theophany."

[4]For example, John Bright, *The Authority of the Old Testament* (Abingdon Press, 1967; reprint ed., Grand Rapids: Baker Book House,
1975); John S. Feinberg, ed., *Continuity and Discontinuity: Perspectives
on the Relationship Between the Old and New Testaments* (Westchester,

IL: Crossway Books, 1988); Walter C. Kaiser, Jr., *The Uses of the Old Testament in the New* (Chicago: Moody Press, 1985); Darrell L. Bock, "Evangelicals and the Use of the Old Testament in the New: Part 1," *Bibliotheca Sacra* 142, no. 567 (July–September 1985):209–23 and "Evangelicals and the Use of the Old Testament in the New: Part 2," *Bibliotheca Sacra* 142, no. 568 (October–December 1985):306–19; Roger R. Nicole, "Patrick Fairbairn and Biblical Hermeneutics as Related to the Quotations of the Old Testament in the New," *Hermeneutics, Inerrancy, & the Bible* (Grand Rapids: Zondervan Publishing House, 1984).

[5]John S. Feinberg, "Salvation in the Old Testament," in *Tradition and Testament: Essays in Honor of Charles Lee Feinberg*, ed. John S. Feinberg and Paul D. Feinberg (Chicago: Moody Press, 1981), 39.

[6]Paul D. Feinberg, "Hermeneutics of Discontinuity," *Continuity and Discontinuity: Perspectives on the Relationship Between the Old and New Testaments* (Westchester, IL: Crossway Books, 1988), 112–14. Feinberg's fifth point, identifying the meaning of an OT passage on the basis of its "use in the NT," is omitted because it lies outside the parameters of this study.

[7]I prefer to distinguish exegesis from hermeneutics as well. Strictly speaking, exegesis is the art of examining the text, while hermeneutics is the art of interpreting the text. The two are intimately related, but they are not the same.

[8]Bright, *Authority*, 78.

[9]See Revelation 13:8.

[10]Bright, *Authority*, 78.

[11]The abundance of soteriological data in the Psalms merits a separate, independent examination. Reluctantly, therefore, I chose to omit Psalmic materials from this investigation (see Conclusion).

[12]Brevard S. Childs, *Old Testament Theology in a Canonical Context* (Philadelphia: Fortress Press, 1985), 7. Note that Childs did not say that OT theology is *exclusively* a Christian discipline.

[13]John Drane, *Old Testament Faith* (San Francisco: Harper & Row, 1986), 15.

[14]Note the lamentable example of David (Ps. 51).

[15]Bright, *Authority*, 45.

1

Creation: The Nature and Character of God

In the beginning God created.

Genesis 1:1

Inevitably, the character of salvation is directly related to the nature of God. An awareness of this relationship is crucial to a correct understanding of the essence of salvation in both Old and New Testaments. The place to begin an investigation of Old Testament soteriology, then, is to analyze and evaluate what the text reveals about the nature of God in the Old Testament. In other words, the paradox produced by the "vengeance-mighty to save" tension of Isaiah 63:1-4[1] must be understood correctly and resolved for the message of salvation to be perceived accurately.

The creation account of Genesis, of course, provides the first data that give insight into the divine makeup. The record furnishes no elaborate philosophical argument for the existence of God, but it does report His unilateral construction of the universe. In so doing, the record also reveals subtle but profound information about the nature and character of the Creator.

Identification of the Creator

The Hebrew word for God in Genesis 1:1, *'ĕlōhīm* (אֱלֹהִים), is the masculine plural form of the noun *'ēl* (אֵל), a common

Semitic term for *deity* in the ancient Near East.[2] *'Ēl*, then, is a generic term for any and all supernatural beings, and the plural form usually connotes the idea of majesty rather than multiplicity.[3] The *'ĕlōhīm* of creation is specified as LORD, however, beginning in Genesis 2:4.

LORD written in all block, capital letters represents the four consonants (יהוה, called the tetragrammaton, from Latin for "four letters") of the personal name of God in the Old Testament and reflects an editorial device used in most English translations. The first Hebrew letter may be transliterated as either *Y* or *J*, while the third may be *V* or *W*.[4] The second and fourth letters are represented by *H*. As will be explained later, these four consonants stand behind the hybrid expression *Jehovah*. In any event, LORD designates the singular personal name of God. We will preserve that identity in the present study by using the unvocalized form of the name, YHWH.

As is well known, the appearance of YHWH coupled with *'ĕlōhīm* has been a prominent feature in the development of the Documentary Hypothesis. A critique of the literary structure and authorship of the Pentateuch is far beyond the confines of this book. Nevertheless, we may note that reputable scholars have called attention to the use of dual names or titles for deities in the ancient Mediterranean world. This practice provides evidence to support the thesis that YHWH *'ĕlōhīm* is an expanded and personal identification of the *'ĕlōhīm* in Genesis 1:1.[5] Independent of the question of composition and textual history, we conclude that the *'ĕlōhīm* of creation has a personal name, YHWH, by which He is to be identified throughout the Old Testament.

Description of the Creator

As the Old Testament record unfolds, the disclosure of the character and nature of YHWH *'ĕlōhīm* expands and intensifies. Still, the opening stanzas of Genesis provide an astounding initial glimpse of the essence and scope of the Creator. The language of the creation account is profoundly simple, but its simplicity must not invite exegetical lethargy. A careful examination of the creation record justifies the following evaluations.

Eternal.[6] On the early side of the formation of matter and the construction of the universe, prior to the inauguration of time and the rolling cycle of seasons, before the first organism quivered or a person gasped an initial breath of air, God existed. Since God was antecedent to all things, it seems reasonably safe to assume that He will survive all things. This introduction to the "precreation" fact of God provided in Genesis is thoroughly compatible with the psalmist's affirmation, "From everlasting to everlasting you are God" (Ps. 90:2). Philosophical speculation may challenge the very concept of *eternal*, but the Old Testament's description of God's extension from eternity to eternity is as close to infinity as the finite human mind can grasp.[7] "In the beginning God. . . . "

Omnipotent. The first verb in the Old Testament, *bārā'* (בָּרָא), clearly reflects the awesome might of God. In fact, this particular form (*Qal* stem) of the verb features God exclusively as its subject throughout the Old Testament. The implication is that no one else has the capacity to perform *bārā'*. Thomas E. McComiskey states that "the word lends itself well to the concept of creation *ex nihilo*, although that concept is not necessarily inherent within the meaning of the word."[8] The *use* of the term, however, strongly supports the nuance of "bringing into existence"[9] without the utilization of previous material. By whatever means or whatever process He used, God's sovereign construction of the physical universe eloquently affirms His infinite power.

Transcendent and Immanent. The creation account presents God as above and beyond all things, as well as before all things. But as J. Wash Watts noted, "at the same time he remains in control of his creation so as to operate within it and manifest himself."[10] God, then, is distinct from matter and nature (pantheism) but is still involved in the total processes of nature.

Personal. God obviously possesses intellect, volition, and emotion: ingredients of personality. Since persons were created in the divine image (Gen. 1:27), human personality is to be construed as a reflection of the Creator's personality. God, then, is not some impersonal force or mechanical principle undergirding the universe. Rather, He is the supreme Person who imparts the capacity for personhood to people, the flower of His creation.

United. Despite the plurality suggested by the form *'ĕlōhîm*, the creation account clearly characterizes God as a singular entity. Reference to the Spirit of God in verse 2 however, appears to contradict that concept.

Hoffmeier has called attention to the fact that the translation "the Spirit of God" for *rūaḥ 'ĕlōhîm* (רוּחַ אֱלֹהִים) "has been seriously questioned in recent years," citing Orlinsky and Luyster as recommending "wind of God" or "mighty wind."[11] While *rūaḥ* may indeed mean "wind" or "breath" (Ex. 14:21), when it occurs in a "construct"[12] connection with either *'ĕlōhîm* or YHWH it usually appears to designate "spirit."[13] Moreover, the absence of meteorological modifiers with *rūaḥ*[14] strongly restricts the possibility that "wind" is intended in Genesis 1:2. The expression "spirit of God," then, would certainly imply a level of intrinsic diversity in the Godhead, rather than some divine energetic activity.

In any event, the cohortative "let us make" in Genesis 1:26 and the attendant plural forms of the pronoun ("our image") also suggest that dimension of variety. However, the dominant use of singular verb forms with *'ĕlōhîm* and the evident singularity of divine purpose in the total account indicate that these distinctions do not reflect division or plurality. No elaborate doctrine of the Trinity can be formulated successfully on the basis of the creation record alone, but the data it provides is remarkably consistent with that theological concept. The creation account seems to indicate a unified diversity within the divine Person.

Rational. God's systematic implementation of the total creation process reveals a reasoned, calculated strategy on the part of the Creator. Imaginative in design and concept, God was able to deal with negative situations, make decisions, and effectively consummate the production of matter, the universe, life, and history. The consistent symmetry of this process, plus the amazingly intricate end-product, strongly suggests that creation was the result of a deliberate, preconceived plan on the part of a Master Architect.

Consequently, the universe hardly seems to be either incidental or accidental.

Moral. In creation God demonstrated His capacity for ethical evaluation. He recognized the merit of His handiwork (Gen. 1:10,18,25,31), the negative aspects of a man in solitude (Gen. 2:18), and the distinction between good and evil (Gen. 3:22). In addition, the integrity of His warning about the tree of knowledge in Eden (Gen. 2:17) indicates His regard for truth. All of these features confirm that God had, and has, the ability to exercise moral judgment. In fact, humanity's own capacity for ethical discernment is a reflection of the divine image.

Benevolent. The Creator's favorable disposition toward the persons He created is clearly revealed in the opening stanzas of Genesis. His provisions of food (Gen. 1:29), companionship (Gen. 2:18), beauty (Gen. 2:8-9*a*), and even clothing after the first couple's disobedience (Gen. 3:21) demonstrate His charitable concern for human welfare. God's appointment of man and woman as "chief executive officers" in nature's hierarchy (Gen. 1:28) further demonstrates legitimate "paternal pride" in His earthly offspring (note Gen. 1:26-27).

Even the divine prohibition and warning (Gen. 2:17) communicate God's concern for human well-being. The prohibition was not penal but protective. As parents warn their children against potential danger and harm, so the Creator attempted to shield His offspring from the lethal act of disobedience that threatened their innocence and very lives. Alas, to no avail! But make no mistake. God attempted to protect humanity from the calamity of defiant sin.

Holy. The curses pronounced on the serpent (Gen. 3:14-15), man and woman (vv. 16-19), and the total ecology of nature (vv. 17-18) indicate God's intrinsic opposition to sin with all of its attendant evil, rebellion, chaos, and devastation. He penalized the serpent for complicity in the human moral insurrection, but note carefully that God held both Adam and Eve responsible for their conduct. In their case, even the justifiable plea "the devil made me do it" did not absolve them of personal accountability for their actions.

The implication is clear. The Creator is holy, and He will not compromise with unholiness. Moreover, He does penalize the guilty. Any theological analysis of the character of salvation (in both Old and New Testaments) must keep these factors in view. God is holy, and sin must be punished. This affirmation is obviously out of sync with the modern age of expanding indulgent permissiveness, but it is nonetheless consistent with the biblical evidence.

Sovereign. The Genesis account clearly depicts the Creator as being in control. Despite the earthly revolution incited by eternity's archvillain, God is the undisputed director of history's total scenario. Individual acts of rebellion are permitted, not because God wills defiance but because He does allow disobedience. Nevertheless, the overall benevolent design will be implemented. By inference, then, one may safely conclude that YHWH God is in full control of His great redemptive plan for humans.

Purposeful. As noted earlier, the creation chronicle suggests a preconceived plan; and the syntactical components of the text support that suggestion. The first chapter of Genesis is liberally sprinkled with verb forms called "jussive" (Gen. 1:3,6,9,11,14,20,24) which may have a distinctive abbreviated spelling and which express the desire of the speaker over external factors (equivalent to the English "let him [her, them] . . ." idiom).[15] These verb patterns, reflecting the intent of the Creator, indicate purpose and design.

The verb construction (*větērā'ĕh*, וְתֵרָאֶה) in the subordinate clause of verse 9, however, is definitely not jussive in form. As Lambdin noted, this type of construction expresses "a purpose or result (Eng. 'so that')."[16] The verb is a "potential subjunctive," and the clause indicates the purposeful strategy of the Master Builder. A preferred translation would be, "in order that (so that) the dry ground may appear."[17] Impersonal, mechanical, random chance is totally alien to the record. A personal will and purpose lie behind each element of creation.

Wise. Finally, the Creation account and the Eden scenario surely indicate that the Creator is more than an eternal repository of knowledge and information; He is not simply an ultimate data base. While God is all-powerful,

His construction of an infinitely complex and intricate universe obviously required more than raw energy.

His response to the tragedy of human insurrection reveals a patient, charitable, and discreet resolve to salvage people from the shambles of despair and death. Rather than eradicate a fledgling race of rebels and replace them with a set of programmed robots, God involved Himself in the human trauma and began immediately to implement a grand design to reclaim sinners (Gen. 3:14-21). Without the incredible particulars of that grand design, even in the somber silence of the empty garden, one can sense the propriety of Paul's exclamation, "Oh, the depth of the riches of the wisdom and knowledge of God! / How unsearchable his judgments, / and his paths beyond tracing out!" (Rom. 11:33). The completion of physical creation and the inauguration of spiritual salvation reveal the superlative wisdom of God.

Summary

The nature of God is an integral feature of His salvation. In evaluating the character of God as reflected in the first three chapters of Genesis, I have tried to resist the temptation to read later disclosures back into the earlier setting. The reader may judge the relative effectiveness of that effort.

As the Old Testament message of salvation unfolds, however, I will attempt to update the divine profile. Inevitably, the expanding redemptive design revealed in the events , disclosures, and affirmations of the biblical record will reflect the nature of the God of salvation. The questions of sin, guilt, punishment, and possible forgiveness must find resolution in the person and character of the Creator. Will the evidence confirm that He is an offended tyrant who is determined to express outrage against the earthly violators of His holiness? Are mercy and grace alien to His nature? Can He forgive? Will He forgive? If so, then on what basis? These issues demand honest consideration as we try to analyze Old Testament redemptive structure in the light of an expanding revelation of the nature of YHWH God.

Notes

[1]A tension revealed elsewhere. Compare Isaiah 61:1-2; Malachi 4:1-2; Exodus 34:6-7.

[2]For a helpful discussion of the possible meaning and use of the term, consult Jack B. Scott, "אלה," *Theological Wordbook of the Old Testament*, ed. R. Laird Harris, Gleason L. Archer, Jr., and Bruce K. Waltke (Chicago: Moody Press, 1981), 1:41-45 (book hereafter cited as *TWOT*). See also Frank M. Cross, "אֵל," trans. John T. Willis in *Theological Dictionary of the Old Testament*, ed. G. Johannes Botterweck and Helmer Ringgren (Grand Rapids: William B. Eerdmans Company, 1974), 1:242-61 (book hereafter cited as *TDOT*). Cross also cited *El* as a proper name among the Semites, noting that "in the Canaanite pantheon *'Il* was the proper name of the god *par excellence*, the head of the pantheon" (242).

[3]See Scott, "אלה," *TWOT*, 1:41-45.

[4]The sixth letter of the Hebrew alphabet is represented in the English Bible by "v" in the proper names David (דָּוִד) and Levite (לֵוִי). It is preserved the same way in "Bar Mitzvah" (מִצְוָה) and is pronounced as "v" in modern Hebrew. See Harry Blumberg and Mordecai H. Lewettes, *Modern Hebrew*, vol. 1, revised ed. (New York: Hebrew Publishing Company, 1974), 369.

[5]See Stanislav Segert, *A Basic Grammar of the Ugaritic Language* (Berkeley: University of California Press, 1984), 46; Cyrus H. Gordon, "Higher Critics and Forbidden Fruit," in *Christianity Today*, ed. Frank E. Gaebelein (New York: Pyramid Books, 1968), 95-96; K. A. Kitchen, *Ancient Orient and Old Testament* (Chicago: Inter-Varsity, 1966), 121.

[6]I am indebted to J. Wash Watts for the first five points of this analysis. See J. Wash Watts, *Old Testament Teaching* (Nashville: Broadman Press, 1967), 10-11.

[7]For nuances in the meaning of *'ōlām* (עוֹלָם), the Hebrew term behind "everlasting" in Psalm 90:2, see Walter Baumgartner and Ludwig Hugo Kohler, *Hebraisches und aramaisches Lexikon zum Alten Testament*, Dritte Auflage (Leiden: E. J. Brill, 1967). See under "עוֹלָם," 3:754-56 (work hereafter cited as KB).

[8]See Thomas E. McComiskey, "בָּרָא," *TWOT*, 1:127.

[9]Ibid. For the range of concrete and metaphorical use of the verb, consult KB, "I ברא," 1:146-47.

[10]Watts, *Teaching*, 11.

[11]James K. Hoffmeier, "Some Thoughts on Genesis 1 and 2 and Egyptian Cosmology," *The Journal of the Ancient Near Eastern Society* 15 (1983):44.

[12]For an explanation of the meaning of a "construct chain" in Hebrew syntax, see Thomas O. Lambdin, *Introduction to Biblical Hebrew* (New York: Charles Scribner's Sons, 1971), 67-72, or my computerized tutorial program, "Guide to Grammatical Forms in Biblical Hebrew," *HAM-MOREH*, Lesson 2.

Creation: The Nature and Character of God

[13]In the light of the parallelism with *nišmat šaddai* (נִשְׁמַת שַׁדַּי, "breath of the Almighty") in Job 33:4, *ruaḥ 'ēl* may mean "breath of God," but hardly "wind." For an extensive list of the uses of רוּחַ, see *Veteris Testamenti Concordantiae* (Tel Aviv: Sumptibus Schocken Hierosolymis, 1967), 1079–80 or *A New Concordance of the Old Testament* (Jerusalem: "Kiryat Sefer" Publishing House Ltd., 1985), 1063–66.

[14]For example, "east wind" (רוּחַ קָדִים) in Exodus 10:13 and "blow" (נָשַׁפְתָּ) in Exodus 15:10.

[15]Wilhelm Gesenius, *Gesenius' Hebrew Grammar*, ed. A. E. Cowley, trans. E. Kautzsch, 2nd English ed. (Oxford: Clarendon Press, 1952), 321–23 (book hereafter cited as GKC).

[16]Lambdin, *Hebrew*, 119.

[17]E. A. Speiser noted this distinction in his translation, "that the dry land may be visible" in *Genesis*, vol. 1, *The Anchor Bible*, 3rd ed., ed. William Foxwell Albright and David Noel Freedman (Garden City: Doubleday & Company, 1981), 3.

2

Eden: The Tragedy of Sin

Now the serpent . . .

Genesis 3:1

Salvation would be nothing but a nebulous and elusive philosophical concept were it not for the savage reality of the human sin problem. The very notion of spiritual deliverance is inextricably connected with the issue of human moral depravity and condemnation. No sin, no salvation! No need for salvation! While some seem to find the notion of human sinlessness to be irresistibly attractive, it is a contrary-to-fact condition, according to the biblical record. No theological or philosophical whitewash obliterates the reality of the deep moral stain of universal sin.

Accordingly, a clear understanding of the nature of the sin problem is essential to a correct perception of God's redemptive design—in both Testaments. God's remedy for sin's malignancy was not sterile bandages, sedatives, or even cosmetic surgery. The magnitude of the divine solution can hardly be appreciated without a full awareness of the genuine horror of the human dilemma. The scope of the sin problem is graphically revealed in the account of Eden's tragedy.

The "Personal Agent" of Sin[1]

As soon as the curtain rises on the stage of history, the archvillain of earth's age-spanning drama is introduced:

"now the serpent. . . . " But the data concerning the mysterious intruder in the garden are so cryptic, so meager. Who or what was this bizarre "reptile" that talked? How did he spin his web of deceit? Was it some fascinating sparkle in his dark, beady eyes that hypnotized Eve? Was it the ingratiating sweetness of his voice that beguiled her? How did he work his damnable "magic"?

Identification. The third chapter of Genesis reports the serpent's presence in the garden without any explanation about his origin, background, or identity. As a matter of fact, he is not specifically identified until the Book of Revelation (12:9). However, his involvement in the disobedience of Adam and Eve and his obvious antagonism toward God strongly suggest that a more sinister presence lurked behind the "serpent-disguise." So a brief examination of other Old Testament terms and symbols of the archvillain may be of help in establishing some acceptable "identification equation."

One popular formula is the "Lucifer" connection, which equates the serpent persona with the "fallen angel" of Isaiah 14:12. On the surface, the equation seems persuasive. Yet an examination of the Isaiah passage reveals some serious flaws in this particular "fallen angel" identification. In the first place, the parameters of the Isaiah context must be considered. Chapters 13—23 contain a series of oracles addressed to specific kingdoms and empires that existed in the Near East during the first millennium B.C.[2] The designated geographical and social entities were concrete historical units. References to their political leaders are quite definite, including the use of names as well as positions (Isa. 20:1). The "Lucifer" notice in chapter 14 is a part of the first oracle in the series, a message directed toward Babylon (Isa. 13:1). The contextual environment, then, appears to be very specific and historical. Nothing suggests an extraterrestrial or celestial setting.

Moreover, the "Lucifer" figure is specifically described as "the king of Babylon" (Isa. 14:4). While the defiant arrogance of the king of chapter 14 is analogous to that of the deposed dragon of Revelation 12, it is also akin to the presumptuous vanity of Babylon's Nebuchadnezzar (Dan. 3:1—4:30). In addition, he is depicted as "the man[3] who shook the earth" (Isa. 14:16). Both designations (king and man) appear to indicate Lucifer's humanity.

The mortality of his nature is emphasized further by an apparent reference to his death (Isa. 14:15)[4] and burial. The concreteness of the death-burial scenario is intensified by the prediction of the desecration of the king's remains. While the bodies of other monarchs might rest in funerary splendor and reverence, the death crypt of Babylon's king would be plundered and his corpse violated (Isa. 14:18-20).[5] Accordingly, the description of Lucifer's humanity, death, and destiny hardly accords with the notion that he is a "fallen angel."

How, then, did such an identification develop? In all probability, the "Lucifer-fallen angel" equation is the result of the transliteration of the Latin translation of the Hebrew term *hēlēl*.[6] Evidently derived from a verb meaning "to shine," the word could well be translated "shining one."[7] As noted in one source,[8] the expression is actually an epithet ascribed to the king of Babylon. Unfortunately, however, in reproducing the Latin term "light bearer" in English, the *King James Version* converted a descriptive noun into a proper name. The name "Lucifer" has continued to attract "fallen angel" connotations,[9] which, in my opinion, exceed the limitations of the context. I conclude, therefore, that the "serpent-Lucifer" equation is not a valid option.

Another possibility is the "king of Tyre" connection associated with Ezekiel 28:12. Again, as in the case of the Isaiah location, the specific message to the "king of Tyre" (Ezek. 28:11-19) is part of a larger series of pronouncements directed against individual political and ethnic units.[10] The section is actually imbedded in a "lament for Tyre" (Ezek. 27:2) that includes a word directed against the "ruler of Tyre" (Ezek. 28:2). In the light of the context, then, one would suppose that a concrete historical personage is designated by the "king of Tyre" label.

Significant items in the text distinguish this passage, however, from the one in Isaiah. In the first place, the "ruler of Tyre" and the "king of Tyre" seem to represent different figures or personalities. Moreover, the description of the "king of Tyre" is remarkably unique. He is said to have been "in Eden" as an "anointed . . . cherub" (Ezek. 28:13-14) and to have "walked among the fiery stones" on "the holy mount of God" (Ezek. 28:14*b*). These esoteric statements appear to characterize an individual who is distinctively different from conventional earthly potentates.

Comments concerning his downfall support this assumption. Sin, pride, and corrupted wisdom led to his banishment (from the garden?) and his being thrown (down) to the earth (Ezek. 28:16-17). His ultimate destiny includes open humiliation and permanent annihilation (Ezek. 28:17-19).

I conclude, then, that the true power behind the throne of Tyre (ruler of Tyre) was the self-infatuated "cherub of Eden" (king of Tyre) who characteristically enlists earthly subjects and monarchs in his rebellion against the divine rule. Accordingly, the premise that Ezekiel's "king of Tyre" was the "cherub in serpent's clothing" has much to recommend it.[11]

Perhaps the most obvious connection, though, is the association that links the personality of the serpent with the supreme antagonist of both God and humans in the Old Testament. Called Satan,[12] this mysterious adversary is depicted as God's opponent and the accuser of people.[13] As noted by Cyrus Gordon and others, however, the Hebrew expression behind the term "Satan" is actually *hassātān* (הַשָּׂטָן),[14] a noun with the article. It is not, strictly speaking, a name but rather a descriptive title. The method of operation and evident intent of Eden's serpent, however, is certainly consistent with that of "the adversary" (Satan) so that equating the two is quite credible. From a canonical perspective, this equation is the proper interpretation as shown in Revelation 12:9.

The interesting thing about attempting to identify the "personal agent" of sin in the Garden of Eden is that not even the New Testament terms that describe him actually supply his name.[15] Gordon has suggested, though, that the "terrible demon" is called *hāby*[16] and that his name does occur (in the Hebrew text) twice in the Old Testament.[17] Even if one rejects Gordon's proposal, it does not follow that the archvillain is both nameless and unknown. Anonymity, as it were, does not obscure his hateful and destructive activity as recorded in Scripture and recognized in human experience.

Intention. The only descriptive term applied to the serpent in the Eden passage is the somewhat mystifying expression "crafty,"[18] a translation of the Hebrew word *'ārūm*, עָרוּם. A careful examination of the term in this context, though, provides a revealing insight into the purpose and design of the "serpent-Satan." The similarity in both appearance (morphology) and sound (phonology) between "crafty" (*'ārūm*, עָרוּם in Gen. 3:1) and "naked" (*'ērōm*, עֵירֹם in Gen. 3:10)[19] reflects a deliberate and significant play on words (paronomasia). Whether these terms share a common origin or not,[20] their association in this context is obviously intentional.

The serpent found man and woman clothed in innocence but naked in body and promptly stripped them of their Edenic purity, leaving them physically and morally nude, exposed, and ashamed in the presence of a holy God. Accordingly, though *'ārūm may* have a positive connotation, it is linked in this account with the wily deceit that led to humanity's moral defoliation. The expression "crafty" then conveys the malevolent nature and malicious intent of the tempter.

As a young pastor, I inadvertently wandered into the children's ward while making a routine hospital visit and encountered for the first time the bewildering confusion of the suffering of the innocent. The little ones were puzzled by their pain—sometimes too small to be able to tell where they hurt, much less understand the philosophical "whys" of it. Disturbed by what I saw, heard, and felt when I emerged from that dungeon of distress into the bright sunlight of life as usual, I wanted to lift my face to heaven and cry, "Why, Lord, why? Who could possibly be pleased with such meaningless misery and pain?"

Others have raised the same or similar questions, and some have concluded that the God of creation must be held directly responsible for all of the ills and inequities of life. The burden of blame must be placed elsewhere. The serpent, not God, invaded the garden to exploit the first people God created, to rob them of fellowship with the Creator, and to unleash the destructive forces of sin and death in human experience. The wily serpent's design was to plunder and destroy, to enslave people in a life of corruption, pain, and decay and, ultimately, to doom and damn. Make no mistake. *He* planned it so.[21]

Walk the corridors of any hospital late at night. If you listen closely enough, with the ears of discernment, you will surely hear the hollow echo of his chill, metallic laughter as he makes his nightly rounds. He, and he alone, enjoys human hurt and grief. He revels in our pain; he luxuriates in our fear and sorrow. For this explicit purpose he entered the garden. Accordingly, no frightful exaggeration of science-fiction imagination compares to the hideous reality of Satan, the "Frankenstein-monster" of the ages. Simon Peter was right on target when he warned, "Be self-controlled and alert. Your enemy the devil prowls around like a roaring lion looking for someone to devour" (1 Pet. 5:8). "Now the serpent. . . . "

Technique. Although the demonic person who appeared in serpent's clothing in Eden has the ability to assume various and misleading guises (2 Cor. 11:14), his basic approach is surprisingly static. He opened the conversation with Eve, for example, with nothing more sinister than a question. Notice that he clearly knew the answer to his question; indeed, his question contained its answer (Gen. 3:1). His was a rhetorical question, not designed to elicit information but rather to sow the seed of suspicion and uncertainty in the mind of the woman. He was preeminently successful.

So, across the ages, he has continued to breed mistrust and doubt in human hearts and minds with nothing more formidable than a question. Somehow the frail human intellect, jaded by its own cynicism, is quick to believe any and every implied charge against divine integrity, with or without evidence. Even those disposed to believe are sometimes confounded because they find no immediate answer for the adversary's question and then assume, erroneously, that there is no reasonable response. No logic, no argument, no evidence, no proof—only a smug, condescending question!

Having established a bridgehead of doubt, the serpent launched a direct attack with his explicit contradiction. The woman had responded to his question by quoting God verbatim (at least to her satisfaction), "You must not eat fruit from the tree that is in the middle of the garden, and you must not touch it, or you will die" (Gen. 3:3). The tempter replied, "You will not surely die" (Gen. 3:4).

His rebuttal contradicted the statement of God and challenged the truthfulness of God. What audacity! Yet, reluctantly, we must concede a degree of accuracy to the satanic charge. The affirmation "You won't *really* die"[22] actually contained an element of truth. When Adam and Eve ate the forbidden fruit, they did not suffer cardiac arrest and drop dead on the spot. They continued to breathe, think, talk, and act. Nevertheless, from the defiant moment of disobedience they became walking, talking corpses, the decay process of death already active in their bodies. It is not surprising to observe that when the "father of lies" told the truth, it was only half truth. Moreover, one is thus reminded that no lie is so insidious as the lie that contains enough truth to make it credible.

The tempter concluded his appeal with the guarantee that their violation of the divine prohibition would make man and woman "like God" (Gen. 3:5). The force of the statement, of course, implies that God was trying to deprive the first couple of something that was their legitimate right to experience. The subtle insinuation is absurd; but again, grudgingly, one must give even the devil his due. After their disobedience, their eyes were opened; and they did come to know the difference between good and evil, *but not like God.*

A small child can learn the meaning of *hot* by plunging a baby hand into a kettle of boiling water, but that learning experience will produce scars that must be carried to the grave. In similar fashion, man and woman acquired the ability to distinguish good from evil at a terrible cost. When the encounter was over, not only were they not *like* God; they were no longer as they once had been. "Now the serpent was more crafty. . . . "

The Nature of Sin

Because of the unique content of the third chapter of Genesis, labels such as "fable," "myth," "legend," and "par-able" have been used to describe its message.[23] The biblical account of the fall contains more than just etiological explanations[24] about natural calamity or the existential reality of human sinfulness. The Genesis account is not some fanciful plot hatched to provide a philosophical or religious rationale for the existence of moral and natural evil. The Bible does, indeed, "give information about the origin of evil" as well as "witness to its character."[25]

However, the record of original sin, with its brutal ring of reality, is so incisive and classic that its lessons and application are universal. Its scope of application does not challenge the record's historical integrity. Instead, its timeless universality confirms the record's authenticity. Accordingly, the analysis of the fall in the garden is almost like an examination of yesterday's indiscretion or tomorrow's disobedience.

Curiosity. Dialogue, action, and description in the text provide concrete data about the fall. These same data also give some insight into the possible emotions and thought processes involved in the event. To be sure, discretion and restraint must be exercised in any attempt to probe the feelings and motives of another, regardless of who is involved. Still, both the situation and the record reveal some hints that can be helpful.

For example, we know that the woman did not understand the nature of good and evil. The serpent's suggestive appeal must surely have stimulated the woman's curiosity concerning not only forbidden fruit but also the possible luxury of moral discernment. How would the inviting food taste? What would be its delectable flavor? What would be the exhilarating sensation of actually *knowing* both good and evil—*just like God*? Surely such notions as these must have buzzed around in Eve's mind.

Alas, how many fatal escapades have been fueled by the heady giddiness of curiosity? While the human penchant for exploration and experimentation has aided mankind's growth and expansion of knowledge, it has also inflicted a devastating toll. Indeed, the bones of the adventuresome clutter the record of human progress. From the fate of the fabled cat to the gallant pioneers of space, curiosity has exacted its deadly price. No doubt, in the Garden of Eden, relatively innocent curiosity was a factor in the sin process that led to humanity's doom.

Doubt. The serpent's questions and contradictions apparently stimulated a gnawing uncertainty and suspicion in the woman's mind. After all, she only had God's word about the possible consequences of disobedience. How could she know for sure that He had spoken truth? How might she determine the accuracy of the serpent's assurance? There was only one way to find out!

Whether Eve actually grappled with these specific questions or not, the report clearly indicates that she came to doubt the integrity of the Creator's explicit warning. Before the specific act of defiance, curiosity was infused with misgivings. As she thinketh in her heart, so shall she be.[26]

Pride. Yet another internal motivation may be projected. Part of the satanic allure had included the prospect of becoming *just like God*. What a dazzling, fabulous thought! The woman observed that not only was the prohibited fruit appealing to the eye but it was "also desirable for gaining wisdom" (Gen. 3:6). On the surface, who could fault either Adam or Eve for wanting to improve their lot, upgrade their mental and moral capacity? Legitimate human ambition for improvement obviously got out of control. What a thin line separates ambition from arrogance! Like the "cherub of Eden" (Ezek. 28:13-14), their hearts became proud (Ezek. 28:17). Adam and Eve yearned for an experiential status that would put them on a par with God. As Milton's tormented demon expressed it, "Better to reign in hell than serve in heaven."[27] It was nearly time for the act.

Defiance. Before the fateful deed, the lethal mixture of curiosity, doubt, and pride stirred the wild intoxication of defiance in the human spirit. How dare God withhold the delicious delicacy of truly knowing good and evil! By what authority would He impose His binding restrictions? Unmistakably, prior to the act of rebellion, the first couple assumed the mind-set of the rebel. The attitude always precedes the act. By whatever means or process, before the overt action, they determined to become the master of their own fate and the captain of their own souls. So the die was cast.

Disobedience. Curiosity, doubt, pride, and defiance, of course, are all internal attitudes. They cannot be precisely determined, only observed tentatively. However, when these attitudes and emotions rage within the human breast, as in the garden, they are inevitably expressed in concrete actions. By eating fruit from the tree in "the middle of the garden," Adam and Eve gave tangible, concrete expression to their internal rejection of the divine government.

Some have questioned the historical reality of the temptation and fall, assuming that the elements of the story are only symbolic in nature.[28] The tangibles of the account do not weaken its credibility or cancel its historicity. To the contrary, the external objective phenomena of the Genesis record accord remarkably with human experience. Sooner or later, the attitude inspires the deed, and the deed requires some thing (or things) external, concrete, tangible, and specific. Moreover, sin does not occur (or even exist) in the abstract. Rather, it requires a definite, temporal environment. Without a specific setting, sin is merely a theological speculation.

All persons are sinful by nature and preference (Eph. 2:3). All people, in due time, express what they are by what they do. No need exists, then, to question either the substance or the significance of the Genesis report. Humanity's fall is not a legendary account that reflects the timeless sin experience of all people. It is the report of the first historical act of sin. Its precise and direct simplicity, plus its classic features, provide a remarkable analogy for any and all subsequent transgressions.

The Results of Sin

The consequences of the indiscretion in the garden were both immediate and far-reaching. Lamentably, with history's initial sin, earth's first pair opened a Pandora's box[29] of death and devastation that would plague all of their descendants. First the deed, then the penalty!

Emotional Disturbance. "Then the eyes of both of them were opened, and they realized they were naked" (Gen. 3:7). Recognizing something of the horrible magnitude of their circumstance, man and woman attempted to hide from the holy presence of God—to no avail. The LORD called to man, "Where are you?" Man replied, "I heard you in the garden, and I *was afraid* (Gen. 3:9-10, italics added).[30] This was the first time a human had ever uttered the word, at least so far as the biblical record reports. What a somber, ominous statement. "I was afraid."

Sin has an insidious way of imposing subtle pressure and strain on human emotions. As in the case of Adam, it stimulates unreasonable and unreasoning fear and anxiety. This is not to claim that every neurosis or phobia is the immediate result of some specific sin, but Adam's fear does reveal that sin damages human personality. The shifting social norms of modern culture may dismiss old-fashioned customs as out-of-date; biblical standards of moral conduct may be rejected as archaic; and any degenerate activity may be excused as an acceptable "alternate lifestyle." These latter-day accommodations do not alter the fact that God's Word condemns sin without equivocation, nor do they protect the human psyche from the emotion-shattering impact of moral impropriety.

Guilt. The couple's sense of shame regarding their nakedness betrayed the inner presence of guilt. Guilt, in turn, prompted them to fashion crude garments to camouflage their nudity and to attempt to flee from the brilliant light of God's purity. Notice the frantic maneuver of the guilty to shift blame and exonerate self. Adam whined, "The woman you put here with me—she gave me some fruit from the tree, and I ate it" (Gen. 3:12). In other words, "God, if it hadn't been for *You* and the *woman*, I wouldn't be in this predicament."

In some early Hollywood movies, the late Oliver Hardy captured the self-justifying attitude of Adam with his oft-repeated admonition to Stan Laurel, "Well, here's another fine mess you've gotten me into!" Invariably, though, the predicament was none of Laurel's doing; it was the result of Hardy's own inept bumbling. The Laurel and Hardy comedy team used the same line again and again to provoke laughter and to remind us of our own foibles. So it is with the burden of guilt. It must be "shared." From the very beginning, humans have tried to shift the blame from self to others.

Note how astutely Eve picked up the little strategy. "The serpent deceived me, and I ate" (Gen. 3:13). So was born the time-honored tradition of "passing the buck." "You," "the woman," "the serpent," but never me! Unfortunately, as the record makes clear, the ploy is fruitless. From the very beginning, man *and* woman were held individually accountable for their personal conduct. No manipulations of conscience can remove the guilt of the guilty.

Alienation. Following the full disclosure of their disobedience, the dejected pair was banished from the garden (Gen. 3:23-24), exiled from beautiful Eden, the only ideal environment they would ever know. More tragically, they were denied companionship with their Creator, separated from the Lord of glory.

Furthermore, one's estrangement from God is not a neutral estate. At the edge of the garden, God positioned cherubim and "a flaming sword flashing back and forth to guard the way to the tree of life" (Gen. 3:24). The terminology of the text exudes hostility. God told the cherubim to "guard," not "guide." No flickering torch illuminated the entrance to the garden to guide earth's rebels back to its pleasures. Instead, a fiery blade was brandished to protect Eden against the insurrectionists.

Yes, human sin does more than separate sinners from God. It produces, in effect, a state of spiritual warfare and enmity. Through sin, people align themselves with the legions of hell and the forces of earthly rebellion. As the Greek term for alienation in the New Testament indicates,[31] estrangement through sin places the sinner in the enemy's camp.

Pain and Sorrow. Sin's immediate consequence inflicted a harsh penalty on both man and woman in the crucial areas of life. For woman, the penalty affected her role as mother and wife, involving pain in childbirth and subjugation to her husband (Gen. 3:16). For man, it complicated his position as "breadwinner," imposing toil and struggle on his efforts to extract foodstuff from the soil (Gen. 3:17-19). In this fashion, then, sin impacted history's first family in the home, in interpersonal relationships, and in the "marketplace."

The common denominator for Adam and Eve, though, was the pain and sorrow factor. The expressions "pains," "pain"

(Gen. 3:16) and "painful toil" (Gen. 3:17) all derive from the same verbal root *'āṣab*.[32] The root "relates to physical pain as well as to emotional sorrow"[33] and encompasses the full range of human trauma, including the grief and distress of death. In short, the destructive influences of sin hit man and woman where they lived, leaving a legacy of hurt, confusion, and distress. What a hellish price to pay!

Contamination. Sin not only imposed a personal penalty; its lethal fallout polluted the entire environment. The very ground became an adversary, resisting all human efforts at cultivation. Briars, weeds, brambles, and cacti started to infest the earth as human rebellion contaminated nature's total economy. The charitable ecology of Eden vanished! History's first family now faced a fallen and perverted order that featured hostile death-dealing conditions, a violent world of chaos and destruction.

Sin also corrupted the moral environment, even contaminating the first children. Cain undoubtedly learned of his parents' conduct. He must surely have known that they disregarded the divine warning, disobeyed, and took the forbidden fruit. So, following their example, he, too, ignored God's admonition, disobeyed, and took—his brother's life (Gen. 4:3-8). The expanding pollution ultimately spawned the noxious seed of Lamech, an arrogant bully who openly boasted of his murderous exploits (Gen. 4:23-24). What a damnable legacy!

Death. Immediately following their rebellion, Adam and Eve were exiled from the garden with the divine commentary that man "must not be allowed to reach out his hand and take also from the tree of life" (Gen. 3:22). The act and the statement combine to communicate the fact of spiritual death. Because of disobedience, people were cut off from access to the God-quality and God-quantity of existence the tree of life represented. The first couple died spiritually as the result of sin and became irrevocably subject to physical death. "Therefore, just as sin entered the world through one man, and death through sin, and in this way death came to all men . . . death reigned from . . . Adam" (Rom. 5:12,14).

Against this backdrop of monumental tragedy God's redeeming activity must be examined and analyzed. No perception of salvation in the Old Testament can be adequate unless it takes into account the magnitude of the monstrous calamity of the fall. The study of Old Testament soteriology must address the issues of temptation and the tempter, the nature and exhibition of the human sin problem, its results and possible solution—all in the context of what the Old Testament explicitly states. As we shall see, where "the serpent was more crafty," the Lord was more gracious.

Notes

[1]I am indebted to Dr. J. Hardee Kennedy for this expression (from unpublished notes).

[2]Note references to Moab (Isa. 15:1), Damascus (Isa. 17:1), Ethiopia (Isa. 18:1), Egypt (Isa. 19:1), Assyria (Isa. 20:1), Dumah (Isa. 21:11), Arabia (Isa. 21:13).

[3]The Hebrew term is אִישׁ. "Most commonly it denotes any individual male" (Thomas E. McComiskey, "אִישׁ," *TWOT*, 1:38.) While the term also distinguishes mankind from animals (Ex. 11:7) and deity (Num. 23:19), it hardly applies to celestial or spiritual beings.

[4]The descent into "the grave" (שְׁאוֹל), however, may also suggest the destiny of the "dragon" (τὸν δράκοντα) in Revelation 20:3,10. If one construes Revelation's "abyss" and "lake of burning sulfur" as the equivalent of "the grave," support for the "Lucifer-Satan" equation results.

[5]Young's proposal that the text indicates the king would be denied burial is unconvincing. See Edward J. Young, *The Book of Isaiah*, 3 vols. (Grand Rapids: William B. Eerdmans Publishing Company, 1978), 1:444-45. R. B. Y. Scott suggested that "it is not clear whether an actual king or a personification of the Babylonian imperial power is intended." See "Introduction and Exegesis: The Book of Isaiah: Chapters 1—39," in *The Interpreter's Bible*, vol. 5, ed. George Arthur Buttrick (Nashville: Abingdon Press, 1956), 258.

[6]The expression is הֵילֵל. The Latin term lucifer (from *lux* "light" and *fero* "bear, carry") follows the Septuagint, ὁ ἑωσφόρος, "Morning-star" (from ἕως, "morn" and φέρω, "carry").

[7]So write Charles A. Briggs, S. R. Driver and Francis Brown, *The New Brown-Driver-Briggs-Gesenius Hebrew and English Lexicon* (Lafayette, IN: Associated Publishers and Authors, Inc., 1978), 237 (book hereafter cited as BDB). KB offers "**Morgenstern**" (morningstar), see under "הֵילֵל," 1:235. For a full discussion of the expression, see Leonard J. Coppes, *TWOT*, 1:217. For a discussion of the passage, see Young, *Isaiah*, vol. 1, 439-46.

[8]See "הֵילֵל **n.m. appel.** shining one," BDB, 237.

[9]See *The New Scofield Reference Bible* (New York: Oxford University Press, 1967), 725.

[10]Observe references to the Ammonites (Ezek. 25:2), Moab (Ezek. 25:8), Edom (Ezek. 25:12), the Philistines (Ezek. 25:15), Sidon (Ezek. 28:21), and Egypt (Ezek. 29:2).

[11]For a helpful discussion, see J. Barton Payne, "שָׂטַן," *TWOT*, 2:875–75. Herbert G. May proposed, "The figure is that of the first man in Eden. He was created perfect in beauty and wisdom, and dressed in the splendor of precious stones. When guilt was discovered in him, he was driven by the cherub from Eden." See *The Book of Ezekiel*, vol. 6 of *The Interpreter's Bible* (Nashville: Abingdon Press, 1956), 220.

[12]Apparently to be associated with the Hebrew verb שָׂטַן, "to resist, oppose." Zechariah's statement וְהַשָּׂטָן עֹמֵד עַל־יְמִינוֹ לְשִׂטְנוֹ ("and Satan standing at his right side to accuse him," Zech. 3:1) seems to connect the "title" to Satan's adversarial activity.

[13]See Zechariah 3:1-2; Job 1:6—2:7; 1 Chronicles 21:1.

[14]Gordon observed, "Satan is not a name. In Hebrew it's . . . 'The Satan.' Now, you can put an article before a common noun. You can say 'the king,' 'the president,' 'the devil'; but you can't say 'the William,' 'the Mary,' 'the Joe.' You don't use articles before proper names. Accordingly, *has-satan* is not his name, but it is an epithet with a definite article in order to avoid his terrible name" (Cyrus H. Gordon, "Egypt and Mediterranean Civilization," paper presented at the Exodus Symposium, Memphis, 1987 [Mimeographed] 6–7). Compare Gordon, "Notes on Proper Names in the Ebla Tablets," in *Eblaite Personal Names and Semitic Name-Giving*, ed. Alfonso Archi (Missione Archeologica Italiana in Siria, 1988), 156.

[15]New Testament terms include ὁ δράκον ὁ μέγας (the great dragon), ὁ ὄφις ὁ ἀρχαῖος (the old serpent), ὁ καλούμενος Διάβολος (the one called the devil—from διαβάλλω, "to slander, accuse"), and ὁ Σατανᾶς (Satan = Hebrew הַשָּׂטָן), Revelation 12:9.

[16]Hebrew חֲבִי, Gordon, "Egypt," 4–6.

[17]Isaiah 26:20 and Habakkuk 3:4. Gordon construes חֶבְיוֹן in Habakkuk to be חֲבִי written with the suffix "on" (וֹן) instead of "hiding place" (BDB, 285) and reads קַרְנַיִם as (pair of) "horns." The association of חֶבְיוֹן with a "demon" described in a Ugaritic tablet as having "a pair of horns and a tail" is challenged by the context in Habakkuk. If קַרְנַיִם does mean "horns," then they are described as emanating "from his hand for him" (מִיָּדוֹ לוֹ).

[18]For a good discussion of the serpent's role in the Eden encounter, see Edward J. Young, *Genesis 3* (Carlisle, PA: The Banner of Truth Trust, 1983), 7–24. For additional perspectives, compare Gerhard von Rad, *Genesis: A Commentary*, rev. ed. (Philadelphia: The Westminster Press, 1972), 87–93 and Victor P. Hamilton, *The Book of Genesis: Chapters 1–17*, in *The New International Commentary on the Old Testament*, ed. R. K. Harrison (Grand Rapids: William B. Eerdmans Publishing Company, 1990), 187–91.

[19]The plural form עֲרוּמִּים occurs in Genesis 2:25, while עֵירֻמִּם appears in Genesis 3:7. In the plural, as Cassuto noted, only a *dagesh* in the *mem* distinguishes "naked" (עֲרוּמִּים) from "crafty" (עֲרוּמִים—Proverbs 14:17); see U. Cassuto, *A Commentary on the Book of Genesis* (Jerusalem: The Magnes Press, 1978), part 1, 143–44.

[20]BDB lists עֵירֹם and עָרוֹם as derived from עוּר "be exposed" (735–36), with עָרוּם connected to the verb עָרַם "be shrewd" (791). An unused root ערם is cited with a reference to an Arabic root *'rm* "strip" (790). The verb עָרָה "be naked" and its derived forms are also listed (788–89). Arabic has a similar dual meaning track but features a singular consonant structure. Is it possible that these multiple forms have a common ancestry? See Roland B. Allen, "עָרֹם," *TWOT*, 2:697–98. Also, compare Hamilton, *Genesis*, 187.

[21]If the identification of Eden's tempter with the "anointed cherub" on "the holy mount of God" (Ezek. 28:14) is correct, mankind's adversary was "created blameless" until "wickedness was found" in him (Ezek. 28:15). Sadly, the calamity in the garden reveals the magnitude of the corrupted cherub's wickedness.

[22]The verb construction לֹא־מוֹת תְּמֻתוּן (an infinitive absolute followed by a finite form of the verb) is vividly emphatic.

[23]For a full discussion of the issue, see Edward J. Young, *In the Beginning* (Carlisle, PA: The Banner of Truth Trust, 1976), 80–87.

[24]Accounts, usually legendary in nature, that explain the origin of something.

[25]Dietrich Bonhoeffer, *Creation and Fall* (New York: Macmillan Publishing Company, 1959), 65.

[26]See Proverbs 23:7 in KJV.

[27]John Milton, *Paradise Lost*, book 1, line 263, *Paradise Lost and Other Poems*, ed. Maurice Kelley (Roslyn: Walter J. Black, 1943), 100.

[28]For example, Cassuto, *Genesis*, part 1, 142. Compare Allen P. Ross, *Creation and Blessing* (Grand Rapids: Baker Book House, 1988), 130.

[29]Pandora, the first woman on earth according to Greek mythology, could not resist the temptation to open a box entrusted to her by the "gods." All of the world's calamities flew out. The fanciful legend may reflect an extrabiblical modification of the Genesis account.

[30]The Hebrew word in verse 10 is (וָ)אִירָא.

[31]The verb ἀπαλλοτριόω suggests alienation in terms of "belonging to another" (see Eph. 2:12).

[32]Hebrew, עֶצֶב. Both עִצָּבוֹן (Gen. 3:17, with suffix עִצְּבוֹנֵךְ in 3:16) and עֶצֶב come from this root. Even God has such pain (Gen. 6:6). In context, the pain of Genesis 3 is the physical pain of birth with an overtone of hard labor (compare Gen. 5:29; Ps. 127:2; Prov. 5:10; 14:23) and the emotional trauma of parenthood.

[33]See Allen, "עָצַב," *TWOT*, 2:687.

3

Salvation Statement

*At that time men began to call
on the name of the LORD.*

Genesis 4:26

Of all the issues associated with the Book of Genesis—
date, authorship, sources, composition, transmission—none
is more pertinent to this book than the question of purpose
or intent. As G. Henton Davies noted, the answer is not necessarily obvious.

> What was the purpose in writing? What led the writer to his
> task? Such a purpose is not stated in the book of Genesis as
> it is, for example, in the first paragraph of the book of Acts.
> The name Genesis, "beginning," serves mainly to identify
> the book, though it secondarily states its purpose. Thus the
> content and the scope of the book must serve to reveal the
> author's purpose.[1]

As noted previously, extreme caution must be exercised
in the attempt to discern the intent of another, whatever
the circumstance. Still, if we are even to approximate the
purpose of Genesis, as Davies observed, we must do so on
the basis of the Genesis text itself. At this point an analysis of the compositional structure of the entire book becomes a significant factor.

While perceptions about the organizational design of
Genesis vary,[2] many students of the text have marked the
significant use of the expression "generations of . . . "[3] as a
clue to the overall composition of the book. In his discussion of the use of the Hebrew term *tōlĕdōt* that stands

behind "generation" (NIV—"account"), Paul R. Gilchrist commented:

> As used in the OT, *tôlēdôt* [sic] refers to what is produced or brought into being by someone, or follows therefrom. In no case in Gen. does the word include the birth of the individual whose *tôlēdôt* it introduces (except in Gen. 25:19, where the story of Isaac's life is introduced by reference to the fact that he was the son of Abraham). After the conclusion of the account in which Jacob was the principal actor, Gen. 37:2 says, "These are the *tôlēdôt* of Jacob" and proceeds to tell about his children and the events with which they were connected.
>
> In line with these usages it is reasonable to interpret Gen. 2:4, "These are the *tôlēdôt* of heaven and earth," as meaning, not the coming of heaven and earth into existence, but the events that followed the establishment of heaven and earth. Thus the verse is correctly placed as introducing the detailed account of the creation and fall of man. It is not a summary of the events preceding Gen. 2:4.[4]

I concur with the foregoing evaluation; *tōlĕdōt* is used as the introduction to a compositional unit rather than as a conclusion. However, I do contest the comment by Gilchrist, "The often repeated statement that the book of Gen. is divided into natural sections by the word *tôlēdôt* does not work out on close examination. Sometimes, as in Gen. 36:9, it merely introduces a genealogical table."[5] Whether *tōlĕdōt* serves as a heading or conclusion, it unquestionably functions as a critical item in the total structure of the book. As the term itself suggests, it reports genealogical data in every case.

The issue, then, is not the fact of genealogical data but the disparity of content or amount of genealogical material contained in the *tōlĕdōt* sections. As Watts's outline confirms, the amount of information reported by the *tōlĕdōt* headings varies radically and reflects a structural analysis of the book that lacks symmetry and balance.

The lack of proportion is obvious, but the real question is, "Why is there such imbalance among these segments?"[7] Is it possible that the underlying purpose of the Genesis account may be observed in and through its asymmetric organization? If the writer(s) and/or editor(s) of the book intended to provide a comprehensive report of creation and the total sweep of early human history, then either *tōlĕdōt* should not be construed as a key to the organization of Genesis, or significant amounts of historical data have been omitted. Is it conceivable that selected historical data were omitted deliberately? If so, upon what basis?

I am convinced that Watts correctly perceived the economy of the *tōlĕdōt* formula:

> The story of early generations then proceeds to picture the ways by which Yahweh God assures fulfillment of his purpose for mankind. The first division, which deals with the generations of the heavens and the earth, shows bad results. The development of all other kinds of creation had been good; but man used his free moral agency to choose the fruit of the tree of the knowledge of good and evil, and sin and death followed. However, the danger of sin and death led some men to call upon the name of Yahweh, and they were assured of salvation. From there on the development of Yahweh worship was the heart of all the stories.[8]

The writer of Genesis, then, was not attempting to provide a comprehensive account of antiquity. Rather, he was evidently tracing a redemptive thread through the intricate fabric of early human history to demonstrate the origin and preservation of the worship of YHWH. In short, the Genesis account is primarily a history of salvation.[9] The "branches" of the early "family tree" which did not contribute to the development of that design were treated summarily and dropped. For example, because they were not essential to the "main plot," the genealogies of Ishmael and Esau were recorded in abbreviated, if not abrupt, fashion and then dismissed (Gen. 25:12-18; 36:1-43). Accordingly, Gilchrist noted correctly that "Gen. 36:9 . . . merely introduces a genealogical table."[10]

The brevity of some *tōlĕdōt* segments, however, does not disqualify the term as a major divisional heading. Instead, it provides a clue to the design of the total composition. So

Watts concluded, "Evidently, the purpose of the book is to tell the story of early generations so as to reveal the salvation provided by Yahweh worship."[11]

This salvation economy prevails throughout the entire Old Testament. Just as the redemptive focus centered on some individuals and families while slighting or ignoring others in the Book of Genesis, the same orientation is indicated later in the Old Testament by the fact that ultimately just the history of the tribes of Israel is reported. The affairs and destinies of other nations are mentioned only to the extent that they impinge on the history of Israel. This is not because other nations were unimportant; but the primary purpose of the Old Testament narrative was, and is, to record the unfolding redemptive acts of God in history. In brief, then, from the very beginning the Old Testament is essentially devoted to the message of YHWH's salvation.

If this be true, one would certainly expect to find in the early chapters of Genesis some word, or at least some hint, about the salvation pattern. Such an expectation is rewarded!

Divine Initiative

While the data are meager and the account is brief, certain details in chapters 3—4 are noteworthy. Notice, for example, that YHWH "was walking in the garden" after the fatal act of human sin.[12] Since the first couple was attempting to hide from the divine presence, God's movement about the garden was not in response to human request or even desire. YHWH's search for and confrontation with His first created people resulted from divine initiative. The consequences of YHWH's encounter with the serpent and Adam and Eve must be evaluated in the light of that fact.

In chapter 4, even before the violent act of fratricide, YHWH attempted to persuade Cain to abandon his murderous plot (Gen. 4:6-7). God thus demonstrated His personal concern in the human sin problem. Before and after the fact, YHWH involved Himself, on His own initiative, in the monumental effort to salvage people from the ruin and chaos of sin. To be balanced and biblical, every perception of the nature of salvation in the Old and New Testament must hinge on this truth.

"First Expression of Redemptive Hope"

As Driver noted, Genesis 3:15 "has been known for long as the *Protevangelium*"[13] or "first gospel." Some interpreters have used this label because of the belief that "it is the first promise in the Bible that a Savior would come to defeat Satan on behalf of man."[14] However, this understanding of the verse is far from unanimous.

Interpretative Opinion. Some have advised a cautious and qualifying position concerning the evangelical content of this verse. Driver himself warned:

> . . . we must not read into the words more than they contain. No *victory* of the woman's seed is promised, but only a perpetual *antagonism*, in which each side, using the weapons which it is natural to it to employ, will seek to obtain the mastery of the other. Only from the general drift and tenor of the passage can it be inferred that the conflict is one in which the "seed of woman" may hope ultimately to have the victory.[15]

Others have rejected gospel content altogether. John Skinner wrote:

> The general meaning of the sentence is clear: in the war between men and serpents the former will crush the head of the foe, while the latter can only wound in the heel. . . . A message of hope and encouragement in the midst of a series of curses and punishments is not to be assumed unless it be clearly implied in the language.[16]

Claus Westermann commented, "The traditional interpretation of the clause ' . . . it will crush your head and you will snap at its heel' as a protoevangelium is therefore impossible, if only because the 'seed' of the woman and the serpent can mean only the generations to come, not an individual (Mary or Jesus)."[17] Cuthbert A. Simpson likewise concluded, "Vs. 15, on the other hand, deals with a psychological characteristic, not only of the serpent but also of man—the ineradicable hostility between them."[18] Walter Russell Bowie's exposition follows Simpson's exegesis:

The serpent now is obviously the snake. In our world of physical experience there is nothing from which men have a more natural revulsion than from the snake. It is secret and stealthy. It strikes without warning and its bite has poison in it. Only a fool will walk carelessly where snakes lurk.[19]

But then, as if sensing the inadequacy of such a simplistic position, Bowie made the following application:

The evil that somehow is in our world cannot be whistled off. It shall bruise man's heel. A man cannot think he will escape the fact of sin by acting as if it were not there. It will strike at him and wound him. When it does wound him the effect must be dealt with drastically, as with the bite of a snake. There may be need of quick, sharp moral surgery to keep the poison of sin from spreading.[20]

Evangelical Character. Whatever the interpretation, one must acknowledge the cryptic, enigmatic content of Genesis 3:15. The circumstantial setting of the verse provides at least a clue to its meaning, however. Remember, the one speaking is YHWH, the Creator who initiated the confrontation with both the people and the serpent. Accordingly, it seems reasonable to assume that anything God said would be consistent with the disclosure of His benevolent nature that is revealed in the total context.

Moreover, the magnitude of the tragic human disaster must be noted. Already, heaven's design for the earthly drama had been shattered; the crowning glory of God's creative pattern had been defiled; human beings were lost, undone, alienated from God, dead in "trespasses and sins." In the light of the demonstrated charitable nature of God and the monstrous calamity of the fall, it hardly seems credible that the Creator would only speak of antipathy toward snakes. Surely something more significant and pertinent than that must be couched in the esoteric language of this text.

I concur, therefore, with those who find a veiled, vague, but unmistakable gospel element in the verse. The divine statement seems to predict a continuing struggle between humanity and satanic influence until another encounter occurs involving "the seed of the serpent" and "the seed of woman." In that confrontation, the "serpent" would "strike" the heel of another representative[21] of mankind; but the "last Adam"[22] would "crush"[23] his head. The imagery of the statement remarkably anticipated the results of Messiah's encounter with Satan.

While a blow to the heel may be painful, it is not normally fatal. An injury to the head, however, may be quite lethal. So when Satan mounted his assault on "the seed of woman," he did inflict intense punishment and pain. He was successful in having the body of the Christ nailed to a Roman cross, drained of blood, and placed in a dark, silent tomb. No doubt, as the shadows of twilight deepened around the sepulchre of Jesus the night of His death, Satan celebrated his fabulous victory. After all, God had made an irreversible blunder by limiting Himself to human flesh, and now He was dead!

Satan had indeed "bruised" the heel of "the seed of woman," but despite the fact that he had done his most "damnable" best, the injury was not fatal after all. The dungeon of death and decay could not permanently imprison the Lord of life and glory. On the first day of the week, angels at the empty tomb reported to His astonished disciples, "He is not here; he has risen!" (Luke 24:6).

The affirmation "he will crush your head" corresponds to the suffering and death of our Lord. Not only did His death atone for human sin, but it also sounded the death knell of the archvillain. In effect, even as He died Jesus hammered the wooden stake of His cross through the heart of hell's fiendish Dracula. To be sure, "the ancient serpent" (Rev. 12:9) continues to thrash about, inflicting destruction and grief; but Satan's tormented frenzy is only the havoc of his death throes. His defeat and doom were forever sealed at the cross.

The wretched couple in Eden could scarcely have understood all of that. Still, YHWH's verdict of ultimate doom to the serpent must surely have stirred hope in the human heart for the first time. Regardless of their awareness or lack thereof, His pronouncement opened the prospect of deliverance from satanic control and domination. That reflects the very essence of salvation. Stripped of all the superficial peripherals—ceremonies, organizations, human piety—salvation is deliverance from the tyranny of sin and Satan. God uttered the very first word of that marvelous deliverance amidst the smoldering ashes of human despair in the Garden of Eden.[24]

Redemptive Illustration

The early Genesis record contains another, more precise salvation notice. "Seth also had a son, and he named him Enosh. At that time men began to call on the name of the LORD" (Gen. 4:26). In this instance, the soteriological message is embedded in an unusual blend of circumstances and names. Although translation does not totally obscure its point, the Hebrew text is a bit more revealing.

Circumstantial Setting. A full record of history's first family is obviously missing, and the exact sequence of events is not necessarily observed. In any event, the birth of the second grandson (Gen. 4:26)[25] occurred "at that time." An understanding of the disturbing nature of "that time" is crucial if one is to appreciate the significance of the final statement of the initial *tōlĕdōt* unit, "Generations of the Heavens and the Earth."

The first report of death in human experience is the account of Cain's deliberate, calculated murder of his brother Abel.[26] No doubt this initial exposure to the morbid trappings of death—violence, blood, a cold gray corpse, rigor mortis, permanent stillness and silence—made a chilling impression on the entire first family. So it was true after all! "For when you eat of it. . . . " As the mute, lifeless body of Abel revealed the ominous truth that people could and would die, perhaps his survivors reflected on the prospect that they, too, would ultimately share the fate of their fallen son and brother. What a dreadful thought! Just maybe—such a monstrous thing might never occur again.

The seed of Cain demonstrated the expanding magnitude of the sin-death syndrome. In time, the arrogant, polygamous Lamech would appeal to the example of his ancestor Cain to justify his own penchant for violence. This man would boast openly of his murderous exploits, without any trace of remorse or evidence of a sense of guilt.[27] Lamech's taking of life, however, did more than mark him as a calloused assassin. It clearly indicated that death was an inevitable—indeed, inescapable—part of life. "At that time. . . . "

Meaning of "Enosh." Though extremely brief in nature, the report of the line of Cain provides striking information about the earliest "accomplishments of civilization,"[28] such as the development of musical skills and metallurgy. The so-called "Sword Song"[29] of Lamech, as U. Cassuto noted, "shows that material progress did not go hand in hand with moral advancement."[30] To the contrary, "The readiness to shed blood, which had been first manifested by Cain, appears in an intensified form in Lamech."[31]

Now, notice two curious items about the context. First, although strict or "tight" sequence in chronology cannot be demanded, the likely temporal disparity between the time of Lamech and that of Enosh must not be overlooked. Lamech was a fifth-generation descendant of Cain, while Enosh was the grandson of Adam (third generation).[32] Especially in the light of the social and cultural developments reported in the Cain *tōlĕdōt*, a considerable lapse of time from the birth of Enoch (to Cain) and the birth of Lamech may be assumed. If this assumption is only generally accurate, Enosh was likely born before the time of Lamech; and the events reported in verses 25-26 are out of chronological order.

The juxtaposition of the Lamech episode and the period when people began to invoke the divine name then suggests a rhetorical rationale. The writer was not trying to report the sequence of events; rather, he was directing the reader's attention to the nature of "that time." It was the first season of the proliferation of death.

Second, an unmistakable play on words (*paronomasia*) is evident in verse 26 in connection with the selection and use of names. In the Hebrew text, the proper name Seth (*šēt*, שֵׁת), which was chosen by Eve (for the son that would "replace" the slain Abel), is derived from the verb (*šāt*, שָׁת) translated "granted."[33] The relationship between the two terms could be reflected in the legitimate translation: "she . . . named him Grant, saying, 'God has granted me another child in place of Abel.'" This deliberate word play on the name Seth would suggest that some significance might be associated with the name Enosh as well.

The suggestion is reinforced by the fact that the word *'ĕnoš* is another term for *man* when it is not a proper noun.[34] The verb that stands behind this common noun occurs some ten times in the Hebrew Old Testament. In nine instances it is a passive participle modifying words such as "wound," "sickness," and "pain."[35] The form is generally translated as "incurable." It is used as a finite verb only once, describing the fatal illness of the infant born to David and Bathsheba.[36] Reflecting circumstances and conditions that terminate in death, the core idea of the verbal root seems to designate the idea of weakness and mortality. Accordingly, '*ĕnoš* is a term for man or humanity that denotes frailty and means "man" in the sense of "mortal" (Pss. 9:20; 103:15; Job 25:4). What a bizarre name for a baby—Enosh—"Mortal"—"The Dying One!"

The circumstantial setting with its expanding exposure to death, however, suggests a basis for the selection of the name Enosh. By this time a gradual and deepening realization must have convinced earth's inhabitants that all mankind was subject to the terminal restriction of death. Even a newborn baby boy was under the fatal curse. Despite the vigor and freshness of infancy, the son of "Grant," like all the rest of his kind, was on his way from the cradle to the grave. So, in evident acknowledgment of everyone's fragile mortality, they named a chubby bundle of vitality Enosh, "The Dying One." "At that time. . . . "

Analysis of the Tetragrammaton. The final word in the first *tōlĕdōt* unit of Genesis is the personal name of the God of creation, YHWH.[37] The background of the passage and play on names in the text strongly suggest that some strategic importance may be attached to the use of the divine name in this situation. This possibility then leads readers of the Bible to a careful examination of the formation and possible meaning of the name YHWH.

As Raymond Abba has observed, "The origin of the name has been the subject of much controversy, and there is as yet no general agreement among OT scholars."[38] The great antiquity of the name, however, seems to be evident:

> There are many indications that the name Yahweh is extremely ancient, although it received a new significance in the exodus period. Its form is archaic, retaining the *v* which was later replaced by a *y* in the verb *hyh* with which the name is connected—a change that took place long before the time of Moses. . . . The tetragrammaton appears in old Semitic script in the ninth-century inscription of Mesha, King of Moab (line 18) and would seem to be the original form of the divine name.[39]

Rejecting Obermann's thesis that the divine name might be a causative participle formed with a *y* rather than an *m* preformative,[40] Barry J. Beitzel summarized several interpretative theories of meaning:

> Actually, the only common denominator among those who endorse this view is that the tetragrammaton springs from the root H W Y. Goitein argues that the root signifies "the Passionate One," whereas Schorr and Bowman aver that the root reflects the meaning "to speak" (cognate to Akkadian *awātu*), hence Yahweh was the "Speaker, Revealer," an epithet particularly eloquent in the Mosaic period. Murtonen, who accepts this reasoning, regards the divine name as a kind of *nomen agentis* with a *y* prefix, meaning "Commander." Klostermann recognized in the same root a negative connotation, declaring that Yahweh means "the Faller," in the sense of one who crashes down or falls from heaven, as a meteor.
>
> But the prominent position has been to associate the tetragrammaton with *hāyāh* (necessarily related to a hypothetical antique verb H W Y), and to suggest the meaning "He Who is the Existing One," "the Absolute, Eternally-Existing One," the One Who is with His people."[41]

Rejecting the "prominent position," Beitzel further insisted:

> What is more, it must be pointed out that a root H W Y is inextant in all west Semitic languages which antedate the Mosaic era. That is to say, Phoenician contains no root H W Y; Ugaritic, despite its attestation of a divine name *yw*, bears no witness to this verbal root; and Amorite Akkadian evidences no root H W Y. The root H W Y is attested only in Aramaic, Syriac, Nabataean and Palmyrian.[42]

That *H W Y* is "inextant" in early west Semitic does not necessarily mean that the root did not occur. It only means that latter-day scholars have not found examples of its occurrence. K. H. Bernhardt commented, "Historically, there may be a relationship with Akk. *ewû*."[43] Although that connection does not constitute a pre-Mosaic west Semitic attestation, it does suggest the antiquity of the root. Moreover, the verb occurs five times in the Hebrew Old Testament.[44]

More recently, Walter J. Kaiser, Jr. summarized the various theories about the form and meaning of the tetragrammaton:

> On the etymology and meaning of the name Yahweh, there is almost no agreement. The bibliography in the last century

alone would fill a whole book, and there seems to be no end in sight. There are several schools of opinion.

1. The name Yahweh has an Egyptian etymology coming from two Egyptian words, *Yah* ("moon") and *we3* ("one"). This view, however, is now totally rejected. . . . A more tenable Egyptian parallel is *p3 nty wn.w.f* ("The one who is who he is"; cf. Cyrus H. Gordon, "He Is Who He Is," *Berytus* 23 [1974]: 27-28).

2. It has no Arabic etymology from *Ya-huwa* ("O He"), a dervish cry. . . .

3. It is a Northwest Semitic root of *hwy* ("to be") in such names as *Yawi-ila*. De Vaux ("Proclamation and Presence"), however, points out that the common root meaning "to be" in Amorite and Ugaritic is *kwn*.

4. It is a Hebrew verbal root from *hāwāy* ("to fall") and thus has the substantive meaning "destruction"; hence Yahweh is the god of storms and thunder. But Exodus does not appeal to this verb. Furthermore, it is only used once in the OT (Job 37:6).

5. Yahweh derives from the Hebrew pronoun *hû'* ("he"), as in Isa. 43:10: "I am he," and Ps. 102:27 (MT28). . . .

6. It is a causative Hebrew verbal root of a *yaqtil/yiqtol* type meaning "he causes to be" or "he is the Creator," but this solution requires a correction in the explanation given in 3:14 in addition to having some philological problems such as distinguishing between the basic and causative forms of verbs with a weak third radical.[45]

While opinions vary as to the components and composition of the name, William F. Albright concluded that it is fashioned from an imperfect form of the Hebrew verb "to be." He adds: "Linguistically the form *yahweh* can only be causative, and to judge from many analogies in Babylonia, Egypt, and Canaan, it is an abbreviation of a longer name or litanic formula."[46] On the basis of that linguistic identification, Albright insisted that although "many different meanings have been attributed to *Yahweh* by scholars who recognized its relative antiquity . . . only one yields any suitable sense: 'He causes to be.' "[47] Albeit reluctantly, Beitzel conceded that Albright's interpretation has represented the "prominent position." Kaiser, on the other hand, proposed, "The most likely etymology and meaning for the name Yahweh is that it is the imperfect form of the root *hwh/hyh*, meaning "he is/will be."[48]

The verbal form of the divine name may also communicate the notion of continuation, with or without a causative force. Bruce K. Waltke and M. O'Connor labeled this function of the imperfect as "customary *non-perfective*" and described it as "marking a verb as designating a repeated action" (i.e., "iterative").[49] Abba correctly noted that element in the tetragrammaton. "Implicit in the divine covenant name is the sense of continuing. The imperfect tense expresses continuity—the eternal constancy of the covenant God."[50]

Actually, the verbal form of the name YHWH may encompass both causative and iterative (frequentative) aspects of *hyh*. Albright's suggested meaning, then, might be expanded to "He ever (always) causes to be (exist)." If the form is not construed as causative, then Kaiser's meaning could be modified to "He (always) is" or "He (ever) will be." Either way, the personal name of the Creator God would suggest that He is the ultimate source of all being, the origin of all existence.

How appropriate, therefore, that people should begin to call on that incomparable, matchless Name "at that time." When people began to understand that they were all under the sentence of death, they turned to their one Source of help, the Fountainhead of all existence—the Author of Life—and called upon Him.

While the expression "call upon the name of the LORD" may mean only the invocation of His name in ritual or ceremony (Gen. 21:33), it obviously means much more than that at the end of "The Generations of the Heavens and the Earth." Indeed, it surely communicates more than the stark fact of the beginning of YHWH worship.[51] It is the first indication of an appeal to the life-giving Name for deliverance from the inexorable curse of death. In the light of the total circumstance of situation and terminology, the original fundamental parameters of divine deliverance in the Old Testament are established.

In other words, this is the first clear-cut statement of salvation in Scripture. What a classic, timeless formula! When people of any age or generation realize that they are "dead in trespasses and sins" and turn to the Source of Life and call upon Him, they are delivered from death and decay. That is the essence of the message of salvation.

Notes

[1]G. Henton Davies, "Genesis," vol. 1, *The Broadman Bible Commentary* (Nashville: Broadman Press, 1969), 102.

[2]For example, compare William Sanford LaSor, David Allan Hubbard, and Frederic William Bush, *Old Testament Survey* (Grand Rapids: William B. Eerdmans Publishing Company, 1983), 69; John J. Davis, *Paradise to Prison: Studies in Genesis* (Grand Rapids: Baker Book House, 1975), 33-36; Claus Westermann, *Genesis*, trans. David E. Green (Grand Rapids: William B. Eerdmans Publishing Company, 1987), 3-4, 93-94, 180, 258-59; and Davies, "Genesis," 119-21.

[3]The NIV has "account" for the Hebrew term תּוֹלְדוֹת. Harrison, in a list of "The Eleven Tablets," has suggested "origins" for the first two "tablets" and "histories" for the remainder. See R. K. Harrison, *Introduction to the Old Testament* (Grand Rapids: William B. Eerdmans Publishing Company, reprint ed. 1982), 548. תּוֹלְדוֹת, derived from יָלַד ("to bear"), literally means "things brought forth." BDB offers "generations" as a translation (410).

[4]Paul R. Gilchrist, "יָלַד," *TWOT*, 1:380. Harrison's theory that the term functions as a "colophon" and constitutes "part of the concluding sentence of each section, thereby pointing back to a narrative already recorded" hardly fits. Note that he has two "editions" of "the histories of Esau" but has no identifying label at all for the last fourteen chapters of the book (a substantial amount of material), *Introduction*, 547-48.

[5]Gilchrist, *TWOT*, 1:380.

[6]Watts, *Teaching*, 3.

[7]An imbalance that intensifies. Compare the size of the report about Esau with the *tōlĕdōt* of Isaac and Jacob.

[8]Watts, *Teaching*, 2-3.

[9]This phrase does not necessarily postulate a *Heilsgeschichte* in which reported events have been "historicised" or "actualised." Compare Gerhard von Rad, *Old Testament Theology*, vol. 2, trans. D. M. G. Stalker (Edinburgh: Oliver and Boyd, reprint 1973), 99-112.

[10]Gilchrist, *TWOT*, 1:380.

[11]Watts, *Teaching*, 3.

[12]Genesis 3:8. The verb מִתְהַלֵּךְ, a *Hitpa'el* participle, suggests "walking to and fro"; see BDB, 235.

[13]S. R. Driver, *The Book of Genesis*, 5th ed. (London: Methuen, 1906), 48.

[14]Leon J. Wood, *Genesis* (Grand Rapids: Zondervan Publishing House, 1975), 35.

[15]Driver, *Genesis*, 48.

[16]John Skinner, *The International Critical Commentary: Genesis* (Edinburgh: T & T Clark, 1976), 80-81.

[17]Claus Westermann, *Genesis: A Practical Commentary*, trans. David E. Green (Grand Rapids: William B. Eerdmans Publishing Co., 1987), 25.

[18]Cuthbert A. Simpson, "Genesis: Introduction and Exegesis," *The Interpreter's Bible*, vol. 1 (Nashville: Abingdon Press, 1982), 508.

[19]Walter Russell Bowie, "Genesis: Exposition," *The Interpreter's Bible*, vol. 1 (Nashville: Abingdon Press, 1982), 508.

[20]Bowie, "Genesis," 508-509.

[21]The word זֶרַע (seed) is a collective noun, and, as in English, may be construed as either singular or plural.

[22]Compare Romans 5:14 and 1 Corinthians 15:45. Milton S. Terry commented that "Adam was a type of Christ because of his representative character as the first man, and federal head of the race (Rom. v, 14)." See Milton S. Terry, *Biblical Hermeneutics*, 9th ed. (Grand Rapids: Zondervan Publishing House, 1974), 338.

[23]"Crush" and "strike" represent יְשׁוּפְךָ and תְּשׁוּפֶנּוּ. Both are from the root שׁוּף ("bruise"); see BDB, 1003. Cassuto's attempt to associate שׁוּף with שָׁאַף seems artificial and strained (Cassuto, *Genesis*, 161).

[24]For a good discussion, see Edward J. Young, *Genesis 3* (Carlisle, PA: The Banner of Truth Trust, 1966), 102-11. Compare Walter Brueggemann, "Genesis," in *Interpretation: A Bible Commentary for Teaching and Preaching*, ed. James Luther Mays (Atlanta: John Knox Press, 1982), 40-54.

[25]Note the birth of Irad to Enoch in Genesis 4:18.

[26]The terse statement "Cain talked with Abel" (Gen. 4:8, KJV) reveals the element of premeditation. Cain must be charged with "murder one."

[27]See Genesis 4:19-24.

[28]Westermann, *Genesis*, 37.

[29]See Genesis 4:23-24.

[30]U. Cassuto, *A Commentary on the Book of Genesis*, trans. Israel Abrahams (Jerusalem: The Magnes Press, reprint ed., 1978), part I, 244.

[31]Driver, *Genesis*, 71.

[32]Lamech would have been in the sixth generation from Adam.

[33]In the Hebrew, the name is שֵׁת and the verb form is שָׁת.

[34]Compare Thomas E. McComiskey, "אנשׁ," *TWOT*, 1:59 and Fritz Maass, "אֱנוֹשׁ," *TDOT*, 1:345–48. Curiously, Gordon J. Wenham noted that אֱנוֹשׁ often "suggests man's weakness, mortality and distance from God," but then concluded that "it is hard to distinguish any semantic difference between אדם and אנושׁ." See Gordon J. Wenham, *Genesis 1–15*, in vol. 1 of *Word Biblical Commentary*, ed. David A. Hubbard, Glenn W. Barker, John D. W. Watts, Ralph P. Martin (Waco, TX: Word Books, Publisher, 1987), 115.

[35]Job 34:6; Psalm 69:20; Jeremiah 15:18; 17:9,16; 30:12,15; Isaiah 17:11; Micah 1:9. In Jeremiah 17:16, it modifies "day," and NIV has "the day of despair." The participle modifies "heart" in Psalm 69:20 and is translated "helpless" (NIV).

[36]See 2 Samuel 12:15. In the KJV the baby is described as "very sick."

[37]Also called the tetragrammaton (see chapter 1 of this book).

[38]Raymond Abba, "The Divine Name Yahweh," *Journal of Biblical Literature* 80 (December 1961): 320.

[39]Abba, "Yahweh," 322.

[40]See Julian Obermann, "The Divine Name Yahweh in the Light of Recent Discoveries," *Journal of Biblical Literature* 68 (1949): 301-23.

Salvation Statement

[41]Barry J. Beitzel, "Exodus 3:14 and the Divine Name: A Case for Biblical Paronomasia," *Trinity Journal* ns (1980): 14-15. Durham suggested "The One Who Always Is" for the meaning of Yahweh. See John I. Durham, *Exodus*, in vol. 3 of *Word Biblical Commentary*, ed. David A. Hubbard and Glenn W. Barker (Waco, TX: Word Books, Publisher, 1987), 453.

[42]Beitzel, "Exodus 3:14," 16-17. Despite his insistence that "it would be virtually unparalleled for a bare verbal form to exist as a divine name" ("Exodus 3:14," 16), in a footnote, Beitzel acknowledged that he had found "one such divine name." The infrequency of a bare verbal form providing the structure for a divine name, however, hardly cancels the possibility that the singular God of creation might possess a unique and distinctive name.

[43]K. H. Bernhardt, "הָיָה," *TDOT*, 3:369.

[44]Consult KB, "II הוה," 1:232. Bernhardt suggests these instances are "aramaizing *hwh*" in light of the verb's seventy-one occurrences in the Aramaic portion of the Old Testament. See Bernhardt, *TDOT*, 3:371.

[45]Walter C. Kaiser, Jr., *Exodus*, in *The Expositor's Bible Commentary*, vol. 2, ed. Frank E. Gaebelein (Grand Rapids: Zondervan Publishing House, 1990), 323.

[46]William Foxwell Albright, *From The Stone Age to Christianity*, 2nd ed. (Garden City: Doubleday/Anchor, 1957), 260.

[47]Albright, *Stone Age*, 259. Abba's rejection of Albright's proposal on the basis of the "tense" function of the imperfect and the exclusive meaning of "pure existence" of the verb "to be" is unconvincing. He is correct that there "is no known example of the verb *hyh* in the hiphil" ("The Divine Name Yahweh," 324-25), but the OT has no example of a *pi'el* causative either. The abbreviated form of יהוה (יָהּ), with an "a" class vowel, supports Albright's construction of the verbal stem. Walker, however, proposed that Yahweh is an expanded form of an older "Yāh" (derived from Egyptian), meaning "'Yāh-One,' *with tacit monotheistic implication*." See Norman Walker, "Yahwehism and the Divine Name 'Yhwh'," *Zeitschrift für alttestamentliche Wissenschaft* 70 (1958): 262-65. For a helpful discussion of the tetragrammaton's possible pronunciation, see George Wesley Buchanan, "Some Unfinished Business with the Dead Sea Scrolls," *Revue de Qumran* 13 (October 1988): 413-20. Buchanan's contention for the pronunciation "Yahowah" or "Yahuwah" does not alter the "a" class vowel under the imperfect preformative (י). In light of the *hiph'il* imperfect pattern of lamed-hey verbs (see יַרְבֶּה in Isa. 55:7), Buchanan's comment "The name 'Yahweh' does not even *sound* Semitic" seems strange. Compare A. R. Millard, "YW and *YHW* Names," *Vetus Testamentum* 30, fasc. 2 (April 1980): 208-12. See also Dennis Pardee, "An Evaluation of the Proper Names from Ebla from a West Semitic Perspective: Pantheon Distribution According to Genre," in *Eblaite Personal Names and Semitic Name-Giving*, ed. Alfonso Archi (Missione Archeologica Italiana in Siria, 1988), 119-51.

[48]Kaiser, *Exodus*, 324.

[49]Bruce K. Waltke and M. O'Connor, *An Introduction to Biblical Hebrew Syntax* (Winona Lake: Eisenbrauns, 1990), 348, 502. Watts described the phenomenon as a "frequentative imperfect"; see J. Wash Watts, *A Survey of Syntax in the Hebrew Old Testament* (Nashville: Broadman Press, 1951), 34-36.

[50]Abba, "Yahweh," 327.

[51]Wenham proposed, "With Delitzsch, König, and Westermann it seems wisest to regard this verse as simply noting the beginning of public worship, a conclusion that receives further support from the Sumerian flood story." See Wenham, *Genesis 1–15*, 116. But the evidence of the Genesis context is more significant than Sumerian parallels. For a discussion of the possible antiquity of the tetragrammaton, see E. A. Speiser, *Genesis*, vol. 1 of *The Anchor Bible*, 3rd ed., ed. William Foxwell Albright and David Noel Freedman (Garden City: Doubleday & Co., 1981), 37-38 and Victor P. Hamilton, *The Book of Genesis: Chapters 1–17*, in *The New International Commentary of the Old Testament*, ed. R. K. Harrison (Grand Rapids: William B. Eerdmans Publishing Company, 1990), 243.

EXCURSUS

The Nature and Function of "Covenant" in the Old Testament

The abundance of scholarly research and writing on the covenant concept in recent years has aptly illustrated the strategic importance of the subject in Old Testament studies.[1] David Noel Freedman noted the impact of this investigation:

> Of the central importance of the covenant theme in the Old Testament there can no longer be any doubt. . . .
> It can therefore be affirmed that the covenant principle is intrinsic to the biblical material and that it defines the relationship of God to his people. Further, the term "covenant" itself was consciously applied by the Israelites to their relationship with Yahweh, from the earliest times.[2]

Attention has focused on the striking parallels between covenant formulas in the Old Testament and similar documents from non-Hebrew cultures during the second millennium B.C.[3] Distinctions do exist between the strongly religious content of Israelite covenants and those of her surrounding neighbors.[4] However, the general covenant phenomena in the ancient Near East support the authenticity of the covenantal patterns recorded in the Pentateuch. Indeed, John H. Walton commented:

> The fact that the biblical covenants most closely resemble the Hittite treaty form certainly gives some credibility to the placement of the covenant documents in the second

millennium B.C. and gives some good arguments against the composition of those documents in the mid-first millennium.[5]

Probably related to the Akkadian term *birtu* ("clasp," "fetter"),[6] the Hebrew word for "covenant" (*běrît*, בְּרִית) designates a commitment or promise that is confirmed by an oath.[7] Accordingly, *covenant* in the Old Testament denotes a pledge or agreement of binding obligation. The use of covenant in association with the message of salvation requires a careful analysis of the covenant-salvation connection. First, a brief survey of the overall use of covenant in the Old Testament is in order.

Function

Within the historical framework of the Old Testament, covenants were invoked to ratify agreements at more than one level. For example, covenants were instituted to formalize alliances between groups or states (1 Kings 5:12). Moreover, a covenant was employed to regulate the relationship between a ruler and his subjects (2 Sam. 5:3). In addition, a covenant might even modify the association of individuals.

Like the boisterous camaraderie between athletes or the desperate bond between warriors who share danger, the brotherly affection between David and Jonathan was a friendship as strong as blood ties. However, Jonathan evidently felt that even that relationship needed the stronger confirmation of covenant status. He requested and received a covenant commitment from David (1 Sam. 20:11-17). It was on the basis of that pledge that David later extended generosity to Jonathan's lame son, Mephibosheth. David's offer of reinstatement of Jonathan's heir was not made because of personal esteem or even lingering affection for the deceased Jonathan. Rather, his magnanimous gesture was based on a sense of obligation to a covenant pledge (2 Sam. 9:1-8).[8]

Still at the individual or personal level, a covenant also applied to the solemn vows of marriage. The pledge of love and fidelity by bride and groom were to be understood as sacred covenant commitments and honored faithfully. Violation of such obligation, therefore, was condemned as "breaking faith" (*bāgadtāh*, בָּגְדְתָּה) with the spouse of your (marriage) covenant (Mal. 2:14-16).

Then, uniquely, the covenant concept was utilized to establish a specific connection between God and people. With all the striking parallels in form and content between the covenants of Israel and those of her neighbors in the ancient Near East, the association of the Hebrew tribes to deity by means of a covenant connection is remarkably distinct. Freedman observed:

> So far as I am aware, the biblical series of covenants between God and man is unique. There are no convincing parallels in the pagan world, whether in the more typical case of God as suzerain binding Israel to serve him or in the more unusual position of God binding himself by oath to the service of his own servants.[9]

In the light of this peculiar arrangement, it is not surprising that the covenant concept has a significant economy in the salvation offered to Israel by her "covenant God."

Application

The multiple translations of *bĕrīt* indicate the term's range of function and latitude in meaning. When *bĕrīt* designated an international alliance between independent states, it actually served as a treaty (1 Kings 5:12). When instituted between a ruler and his subjects, *bĕrīt* might be construed as an official edict or ordinance. The *bĕrīt* which David negotiated with the Hebrew elders when he finally became king over all Israel (2 Sam. 5:3) was likely a mutual agreement. NIV's translation, "compact," is a happy choice.[10] When used at the individual level, *bĕrīt* designated what might best be described as a personal agreement or pledge.[11]

Terminology

An interesting feature in the phenomenon of covenant is the assortment of verbs related to *bĕrīt*. They include *śīm* (שִׂים, "place"), *nātan* (נָתַן, "give"), and *hēqīm* (הֵקִים, "establish") for the inauguration of a covenant and *šāmar*

(שָׁמַר, "keep"), *nāṣar* (נָצַר, "guard"), or *'āzab* (עָזַב, "forsake") denote covenant observance (or the lack of it).

The term *kārat* (כָּרַת, "cut"), however, was the conventional word used to indicate the initiation of a covenant arrangement. The slaying of animals in association with covenant ceremony[12] obviously inspired the idiom *kārat bĕrīt* ("cut a covenant"), and the expression may be described as "pregnant with theological meaning." Carl Schultz is likely correct in interpreting the animal-slaying ritual as depicting "the self-destruction of the one making the contract in an analogous way: that the fate of the animal should befall him in the event that he does not keep the *bĕrît*."[13]

Types

A crucial issue in the analysis of Old Testament covenants is the question of conditionality. The possible range of conditionality is reflected in M. Weinfeld's list of options that include (1) a commitment by the subject of the *bĕrît*, (2) an obligation imposed by the subject of the *bĕrît*, (3) a mutual obligation made by two parties, or (4) a mutual obligation sponsored by a third party.[14]

As Waltke has observed, the Old Testament covenants between YHWH and people fit into one of Weinfeld's first two categories. He noted that the first type may be called unconditional and the second conditional. However, he warned that while "the distinction is valid . . . the terms *unconditional* and *conditional* may be misleading."[15] The warning is well taken, for both the concept of conditionality and the nomenclature used to label it as such are subject to considerable ambiguity. In this book an attempt will be made to minimize confusion by adopting Weinfeld's two designations: "obligatory" and "promissory."[16]

Obligatory. Some covenant formulas include specific conditions (or a condition) which one or both contractual parties must honor (as in Weinfeld's third option). However, as Waltke noted, the Old Testament covenants between God and people exclude this kind of mutual agreement.[17] Accordingly, the God-person covenants which are vital to understanding the message of salvation usually feature an obligation imposed by the subject, God (as in Weinfeld's second option). This type of covenant is quite obviously conditional in that certain requirements must be satisfied for the covenant to be in force. As further evidence will indicate, though, even promissory covenants (Weinfeld's first option) have conditional elements. So descriptive terminology may be somewhat inadequate.

Weinfeld labeled the obligatory covenant as "treaty."[18] Freedman described it as "a covenant of human obligation."[19] McComiskey preferred the designation "administrative covenant" (as opposed to "promissory"),[20] though his analysis is more theological than structural. In any event, some covenant formulas contained certain specifications or conditions which must be honored for its provisions to be available—conditions which had not already been met. These covenants will be labeled "obligatory," and their importance to the matter of soteriology must not be overlooked.

Promissory. Weinfeld described this type of covenant as a "grant."[21] While essentially unilateral in nature without the imposition of designated requirements, the "grant" covenant was not actually unconditional. As he noted, "the grant is a reward for loyalty and good deeds already performed."[22] In reflecting on the unconditional aspect of the Davidic covenant, Waltke remarked, "YHWH's grant to David places no obligations on David for its enactment or perpetuation. It is unilateral, and in that sense unconditional." But he added, "David, through his loyalty to YHWH, had created the spiritual climate favoring this covenant."[23]

In summary, one may conclude that a promissory covenant (or grant) was unconditional in the sense that no additional requirements were demanded. At the same time, the grant covenant was conditional, but the covenant requirements were already satisfied so that no further stipulations were necessary.

Elements

While both of the foregoing Old Testament types have parallels in the ancient Near East,[24] the biblical covenants have their own notable characteristics. Moreover, although all of the following components may not occur in every covenant formula, they are important when they are present. Consider, then, these possible elements within the covenant structure:[25]

Historical Introduction (Ex. 19:4)
Stipulations (Ex. 19:5; Deut. 28:1)
Invocation of Solemn Witness (Deut. 30:19)
Blessings and/or Curses (Deut. 28:1-68)
Agreement (Ex. 19:8; 24:3,7).

Features

In addition, the following attendant features may be encountered. Again, not all of them were present in every covenant context, but they did occur on occasion. For example:

Solemn Meal (Gen. 26:28-30)
Oath (Gen. 26:31)
Erection of Memorial Markers (Gen. 31:51-52)[26]
Institution of Signs
    Bow (Gen. 9:17)
    Circumcision (Gen. 17:11)
    Sabbath (Ex. 31:13)
Ratification Rite (Gen. 15:9-17; Jer. 34:18)
Covenant Codification (Ex. 24:4).

Old Testament Covenants

Not all of the covenants reported in the Old Testament demand attention in the study of soteriology. Some are vital to the study, though, and others must be examined before they can be legitimately eliminated.

Covenant with Adam. Based on Hosea 6:7, the idea of an "Adamic" covenant has been posited, but terminology and concept are not uniform in discussions which address this covenant idea. Some prefer the designation "covenant of works,"[27] while others refer to it as the "Edenic Covenant."[28] Rejecting "an implied Covenant of Works concluded by the Deity with Adam,"[29] W. J. Dumbrell prefers a "Covenant with Creation" which "will involve nothing less finally than the redemption of all creation."[30]

I agree with Dumbrell's perception of God's design and economy for creation, but the Genesis data hardly conform to his analysis. Dumbrell wrote that "the substance of the covenant with which we are concerned is clearly a commitment *implicit* in the total creation account of Genesis 1:1–2:4a. Such a commitment was intended to achieve the purpose of creation"[31] (italics added). In his summary, he then concluded (italics added):

> The *implications* of a covenant *implied* by the fact of creation itself were then drawn out. There could be only one biblical covenant, of which the later biblical covenants *must* be sub-sets.[32]

The highly tenuous nature of Dumbrell's argument is revealed by the recurrent use of tentative terms ("implicit," "implications," and "implied"). It is difficult to understand how any consequence "must" develop from such uncertain circumstances.[33]

Dumbrell's unique approach illustrates the highly ambiguous notion of a covenant in the Creation-Eden-Adam context. John Murray, preferring the concept of an "Adamic administration," questioned the label "The Covenant of Works" (with Adam?) and observed: "It is not designated a covenant in Scripture. Hosea 6:7 may be interpreted otherwise and does not provide the basis for such a construction of the Adamic economy."[34] In the light of the conflicting and inconclusive scriptural evidence, Fred H. Klooster's appraisal is persuasive:

> For such reasons I do not consider it legitimate to speak of a covenant of creation, an Edenic Covenant, an Adamic Covenant, a covenant of works, or a covenant of redemption as has been done by many in the past. Covenanting involved a unique oath-taking arrangement, and the term may not be imposed where Scripture does not itself do so or provide the precise elements that warrant it.[35]

Since neither covenant nomenclature nor content may be precisely identified in the Creation-Adam-Eden context, I have analyzed the message of salvation in the early chapters of Genesis without reference to a covenant connection.

Covenant with Noah. As noted previously, the covenant with Noah was limited to a guarantee that there would never again "be a flood to destroy the earth" (Gen. 9:11). Because of its restricted scope, that covenant does not bear directly on the theme of Old Testament soteriology.

Covenant with Abraham (Gen. 15:1-21). This covenant will be examined in the next chapter.

Covenant of Holiness (Ex. 19—24); *Covenant of Entry* (Ex. 34:10-17); *Covenant of Possession* (Deut. 28—30). These three covenants with Israel will be examined and compared later in the same unit of study.

Everlasting Covenant (Isa. 24:5; 55:1-13; 59:16-21). This formula (*bĕrît 'ōlām*) will be discussed in detail in a later chapter.

New Covenant (Jer. 31:31-34). This, too, will be evaluated later.

The foregoing covenants are of critical significance in this book and will be considered at the appropriate juncture. Other covenants are contained in the Old Testament, including the Priestly Covenant (Num. 25:11-13), the Covenant of Joshua (Josh. 24:2-27), the Covenant of Jonathan and David (1 Sam. 20:11-17), and the Davidic Covenant (2 Sam. 7:12-16; Ps. 89:3-37).[36] While these covenants are of relative importance (especially the Davidic Covenant), since they do not impact directly on our investigation they will not be evaluated.

Notes

[1]For example, note Delbert R. Hillers, *Covenant: The History of Biblical Idea* (Baltimore: Johns Hopkins Press, 1969); W. J. Dumbrell, *Covenant and Creation* (Nashville: Thomas Nelson Publishers, 1984); and Thomas Edward McComiskey, *The Covenants of Promise* (Grand Rapids: Baker Book House, 1985); Trent C. Butler, "Covenant," *Holman Bible Dictionary*, ed. Trent C. Butler (Nashville: Holman Bible Publishers, 1991), 308-312.

[2]David Noel Freedman, "Divine Commitment and Human Obligation," *Interpretation* 18 (1964): 419.

[3]See George E. Mendenhall, "Covenant Forms in Israelite Tradition," in *The Biblical Archaeologist Reader*, vol. 3, ed. Edward F. Campbell, Jr. and David Noel Freedman (Anchor Books ed., New York: Doubleday & Company, 1970), 25-53; Dennis J. McCarthy, *Treaty and Covenant* (Rome: Biblical Institute Press, 1978), 277-98; and John H. Walton, *Ancient Israelite Literature in Its Cultural Context*, 2nd print-

Salvation Statement

ing (Grand Rapids: Zondervan Publishing House, 1990), 95-107; Meredith G. Kline, *Treaty of the Great King* (Grand Rapids: William B. Eerdmans Publishing Company, 1963).

[4]Notice the decidedly political and military tone of (Hittite) stipulations such as "Do not join plots," "Send troops," and "Covet no Hittite land." See McCarthy, *Treaty*, 82.

[5]John H. Walton, *Ancient Israelite Literature in Its Cultural Context*, 2nd printing (Grand Rapids: Zondervan Publishing House, 1990), 107.

[6]For discussion, see M. Weinfeld, "בְּרִית" *TDOT*, 2:253-56 and Elmer B. Smick, "ברה," *TWOT*, 1:128-30.

[7]Klooster wrote that "a covenant is basically an oath-bound promissory relation." See Fred H. Klooster, "The Biblical Method of Salvation: A Case for Continuity," in *Continuity and Discontinuity*, ed. John S. Feinberg (Westchester, IL: Crossway Books, 1988), 149; Weinfeld affirmed that "*berith* as a commitment has to be confirmed by an oath" in "בְּרִית" *TDOT*, 2:256.

[8]Note especially verses 1, 3.

[9]Freedman, "Divine Commitment," 420.

[10]KJV has "league."

[11]Note NIV's "agreement" in 2 Samuel 3:12.

[12]See Genesis 15:9-11; Exodus 24:5-6; Jeremiah 34:18. The idiom "to kill a donkey foal" denoted the concluding of a covenant at Mari. See Moshe Held, "Philological Note on the Mari Covenant Rituals," *Bulletin of the American Schools of Oriental Research*, no. 200 (December, 1970), 33. To "cut the throat of a sheep" described covenant ritual at Alalakh; McCarthy, *Treaty*, 87. Also see Speiser, *Genesis*, 112.

[13]Carl Schultz, "כָּרַת," *TWOT*, 1:457.

[14]Cited by Bruce K. Waltke, "The Phenomenon of Conditionality within Unconditional Covenants," in *Israel's Apostasy and Restoration*, ed. Avraham Gileadi (Grand Rapids: Baker Book House, 1988), 123.

[15]Ibid., 124.

[16]M. Weinfeld, "The Covenant of Grant in the Old Testament and in the Ancient Near East," *Journal of American Oriental Schools* 90 (1970): 184.

[17]Waltke, "Conditionality," 124.

[18]Weinfeld, "Covenant of Grant," 185.

[19]Freedman, "Divine Commitment," 420.

[20]Thomas Edward McComiskey, *The Covenants of Promise* (Grand Rapids: Baker Book House, 1985), 139.

[21]Weinfeld, "Covenant of Grants," 185.

[22]Ibid.

[23]Waltke, "Conditionality," 130-31.

[24]See Freedman, "Divine Commitment," 427.

[25]Note the similarity to McCarthy's analysis (of Hittite vassal treaties) that includes: titulary, history, stipulations, document clause, god list, blessings and curses. See McCarthy, *Treaty*, 51-52. Compare Mendenhall's list: preamble, historical prologue, stipulations, provision

for deposit, lists of gods as witnesses, and curses and blessings; Mendenhall, "Covenant Forms," 32-35. Walton provided this format: introduction of speaker, historical prologue, stipulations, statement concerning the document, divine witnesses, and curses and blessings; compare Walton, *Israelite Literature*, 101.

[26]In the covenant (treaty) between Jacob and Laban, the *gal* (גַּל, "heap") or *maṣēbā* (מַצֵּבָה, "pillar") probably served as a boundary marker. See Joshua 24:25-27 for the use of a stone marker as a "witness."

[27]McComiskey, *Covenants*, 213.

[28]Fred H. Klooster, "The Biblical Method of Salvation: A Case for Continuity," in *Continuity and Discontinuity*, ed. John S. Feinberg (Westchester, IL: Crossway Books, 1988), 150.

[29]W. J. Dumbrell, *Covenant and Creation: A Theology of Old Testament Covenants* (Nashville: Thomas Nelson Publishers, 1984), 43.

[30]Ibid., 33.

[31]Ibid.

[32]Ibid., 43.

[33]Dumbrell's argument evidently developed from his interpretation of "establish my covenant" (הֲקִמֹתִי אֶת־בְּרִיתִי) in Genesis 6:18. His insistence that where this formula occurs "the institution of a covenant is not being referred to but rather its perpetuation" (Dumbrell, *Covenant*, 26) loses continuity in the Noah-flood context. The content of the (grant) covenant is: "Never again will all life be cut off by the waters of a flood; never again will there be a flood to destroy the earth" (Gen. 9:11). Such covenant content is totally absent from the creation record.

[34]John Murray, "The Adamic Administration," in *Collected Writings of John Murray* (Carlisle, PA:Banner of Truth Trust, 1977), 2:49.

[35]Klooster, "Salvation," 150.

[36]In the light of our previous reluctance to insert a covenant concept into the creation account, we would hesitate to designate the promise to David (in 2 Sam.) as covenant were it not for the fact that it is so indicated in Psalm 89. Also, see 2 Samuel 23:5.

4

Our Father Abraham

Abraham believed the LORD,
and he credited it to him as righteousness.

Genesis 15:6

Abraham is a striking figure in religious history. Revered by Jew, Muslim, and Christian alike, he occupies an exclusive niche of respect common to three of the world's major religions. This special position of honor alone would suggest that Abraham played a significant role in the development of the salvation strategy revealed in the Old Testament. That perception is confirmed by Paul's appeal in the New Testament to the example of Abraham in support of his insistence on faith as the singular basis of salvation (Rom. 4:1-25; Gal. 3:6-16). In the light of Paul's argument, an analysis of Abraham's relationship to YHWH is vital to a correct perception of the nature of redemption in both Testaments.

The Significance of the Promises to Abraham

Early in Abraham's pilgrimage YHWH made a marvelous and complex promise to the son of Terah: "Leave your country, your people and your father's household and go to the land I will show you. I will make you into a great nation and I will bless you; I will make your name great, and you will be a blessing. I will bless those who bless you, and whoever curses you I will curse; and all peoples on earth will be blessed through you" (Gen. 12:1-3).

While this multifaceted promise did not constitute a formal covenant, it did provide the foundation for the covenant that would be ratified with Abraham later and was the basis for subsequent covenants with Israel and David. It also furnishes a broad outline to the overall redemptive design revealed in the Bible, causing its specific provisions to be worth noting.

Inheritance. In addition to the pledge of ultimate blessing and greatness (Gen. 12:2), the legacy promised to Abraham included both a place and a people. He had been instructed by YHWH to leave his native land and family— no trivial requirement in any time or place; but the burden of separation and isolation imposed by the divine command must have been especially severe in the ancient setting. Though commerce and cultural interchange were more advanced in the time of Abraham than we might have once supposed, still, by modern standards travel and communication were radically primitive. To comply with the divine instruction was no minor accomplishment.

YHWH promised Abraham a replacement on each count. He would lead Abraham to another land, nameless and unspecified at first, but a region that would ultimately be an everlasting possession for his offspring (Gen. 13:14-15). YHWH also promised that Abraham's family was to be a "great nation" that would emerge from his own body (Gen. 12:2; 15:4). So both a land and a people were guaranteed to Abraham as the inheritance of obedience.

Providence. Moreover, YHWH promised to reward Abraham's obedience with appropriate benefits. The harsh winds of time would neither erode the memory of his faith nor erase the testimony of his faithfulness. His role in God's grand redemptive design for history would not be swallowed up by oblivion. He would be remembered. His legacy would endure. "I will make your name great."

A special protective watchcare was also affirmed. "I will bless those who bless you, and whoever curses you I will curse." YHWH promised to superintend Abraham's pilgrimage, to guard, to defend, and to make him prosperous. He thus became a designated object of divine care and protection.

Destiny. In addition, God pledged that Abraham would occupy a distinctive and universal position in His salvation strategy: "All peoples on earth will be blessed through you." This facet of the promise elevates its importance and application beyond narrow ethnic or sectarian considerations. Announced to an obscure Semite in a dim, distant locale of an almost forgotten past, the pledge transcends time and favoritism with its magnificent prospect of universal benefit and blessing.

An Analysis of the Covenant with Abraham

YHWH's promise needs no additional pledge or guarantee to assure its certainty. God did not need to confirm His promise with a covenant oath for it to be valid and trustworthy. That YHWH did, nevertheless, affirm His promise to Abraham with a formal covenant commitment (Gen. 15:9-18) underscores the significance of the promise. It further suggests that the covenant was implemented more for human benefit than from divine necessity. The covenant pledge must surely have strengthened Abraham's confidence. More than incidentally, it also provides valuable insight into the Old Testament message of salvation.

Ratification Rite. Consonant with treaty patterns of the ancient Near East, a brief historical prologue introduced the formal covenant ceremony with Abraham (Gen. 15:7).[1] Following the succinct reminder of the events which had led to the present circumstance, God instructed the emigrant from Ur to prepare three animals and two birds for a ritual which would formalize the LORD's official covenant relationship with Abraham. The enigmatic and haunting scene that followed would merit an independent analysis, but other features of the covenant enactment are of greater importance to this study.[2] Whatever the possible symbolism of the various elements of the ratification rite, the total scenario emphasized the solemn magnitude of the new formal arrangement between Abraham and YHWH.

Disclosure. Following obedient preparation and placement of the animal and fowl carcasses,[3] as evening shadows lengthened, Abraham sank into a deep, frightening, coma-like sleep.[4] The glow of divine presence promptly illuminated the dark valley of dreadful slumber, however. YHWH then informed Abraham concerning the design and time-table for covenant fulfillment. Abraham, according to promise and covenant, would indeed become the father of a great people (Gen. 15:5); but his descendants would not immediately occupy the terrain which had been promised as the permanent homeland for his seed (Gen. 13:14-17).

Rather, according to the disclosure, his heirs must first endure four hundred years of brutal abuse as "refugee-slaves" in a foreign land. The assurance that Abraham himself would live to "a good old age" and ultimately die "in peace" may have provided only scant comfort in light of the distressing announcement about the miserable fate of his seed.

The rationale given for the postponement of occupation of the land of Canaan by Abraham's offspring is striking: "for the sin of the Amorites has not yet reached its full measure." This enigmatic utterance demands examination. The questions "who?" and "why?" must be addressed.

First, who were the Amorites?[5] On the threshold of Israel's departure from Egypt, after the four-hundred-year sojourn, the Amorites were mentioned among the peoples dwelling in the land of Canaan (Ex. 3:8-10). The specific designation of individual racial or "national" groups (for example, "Hittites") would suggest that the term "Amorite" was an ethnic or national label.

However, the word was also used with a broader connotation. As E. A. Speiser observed, the term was "normally the name of a specific people . . . , but sometimes also the collective term for the pre-Israelite population of Canaan."[6] This double level of meaning is reflected in Joshua's use of the word (Josh. 3:10; 5:1), so one may conclude that the term can function as a synonym for "Canaanite." Obviously, the expression was so used in YHWH's word to Abraham and constituted a statement, in effect, about the ultimate fate of all the inhabitants of Canaan.

Second, why was the occupation of Canaan by Abraham's seed (Israel) to be delayed so long, especially in light of the distressing circumstance of the projected postponement? The answer is clear: "for the sin of the Amorites has not yet reached its full measure." Already in the time of Abraham, the reprobate character and conduct of the inhabitants of Canaan were reprehensible to the God of creation. Their sin demanded retribution.[7] However, even at the considerable expense of Abraham's progeny, penal judgment on the Amorites would be postponed—for four hundred years.

This dictum of delay reveals two significant truths: (1) Despite the Amorites' preoccupation with deities fashioned by human minds and hands, YHWH held them accountable to Himself for their sin. (2) YHWH was willing to extend ample time and opportunity for the Amorites to repent and forsake their sin. So enshrouded in the dark shadows of Abraham's hypnotic sleep is the two-fold message that the God of the patriarch (and later Israel) was (and is) the God of all peoples and that He is gracious and patient.

Prerequisite. Conspicuously absent from the account of the covenant ratification procedure is any mention of requirement or stipulation. This studied omission would lead to the conclusion that no condition was required of Abraham. Accordingly, as Weinfeld noted correctly, the covenant with Abraham is to be construed as "promissory."[8] As noted earlier, however, even a promissory covenant is not necessarily totally unconditional.[9] This covenant, like the later one with David, was enacted because its requirements were already satisfied and no further stipulations were needed. What were the demands of this unique relationship, and in what way was Abraham qualified for special covenant status?

The overture to the covenantal account contains the assurance that the "great nation" which had been promised (Gen. 12:2) would be the natural progeny of Abraham, not the descendants of an adopted heir (Gen. 15:2-5). That affirmation is followed by the significant statement, "Abram believed the LORD, and he credited it to him as righteousness" (Gen. 15:6). The statement is extraordinary on two counts: (1) the meaning of "believed" and (2) the circumstance of Abram's belief.

Mighty to Save

The Hebrew verb translated "believed"[10] is associated with a cluster of morphologically and semantically related words.[11] In the light of the general aura of meaning common to these multiple terms, Jack B. Scott is undoubtedly correct in claiming, "The basic root idea is firmness or certainty."[12] Allen P. Ross offered this appraisal of the verb's stem distinctions:

> So words in the *qal* describe trustworthy people or things, usages of the *niphal* stress reliability, security, or steadfastness, and almost all of the *hiphil* uses denote a firm confidence or the act of believing.[13]

The form of the verb is *hiphil* in this instance and therefore, as Ross has suggested, denotes the exercise of "firm confidence." The notion of belief associated with the verb, then, is considerably more profound than a view of belief that indicates mere intellectual assent. Hirsch astutely noted that this particular construction:

> . . . represents a much deeper concept than mere belief. It suggests total submission in the sense that one places his total confidence and seeks all his guidance and attitudes in God.[14]

The point is clear. Abram exercised saving faith in terms of trust, surrender, and commitment.[15]

In the light of the syntactical structure of verse 6, the circumstance of Abram's faith is as profound as the fact of it. David Noel Freedman commented on the importance of the faith element: "Here, as elsewhere, a covenant of divine commitment is preceded by an act of faith or devotion."[16] If Freedman is correct—and the context certainly supports his appraisal—then Abram's faith constituted an indispensable precondition for covenant enactment. What precedes the statement of faith, though, is also important.

The report of YHWH's reassurance to Abram that his heir would be "a son coming from your own body" concluded, "Look up at the heavens and count the stars—if indeed you can count them. . . . So shall your offspring be" (Gen. 15:5). Verse 6, following immediately, would suggest that Abram's faith was in response to the preceding promise. The syntactical form of the verb "believed," however, precludes that interpretation. The precise nuance of the syntax formula used in this instance, the conjunction *vav* plus a perfect form of the verb, is a matter of some dispute among Hebrew grammarians;[17] but the construction definitely does not suggest sequence or development. Ibn Caspi noted this distinction:

> There was nothing new in this trust, it means that this unswerving faith which he now displayed had been innately a part of him for a long time. Had the meaning been that he trusted from that moment on, the Hebrew would have read *vaya'ămēn*.[18]

Observing that the NIV leaves the conjunction untranslated "to avoid the implication that verse 6 resulted from or followed chronologically verse 5," Ross added:

> If the writer had wished to show that this verse followed the preceding in sequence, he would have used the normal structure for narrative sequence (וַיַּאֲמֵן), "and [then] he believed"—as he did within the sentence to show that the reckoning followed the belief (וַיַּחְשְׁבֶהָ), "and [so then] he reckoned it." We must conclude that the narrator did not wish to show sequence between verses 5 and 6; rather, he wished to make a break with the narrative in order to supply this information about the faith of Abraham.[19]

The account is explicit; Abraham trusted in YHWH. The patriarch's faith was more than a disposition prompted by a reaction to a single promise. Rather, his faith represented an attitude of confidence and commitment that determined his response to any and all promises or commands from YHWH.[20] The insertion of the monumental faith statement into the narrative as an introduction to the inauguration of the covenant, however, would indicate that Abraham's faith was the prerequisite to covenant enactment—a condition which had already been met. Faith was the basis, not the result, of the Abrahamic covenant.

Significance of חָשַׁב. The verb translated "credited" is a term with a rather wide semantic range. For example, it may mean "think" (Isa. 10:7, KJV), "devise" or "plan" (Ezek. 38:10), and "esteem" (Isa. 53:3), as well as "charge" or "impute" (2 Sam. 19:19, KJV). Leon J. Wood concludes, "The basic idea of the word is the employment of the mind in thinking activity."[21] The quality or item to be ascribed is in the mind or thought of the one who makes the evaluation.

Accordingly, the assignment of righteousness to Abraham must be understood as essentially an internal evaluation by

YHWH. That appraisal was not a totally unconditional, unilateral decree; it was contingent on the faith of Abraham. Whereas Abraham's exercise of faith was not syntactically connected to the preceding promise, the divine imputation of righteousness was the direct consequence of his faith.[22] The righteousness of Abraham was neither intrinsic nor inherent. It was imputed on the basis of his trust.

Summary

An awareness of the correlation of faith and righteousness in the experience of Abraham leads to a fuller appreciation of the covenant which YHWH established with the expatriate from Ur. Ultimately universal in its application, that ancient covenant extends redemptive influences across temporal and ethnic barriers to bless peoples far removed from the original setting. Fred H. Klooster's evaluation is noteworthy:

> The Abrahamic Covenant, often called the covenant of grace, is an everlasting covenant. It continues through the rest of history, was adapted to the post-Sinaitic situation of the theocratic nation, and was eventually fulfilled in the blood of Christ, the New Covenant predicted by Jeremiah 31. This is the covenant of grace in which God still embraces believers. . . . It was not the introduction of a new dispensational test.[23]

Although the focus of interest in this investigation is the Old Testament message to its original audience, Paul's New Testament interpretation of Genesis 15:6 is applicable and must be considered. The converted Pharisee, whom one may construe to be the consummate exegete of the Old Testament, appealed to the commitment of Abraham in formulating and defending his theological thesis of salvation by faith alone.[24]

Paul, in interpreting Genesis 15:6, concluded that the ultimate ancestor of Jewry was "justified" on the basis of faith and only faith. Before the institution of tabernacle or temple ceremony, before the sacrifices of the Levitical system, before the moral dictums of the Law, before Moses or Sinai, before the exodus, before the rite of circumcision—indeed, before the establishment of covenant—"Abram believed the LORD, and he credited it to him as righteousness."

Abraham was not considered righteous on the basis of personal piety, nor was he exonerated from moral guilt because of compliance with religious ritual. Righteousness was imputed to him as a direct and specific consequence of his faith. We therefore conclude with Paul that Abraham was "saved" on precisely the same basis as persons are saved today—by grace through faith.

Notes

[1]See the Excursus, footnote 5.

[2]For a discussion of the procedures described in Genesis 15:9-12, see Gerhard F. Hasel, "The Meaning of the Animal Rites in Genesis 15," *Journal for the Study of the Old Testament* 19 (1981): 61-78.

[3]Marked by the mysterious attack of "birds of prey" (עַיִט), Genesis 15:11.

[4]The noun used is תַּרְדֵּמָה. See Jonah 1:5.

[5]Genesis 15:16 has the collective singular הָאֱמֹרִי.

[6]Speiser, *Genesis*, 113.

[7]See J. Arthur Thompson, "Canaan, Canaanites," *The Zondervan Pictorial Encyclopedia of the Bible*, ed. Merrill C. Tenney (Grand Rapids: Zondervan Publishing House, 1977), 1:701-708. For a concrete illustration of the immoral influences of Canaanite religion, see the example of deity described in the "Baal" Epic," G. R. Driver, *Canaanite Myths and Legends* (Edinburgh: T & T Clark, 1956), 72-118.

[8]M. Weinfeld, "The Covenant of Grant in the Old Testament and in the Ancient Near East," *Journal of the American Oriental Society* 90 (1970): 184.

[9]See the Excursus in this book.

[10]Here, in the *Hiph'il* stem, הֶאֱמִן.

[11]The list includes: אֹמֶן, אָמֵן, אָמָן, אֹמְנָה, אֱמוּנָה, אֲמָנָה. See BDB, 52-54.

[12]Jack B. Scott, "אָמַן," *TWOT* 1:51.

[13]Allen P. Ross, "The Biblical Method of Salvation: A Case for Discontinuity," *Continuity and Discontinuity*, ed. John S. Feinberg (Westchester, IL: Crossway Books, 1988), 354-55.

[14]Hirsch, *Bereishis*, trans. Rabbi Meir Zlotowitz, vol. 1 (Brooklyn: Mesorah Publications, 1986), 512.

[15]Meredith G. Kline's proposal that הֶאֱמִן in this text is delocutive ("Abram's Amen," *The Westminster Theological Journal* 31 [1968]: 1-11; see also Delbert R. Hillers, "Delocutive Verbs in Biblical Hebrew," *Journal of Biblical Literature*, 86 [1967]: 320-24) is unconvincing, but the expression reveals a profound trust on the part of Abram in any

Mighty to Save

event. Note its use in Micah 7:5 and Psalm 78:22 in parallel with בָּטַח, "trust."

[16]David Noel Freedman, "Divine Commitment and Human Obligation," *Interpretation* 18 (1964): 422.

[17]For example, Waltke and O'Connor noted, "Scholars are agreed that the *wə* in the *weqataltí* construction usually (though not always) signifies succession (temporal or logical), but they are not agreed about the meaning of the suffix conjugation in this construction"; see *Syntax*, 523.

[18]Hirsch, *Bereishis*, trans. Rabbi Meir Zlotowitz, vol. 1 (Brooklyn: Mesorah Publications, 1986), 512.

[19]Ross, "Salvation: Discontinuity," 168. Brueggemann, on the other hand, construes Abraham's exercise of faith as the result of the preceding promise. See "Genesis," 144.

[20]See the offering of Isaac in Genesis 22.

[21]Leon J. Wood, "חָשַׁב," *TWOT* 1:329-30. Note full discussion of use of the verb and associated nouns.

[22]Waltke and O'Connor described this function of the imperfect, "*Wayyqtl* signifies logical succession where a logical entailment from (a) preceding situation(s) . . . is expressed"; see *Syntax*, 547.

[23]Fred J. Klooster, "The Biblical Method of Salvation: A Case for Continuity," *Continuity and Discontinuity*, ed. John S. Feinberg (Westchester, IL: Crossway Books, 1988), 150.

[24]Romans 4:1-5,10-14; Galatians 3:6-9.

5

Redemptive Illustration at Jabbok

Your name will no longer be Jacob, but Israel.

Genesis 32:28

The theory that people are automatically saved on the basis of ancestry and environment persists despite monumental evidence to the contrary. Whether stated or not, this position assumes that being born into the right family and reared in a proper religious atmosphere will surely produce an acceptable relationship with God. Jacob, as no other character in the Bible, totally demolishes this theory.

Son of the "promised seed," Isaac, and grandson of the patriarch Abraham, Jacob certainly came from acceptable stock, the heir of an impeccable earthly bloodline. With this unique family connection, Jacob grew to manhood in the religious aura of a special covenant relationship with YHWH. If any individual within or outside Bible history could qualify for salvation on the basis of ancestry and environment, it would have to be Jacob. Yet, as the Genesis narrative reveals with almost painful candor, Jacob, along with his twin brother Esau, was essentially a carnal individual. He demonstrated no real evidence of genuine spiritual piety or sensitivity. Something more noble than birth and more revolutionary than religion would be required of Jacob.

Early Years in Canaan

The account of the events leading to the marriage of Isaac and Rebekah (Gen. 24:1-67) reflects the oriental custom of marriage arrangement that has persisted to the present era.[1] The providential union of this noble pair, however, was not without strife and tension. Indeed, their ancient home, at least at times, seems to encompass all the subtle conflict and stress that plague family life even today.

Factors at Birth. Jacob was the younger of twin sons born to Rebekah. While the birth of twins is uncommon enough, the unique delivery of Rebekah's two sons prompted this report: "When the time came for her to give birth, there were twin boys in her womb. The first to come out was red, and his whole body was like a hairy garment; so they named him Esau. After this, his brother came out, with his hand grasping Esau's heel; so he was named Jacob" (Gen. 25:24-26).

Obviously, the unusual birth circumstances influenced the choice of names for the two boys. The NIV suggests that *"Esau* may mean *hairy,"*[2] but the equation is rather tenuous. The name Jacob, on the other hand, clearly relates to the word for "heel" in the Hebrew text. The transparent play on words has led to the proposal that *Jacob* means *"he grasps the heel"*[3] or "heel-catcher." As the NIV's alternate translation suggests, however, (*"he deceives,"* Gen. 25:26),[4] the name attached to Rebekah's younger son may include a more subtle, even negative, connotation.

Esau's "play" on Jacob's name reveals that unflattering level of meaning. As a robust, manly youth (Gen. 25:27), Esau frivolously bartered away his birthright to his younger brother (Gen. 25:29-34), apparently insensitive to the spiritual ramifications of his action. Notwithstanding, when he learned of Jacob's subsequent ploy to appropriate the paternal blessing that belonged to the firstborn, Esau was justifiably furious. The offended elder brother fumed, "Isn't he rightly named Jacob? He has deceived me these two times: He took my birthright, and now he's taken my blessing!" (Gen. 27:36).

The verb translated "deceived" is fashioned from the same consonantal root upon which the name Jacob was built. Accordingly, one could preserve Esau's pun by constructing an artificial verb so as to reveal that connection: "Isn't he rightly named Jacob? He has 'jacobed' me these two times." Just as legitimately, the flavor of the verb could be reflected in the proper name: "Isn't he rightly named 'Deceiver'? He has deceived me these two times."

While the word cluster associated with this consonantal root indicates a somewhat puzzling range of meaning,[5] Esau's bitter appraisal demonstrates his own negative feeling for the meaning of the verb and the treacherous character of his brother. Though it is surely linguistic accident, his evaluation of Jacob as the equivalent of a first-class "heel" makes a thoroughly understandable idiom in English. Why the Hebrew verb would convey such an uncomplimentary notion is unclear, but it is at least possible that Jacob himself infused that flavor into it.[6] In any event, although succeeding generations would remember Jacob as a member of the illustrious patriarchal triumvirate, his elder brother considered him to be deceitful and devious. He hardly seemed to be made of the "right stuff," at least in the days of his youth.

Divine Election. The manipulative character of the youthful Jacob challenged the noble destiny that the LORD had predicted. During Rebekah's pregnancy, the LORD assured her: "Two nations are in your womb, / and two peoples from within you will be separated; / one people will be stronger than the other, / and the older will serve the younger" (Gen. 25:23).

That pronouncement surely implied that the younger of Rebekah's sons would exhibit superb moral character and embody the positive religious disposition of his father and grandfather. Jacob's projected superiority over Esau is demonstrated later in the biblical revelation, "Yet I have loved Jacob, but Esau I have hated" (Mal. 1:2-3).[7] Jacob did exhibit an interest in the family birthright and blessing, to be sure; but his conniving efforts to secure those benefits betrayed the selfish nature of his motives. Jacob's divine nomination to be the agency through which YHWH would honor His covenant pledge seemed to be canceled by the "deceiver's" lack of moral qualifications.

A Study in Contrast. The two sons of Isaac and Rebekah were apparently almost total opposites. Their lifestyles were different; Esau was the athletic "outdoor type," while Jacob "was a quiet man, staying among the tents" (Gen. 25:27).[8] Their affections were different. Esau's inordinate fondness for "red stew" not only contributed to the "sale" of his birthright to Jacob but also inspired his nickname, Edom or "Red."[9] Esau's careless indifference to the significance of that transaction clearly indicates his limited sense of values. Jacob did play on his brother's weakness, but his opportune maneuver reflected his perception of the importance of the birthright. This importance was totally ignored by Esau.

A Night at Bethel

As might be expected, the potentially dangerous disparity in personality and interest of the two brothers, compounded by the "trigger-mechanism" of parental favoritism (Gen. 25:28), eventually exploded like an emotional hand grenade. When Esau learned of the "grand deception" Jacob perpetrated, he vowed murderous revenge (Gen. 27:1-41).[10] So violent was Esau's reaction that Jacob found it necessary to flee for his very life. Following his parents' advice, the younger son departed for the home of his kinsman, Laban, in distant Paddan Aram.[11] En route, Jacob stopped for the night at "a certain place," a night and a location to be immortalized in Hebrew history.

When the vagabond exile sank in troubled sleep, he had a dream in which he saw "a stairway . . . reaching to heaven . . . and the angels of God . . . ascending and descending on it" (Gen. 28:12). Furthermore, in the visionary experience YHWH extended the covenant blessings to Jacob that He had previously promised to Abraham and Isaac, adding this important expansion:

"I am with you and will watch over you wherever you go, and I will bring you back to this land. I will not leave you until I have done what I have promised you" (Gen. 28:15).

Waking up, Jacob was overwhelmed by the magnitude of the unexpected encounter and concluded, "How awesome is this place! This is none other than the house of God; this is the gate of heaven" (Gen. 28:17). He then set upright the stone that he had used for a pillow, anointed it as a "pillar" or monument,[12] and made a solemn vow of loyalty to YHWH—provided certain benefits were guaranteed. He called the place Bethel, the "house of God."

In Paddan Aram

The record of Jacob's sojourn with Laban in Paddan Aram, among the Eastern peoples (Gen. 29:1), provides another interesting chapter in domestic tension and family stress. The ambitious, aggressive visitor from Canaan pretty well met his match in his equally devious relative, Laban. The two men sparred and feinted like skilled boxers, each trying to take advantage of the other's vulnerability. Laban, exploiting Jacob's love for his younger daughter, duped him into marrying both Rachel and Leah (Gen. 29:16-30). Furthermore, in the process, he exacted fourteen years of labor from Jacob as the price of "marriage privilege."

The relationship between Jacob and his two wives could well inspire a report entitled "The Case for Monogamy." Conventional sibling rivalry between the sisters intensified as they competed for the affection of their shared husband. Strife, jealousy, and pettiness plagued the heart and home of Jacob (Gen. 29:31—30:24). What a price to pay for the love of a woman!

In time, following the birth of many children and the accumulation of considerable wealth (Gen. 30:43),[13] Jacob took his family "along with all the goods" (Gen. 31:18) and departed Paddan Aram for Canaan. Like his earlier flight from home, Jacob's departure from Haran[14] was accompanied by controversy and deceit. He did not disclose his intentions to his father-in-law; not until the third day was Laban told that "Jacob had fled."

On learning of that development, Laban pursued Jacob and his party for seven days before catching up with them "in the hill country of Gilead" (Gen. 31:17-23). There he rebuked Jacob. "What have you done? You've deceived me,[15] and you've carried off my daughters like captives in war" (Gen. 31:26). From Canaan to Paddan Aram and from Paddan Aram to Gilead, the younger son of Rebekah and Isaac lamentably lived up to his name, Jacob—"Deceiver." Next stop: Jabbok!

From Jacob to Israel

In a final confrontation, characterized by charge and countercharge (Gen. 31:26-43), the fractious in-laws reached an uneasy truce by making a covenant. Laban extracted an agreement from Jacob to treat his daughters fairly and humanely, while Jacob, in turn, inserted a "mutual non-aggression clause" in the treaty arrangement (Gen. 31:44-54). Then, bidding his daughters and grandchildren farewell, Laban turned back toward Haran. Jacob resumed his journey to Canaan.

Before the traveler would reach the land of his birth, however, he would spend another eventful night "on the road." At a ford to the river Jabbok, Jacob would have an experience to surpass even that of Bethel. Following the occurrence, he would thereafter be known as Israel.

The chronicle of Jacob's memorable encounter at Jabbok is both striking and tantalizing. The account provides some amazing details, while omitting other matters that cry out for explanation. Hauntingly similar to an incident in the life of another Hebrew traveler (of a far later time),[16] the midnight struggle between "Deceiver" and his unnamed assailant provides much more than a bizarre episode from the ancient Near East. It captures, in essence, the indispensable ingredients of a "new birth" experience (long before the nocturnal conversation between Nicodemus and the Teacher from Nazareth). Moreover, the report beautifully isolates these essential elements for analysis.

Extremity. As Jacob came nearer to the land of his birth, he obviously recalled the turbulent circumstances that had led to his departure some twenty years earlier (Gen. 31:41). Never one to leave a situation to blind chance, he dispatched a reconnaissance patrol to search for Esau and determine what kind of reception he might anticipate.

Imagine, then, his consternation when the patrol returned with a disturbing report. "We went to your brother Esau, and now he is coming to meet you, and four hundred men are with him" (Gen. 32:6). Four hundred men? That's much too large a group to constitute a welcome committee. No doubt, in his mind's eye, Jacob could readily envision the appearance of the approaching party—four hundred mounted Bedouin, armed to the teeth, racing across the sands! What a frightening prospect! The band of four hundred "warriors" assumed the proportions of a "lynch party" rather than a receiving line. So Jacob approached the Jabbok in "great fear and distress" (Gen. 32:7).

In one final spasm of self-preservation, the distraught Jacob divided "the people who were with him into two groups" in the wistful hope that part of them might escape the vengeful wrath of Esau. One can almost see him as he paced back and forth in his tent that evening, wringing his hands in anguish and lamenting his brother's anticipated lack of forgiveness. The degree of his anxiety is reflected in his desperate plea to YHWH; "Save me, I pray, from the hand of my brother Esau, for I am afraid he will come and attack me, and also the mothers with their children" (Gen. 32:11).

Could it be? Had the "master of manipulation" finally exhausted his bag of tricks? Had the crafty strategist been outflanked? Yes, it was true. The LORD had Jacob in "checkmate." Jacob was "out of moves."

In any time frame, in any generation, the essential first step to a life-changing encounter with the LORD is the recognition of one's own hopelessness apart from divine deliverance. As in the case of Jacob, that awareness may be triggered by some external emergency or calamity. In other situations, the troubled anxiety may be totally internal and subjective in nature. Whatever the circumstance, until one comes to perceive his or her urgent need of the LORD's salvation, the prospect of His intervention is remote indeed.

The conventional religious terminology for this essential distress of spirit is "conviction." The term is usually employed to designate an inner emotional and intellectual state, stimulated by the Holy Spirit, that leads one to recognize the magnitude of personal sin and a need for pardon. While that internal aspect of the experience is certainly present in every "conviction" situation, it is likewise true that external circumstances may activate and intensify the inward sense of guilt, alienation, helplessness, and need. In any event, whatever the stimulus, the sense of urgent need exhibited in the extremity of Jacob is an unavoidable prelude to the LORD's grand intervention. Label it "conviction."

Confrontation. Striving frantically to placate the expected wrath of his brother, Jacob sent a lavish present of animals to Esau with the thought, "I will pacify him with these gifts I am sending on ahead" (Gen. 32:13-20).[17] Then, that night, Jacob sent his family across the stream, remaining behind alone. The ensuing episode is introduced by the cryptic affirmation, "A man wrestled with him till daybreak" (Gen. 32:24). As has been noted, the expression "man" (אִישׁ), considering the unique circumstance, fails to specify either the identity or the nature of Jacob's strange adversary.[18] Moreover, the terse statement ignores a reference to any provocation that might have triggered the desperate night-long struggle.

Westermann's proposal that the line suggests "a surprise attack resembling a robbery or murder" so that Jacob's opponent is depicted as a "robber" or "a night or river demon," is hardly consistent with the character and details of the context.[19] Still, he makes a valid point: "We are not dealing with a wrestling match agreed to by both parties."[20] The concise language of the account does, indeed, imply a sudden and unexpected encounter that could be described, at least from Jacob's standpoint, as an attack.

The duration and result of the encounter indicate the violent intensity of the hand-to-hand battle. The fight lasted all night, "till daybreak"; and Jacob was left at least partially crippled for the remainder of his life. Make no mistake; this was no choreographed pantomime. It bordered on mortal combat.

Who was the "nameless adversary" of the "desperate nocturnal struggle?"[21] By daybreak, despite his opponent's refusal to supply his name, Jacob perceived that his antagonist was decidedly more than human. Was the beleaguered traveler excessively impressed with the battle skills of his attacker, or does the evidence confirm his appraisal?

Remember the context. Even as Jacob maneuvered to evade the vengeance of Esau, he apparently sensed the futility of his stratagem and turned to the Lord for help (Gen. 32:9-12). This shift in focus from self-made devices to divine assistance captures the essence of the New Testament's "change of mind"[22] concept. The Deceiver's plaintive plea represented a radical transition.

In the light of YHWH's design that was previously revealed at Bethel, one would presume that the LORD would not ignore Jacob's dire appeal. Moreover, if the covenant God should intervene in Jacob's behalf, His involvement might well reflect the tension between His own holy nature and the selfish ego of Laban's son-in-law. Indeed, whenever Holy God and sinful person meet, something dramatic and traumatic results.

Surely, then, the midnight assailant was no nameless wandering nomad, a renegade warrior bent on random violence. Nor was he some desert bandit who simply stumbled into an opportunity for plunder. No, the thrust of Jacob's plea before the encounter and the striking nature of the event combine to support his evaluation that the shadowy opponent was some tangible, physical manifestation of deity. In the gray light of dawn, Jacob was convinced that he had met God face to face, though the stranger's name was never uttered, his identity never explicitly revealed.[23]

Just so, a salvation "experience," in the biblical sense, is not the consequence of superficial alterations. It involves more than intellectual agreement to certain theological propositions, as important as theological truth may be. It is not the result of cosmetic changes in lifestyle; it is not initiated by the development of religious associations. The perception of truth, holy living, and identification with the community of faith are important; but they do not, in and of themselves, produce or guarantee spiritual transformation. Jacob must meet God in personal encounter before he can become Israel.

Supplication. Like gladiators locked in deadly struggle, the two figures thrashed about in the darkness, making no sound but the noise of their scuffling, punctuated by muted grunts of exertion. Then his opponent broke the verbal silence. "Let me go, for it is daybreak." Jacob replied, "I will not let you go unless you bless me" (Gen. 32:26). Finally, communication took place. In responding to the request for release, Jacob was, in effect, talking to God.

Conversation with God is usually described as prayer; however, Jacob's words hardly qualify as prayer. His abrupt reply is totally absent of conventional prayer protocol, none of the polite "thees," "thous," or flowery ornamentation associated with acceptable religious formulas. Nevertheless, with or without the formal niceties, his communication with God must still be defined as prayer.

What a presumptuous prayer! How dare he speak to God in any circumstances with such audacity? To be sure, Jacob was certainly capable of presumption. A careful examination of the Bethel experience reveals Jacob's capacity for impertinence. There Jacob made a vow:

"If God will be with me and will watch over me on this journey I am taking and will give me food to eat and clothes to wear so that I return safely to my father's house, then the LORD will be my God and this stone that I have set up as a pillar will be God's house, and of all that you give me I will give you a tenth" (Gen. 28:20-22).

The clear evidence that he was attempting to strike a bargain with God discloses the impudence of Jacob's prayer-vow at Bethel. He extended his offer of allegiance and promise of financial contribution on the condition that God would guarantee "health, wealth, and prosperity" up front. The "manipulator" was negotiating for benefits and privileges by offering loyalty to God, as if he were doing the Lord of Glory a monumental favor. Yes, Jacob certainly had the capacity for presumption.

Nevertheless, to infer that his "request" at Jabbok is a further demonstration of selfish ambition is not necessarily justified. That Jacob's adversary did not seem to be offended or insulted by the statement is noteworthy. Perhaps Jacob's reply contained something more profound. Von Rad correctly observed, "Now one must assume that

Jacob has discovered something of the divine nature of his opponent." It does not follow, however, that he (Jacob) was attempting "to wrest a blessing from him, viz. divine vitality."[24] How, then, may one understand the seemingly audacious words of the battered wrestler?

The context would at least suggest that Jacob's focus of distress had shifted. Anxiety about deliverance from Esau's feared assault on his treasure had evidently yielded to a more fundamental concern for sheer survival. One can only surmise the thoughts behind the words. Perhaps Jacob had recognized that the pending showdown with Esau was the consequence of his own devious action and finally realized that he was his own worst enemy. Moreover, he may have sensed that the divine adversary could not only master him physically but could also conquer the enemy within, Jacob's basic nature.

He had three choices in the circumstance: (1) cast himself on the unpredictable mercy of Esau, (2) continue to trust in his own wits and dwindling devices, or (3) cling to God as his one and only hope. Jacob's plea clearly indicates that he chose the latter. Rather than exuding arrogant ambition, his words demonstrate the degree of his desperation.

Later in the Old Testament flow of revelation, the LORD declared, "You will seek me and find me when you seek me with all your heart" (Jer. 29:13). When the earthly rebel is through with his fun and games and is ready to do business with God in truth and candor, then He is available. The younger son of Isaac and Rebekah finally reached that point of earnest and urgent sincerity. In effect Jacob said, "You are the only hope I have. I cling to you and you alone." No conditions, no agreements, no negotiations— only unequivocal commitment!

Admission. Apparently ignoring his affirmation, the antagonist responded by asking Jacob for his name. If his opponent was divine indeed,[25] He must surely have known Jacob's name. Why then the question? Von Rad's explanation is on target:

> In the entire section which follows one must bear in mind that the ancients did not consider a name as simply sound and smoke. On the contrary, for them the name was closely linked with its bearer in such a way that the name contained

something of the character of the one who bore it. Thus, in
giving his name, Jacob at the same time had to reveal his
whole nature. The name Jacob (at least for the narrative) actually designates its bearer as a cheat.[26]

Jacob could not even identify himself without making a
tacit acknowledgment of his character. "You know me,
Lord. I'm Jacob, the Supplanter, Schemer, Deceiver." By
his name, he designated both who and what he was.

Not all people are named Jacob, but all have Jacob-like
qualities. Jeremiah's well-known diagnosis of the human
sin problem highlights that fact: "The heart is deceitful
above all things and beyond cure. / Who can understand
it?" (Jer. 17:9). The word "deceitful" עָקֹב is derived from
the same root associated with the name Jacob, thus indicating that the core of mankind's moral problem is a
treacherous Jacob-like heart.

So it is that, if one is to experience spiritual transformation, he or she must first be willing to admit one's sinful
condition and acknowledge the presence of the "Jacob factor." A personal encounter with a pure and holy God is not
the time to plead self-righteousness or pretend, "I'm doing
the best I know how." No, this is the time to tell it like it is.
Later, in the New Testament, John warned, "If we claim to
be without sin, we deceive ourselves and the truth is not in
us" (1 John 1:8). With the very utterance of his name,
Jacob, in effect, confessed his sinful condition.

Alteration. In response, the divine Adversary declared,
"Your name will no longer be Jacob, but Israel, because you
have struggled with God and with men and have overcome"
(Gen. 32:28). The enigmatic reply raises two pertinent
questions: (1) What is the meaning of the new name "Israel," and (2) what is the significance of the name change?

The components of the name are relatively clear. It is a
compound term composed of the masculine singular form
of the word for God (אֵל) and the verb *śārāh* (שָׂרָה), meaning
"persist" or "persevere."[27] The issue in question is whether
God is the subject or object of the force of the verb. Edward M. Curtis observed:

> On the basis of the explanation of the name given in v. 29 (28
> English) many have concluded that the name means "he strug-
> gles with God" or "he prevails with God." This, however, runs
> against the analogy of other names involving an imperfect

verb and a theophoric element since in virtually all those instances the theophoric element is the subject of the verb rather than the object. . . . The name then probably means something like "may God struggle/fight" or "may God prevail."[28]

The pattern, represented by such classic examples as the names Ezekiel and Ishmael,[29] clearly supports the interpretation that God is the agent of the verbal action in the name Israel rather than the recipient. However, one cannot ignore the force of the context.

Throughout the Old Testament, a causal clause often provides an explanation for the selection of a given name.[30] The use of that formula in verse 28 indicates that both the meaning and propriety of the name Israel are being clarified. Accordingly, the Opponent's use of the verb associated with Jacob's new alias is a critical factor in the decipherment of its meaning. The significant feature of the verb used as the predicate in the causal clause is its grammatical form, second masculine singular.

In the light of this designation, *Jacob* is unmistakably the subject of the verb, since no other personal antecedent is found in the context. That would strongly imply that *Jacob* is the unspecified agent of the verbal action in the new name. Moreover, the prepositional phrase "with God" follows the predicate,[31] indicating objective rather than subjective force. The explanatory subordinate clause then makes little sense unless the "he prevails with God" meaning of Israel is adopted.

Actually, the verb in question occurs only three times in the Old Testament, once here and twice in Hosea 12:3-4.[32] Hosea's use of the verb is confined to his reflection of the Jabbok encounter, and in both instances *Jacob* is clearly the subject of the verb.[33] The evidence is persuasive that, patterns to the contrary notwithstanding, Hosea understood Jacob to be the subject of the verb force in the name Israel. Accordingly, Driver's definition of the name as "Perseverer with God"[34] or even "Prevailer with God" may be a happy choice.

What, then, is the significance of the name change? Whatever the grammatical or syntactical value of the new name, its assignment to Jacob is obviously of profound relevance. J. Barton Payne provided this evaluation:

Mighty to Save

> The name *yiśrā'ēl* was bestowed upon Jacob by the Angel of
> Yahweh . . . himself, after he had wrestled with him all
> night. . . . Jacob's struggle was spiritual, in prayer . . . as well
> as physical. And in it the patriarch "prevailed."[35]

Speiser commented on the profound influence of the Jabbok event:

> Significantly, Jacob is henceforth a changed person. The man
> who could be a party to the cruel hoax that was played on his
> father and brother, and who fought Laban's treachery with
> crafty schemes of his own, will soon condemn the vengeful
> deed by Simeon and Levi (xxxiv) by invoking a higher con-
> cept of morality (xlix 5-7).[36]

Driver captured the import of the total experience in
this moving summary:

> The struggle at Peniel is the turning-point in Jacob's
> life. . . . He is on the point of re-entering the land which he
> left 20 years before (xxi. 41); he is about to meet his brother,
> whom he had wronged and deceived; memories of the past
> crowd upon him; his conscience smites him, and he is 'greatly
> afraid.' But God is his real antagonist, not Esau; it is God
> whom his sins have offended, and who here comes to contest
> His right. These thoughts and fears are, as it were, materi-
> alized in his dream. He struggles with his mysterious an-
> tagonist; and he struggles with such persistence and effect
> that his antagonist cannot overcome him, until by a divine
> touch he paralyses his natural strength. Even then Jacob's
> tenacity of purpose remains unimpaired; he is conscious that
> he has a heavenly visitant in his embrace. . . . But he only
> gains the blessing after his natural self has been rendered
> powerless. The moment marks a great spiritual change in
> Jacob's character. He feels his carnal weapons become lamed
> and useless; they fail him in his contest with God; as the re-
> sult of his struggle his natural self is left behind, he rises
> from it an altered man.[37]

In similar vein, Nahum M. Sarna concluded, "The major
significance of the episode derives, of course, from the
change of name that resulted."[38] The substitution of Israel
for Jacob, with all the obvious symbolism of the two names,
was the external label that indicated an internal modification. After the battle of Jabbok, the younger son of Isaac
was never quite the same. His attitude was different, his
disposition more kind, gentle, and less demanding. He
even walked differently! From that memorable night forward he limped "because of his hip" (Gen. 32:25, 31-32).
The name change is the signet of his character alteration.

The transition from Deceiver to Prevailer with God, of course, inevitably calls to mind the word from Patmos of "a white stone with a new name written on it" (Rev. 2:17). In Western culture, a formal change of name is a rather infrequent occurrence. However, in non-Christian societies, new believers sometimes adopt a biblical name as an indication of a new birth and a new loyalty. Considering the Jacob-Israel transition, perhaps the procedure is an appropriate way to commemorate a change of heart and life. In any event, the angel's pronouncement at Jabbok indicates a spiritual metamorphosis in the heart of Jacob.[39]

Recognition. After the experience, Israel (Jacob) named the place Peniel with the explanation, "It is because I saw God face to face, and yet my life was spared" (Gen. 32:30). Following the name selection motif mentioned above, his causal clause clarifies the site-name choice, for Peniel means "Face of God."[40] On the basis of this statement alone, independent of other confirming factors, one may conclude that Jacob's opponent was some concrete, physical manifestation of deity. Whatever term or interpretation the modern reader may attach to the mysterious figure, Jacob was himself convinced that he had encountered God face to face.

Israel's straightforward confidence about the identity of the midnight intruder and the nature of the Jabbok event beautifully anticipates the salvation assurance projected by John: "I write these things to you who believe in the name of the Son of God so that you may know that you have eternal life" (1 John 5:13). Even as he limped away from Peniel, perhaps leaning for support on a makeshift cane, the former Deceiver knew that he had had an experience with God and would never be the same.

The strange dream at Luz, on the way to Paddan Aram, prompted Jacob to call the location Bethel, the "house of God." No doubt the experience was a vital factor in Israel's preparation for his unique role in the divine salvation strategy, but the grand transition occurred at the ford of Jabbok. At Bethel he entered the house of God. At Peniel he met the Master of the house, face to face.

Accordingly, though the time and circumstance of the Jabbok event are radically different from those of Paul's

Damascus Road incident, the two happenings are not totally dissimilar. The transformation from Jacob to Israel
surely anticipates the later transition of Saul to Paul.

Notes

[1]For example, the role of the "matchmaker" in Japan. See *Kenkyusha's New Japanese-English Dictionary*, 1954 ed., s.v. "nakadachi"
and "nakōdo." For insight into the Japanese family and marriage tradition, compare Lafcadio Hearn, *Japan: An Attempt at Interpretation*, 3rd
ed. (Tokyo: Charles E. Tuttle Company, 1962), 55-79 and Alexander
Campbell, *The Heart of Japan* (New York: Alfred A. Knopf, 1961), 67-
69, 289-90. Hearn's allusion to Jacob and Rachel (64-65) is intriguing.

[2]In footnote to Genesis 25:25. This assumes a connection between
שֵׂעָר and עֵשָׂו. KB concludes that the etymology of the term is uncertain.
See under "עָשָׂו," 3:845.

[3]See the footnote to Genesis 25:26 in NIV. The association is between עָקֵב and יַעֲקֹב.

[4]The full note reads, "Jacob means *he grasps the heel* (figuratively,
he deceives)."

[5]See BDB, 784-85 and J. Barton Payne, "עָקַב," *TWOT*, 2:691-92.

[6]Especially in light of the force of the adjective עָקֹב (Jer. 17:9), the
NIV translation "deceive" is preferable to the archaic "supplant" (KJV)
and the "follow at the heel" or "overreach" of BDB, 784. Jeremiah's later
use of the verb ("Every brother is a deceiver, Jer. 9:4, NIV) is reinforced
by the parallel expression, "and every friend a slanderer." Accordingly,
von Rad's speculation that "Esau in his anger misunderstands his
brother's name etymologically" (*Genesis*, 278) lacks credibility.

[7]Compare Romans 9:13.

[8]NIV's translation of אִישׁ תָּם as "quiet man" is interesting. See also
von Rad, *Genesis*, 264. Compare Speiser's "retiring man" (*Genesis*), 194.

[9]Genesis 25:29-34. As is well known, אָדֹם and אֱדוֹם share the same
semantic root.

[10]Notice the doting involvement of Rebekah.

[11]Rebekah convinced Isaac that Jacob should marry one of the
"daughters of Laban" instead of a "Canaanite woman" (Gen. 27:46—
28:2), but the true reason for her proposal undoubtedly was fear for
Jacob's life (Gen. 27:41-45).

[12]Hebrew מַצֵּבָה.

[13]For Jacob's own appraisal of his "net worth," compare Genesis
32:4-5.

[14]The specific location of Laban's home in Paddan Aram (Gen. 29:4).

[15]Literally, "you have stolen my heart," words which Esau could just
as easily have uttered. Laban did not use the verb associated with
Jacob's name.

[16]Compare the experience of Saul of Tarsus (Acts 9:3-5).

[17]The literal statement in verse 20 is, "I will cover his face."

[18]Note Speiser's translation "some man" (*Genesis*, 253) and Westermann's parenthetical "[that is, 'someone']" in *Genesis*, 229. Von Rad observed, "The word 'man' is open to all possible interpretations" (*Genesis*, 320).

[19]Westermann, *Genesis*, 229.

[20]Ibid. For a full discussion of various theories concerning the "man" at Jabbok, see Allen P. Ross, *Creation and Blessing* (Grand Rapids: Baker Book House, 1988), 546-49.

[21]Speiser, *Genesis*, 256.

[22]The Greek term μετάνοια (*metanoia*), generally translated "repentance" (see Acts 20:21).

[23]To propose that God, in a temporary physical form, wrestled with Jacob does not warrant the evaluation that the story is close to "all those sagas in which gods, spirits, or demons attack a man and in which then the man extorts something of their strength and their secret" (von Rad, *Genesis*, 321). The consistent moral character of the Old Testament sets this account uniquely apart from such superstitious legends.

[24]Von Rad, *Genesis*, 321. The objectionable feature of von Rad's sentence is the verb "wrest" that implies "divine vitality" can be seized, rather than received. Equally unacceptable is Westermann's evaluation: "In this context, such a blessing can mean only that the attacker must give him some of his superhuman power" (*Genesis*, 229).

[25]Perhaps the Old Testament identification, "the Angel of YHWH," would be an appropriate label.

[26]Von Rad, *Genesis*, 321.

[27]See BDB, 975. R. Laird Harris added, "The verb *śārâ* limits itself to contexts which discuss the struggle of Jacob as he wrestled with the Angel of Yahweh at Peniel in Transjordan" ("שָׂרָה," *TWOT* 2:883). Note also the semantic association with שָׂרַר and שַׂר. (Compare Gary G. Cohen, "שָׂרַר," *TWOT*, 2:884 and KB, "שׂרר," 4:1269.)

[28]Edward M. Curtis, "Structure, Style and Context as a Key to Interpreting Jacob's Encounter at Peniel," in *Journal of the Evangelical Theological Society* 30, no. 2 (June 1987): 134.

[29]Hebrew words meaning "God strengthens" and "God hears" respectively.

[30]For example, Genesis 4:25; Exodus 2:22; 1 Samuel 1:20; Isaiah 8:3-4; Hosea 1:6, 9.

[31]Plus "with men."

[32]In the Hebrew text, Hosea 12:4-5. The pointing of the verb (v. 5) is debated. KB proposes וַיִּשַׂר for וַיָּשַׂר (the Masoretic Text actually has וַיָּשַׂר). See under "I שׂרה," 4:1262. Compare Payne, "שָׂרָה," *TWOT*, 2:883 and Driver, *Genesis*, 295.

[33]The first verb has either the preposition "with" or the direct object marker (identical forms in this situation, see BDB, 84-85) followed by אֱלֹהִים, while the second features the preposition אֶל with מַלְאָךְ.

[34]Driver, *Genesis*, 295. For other options, see Ross, *Creation and Blessing*, 554-55. Manfred Krebernik called attention to the analogue of

personal names from Ebla. "A great number of personal names are composed of a prefixed verbal form and a noun, the verbal form usually preceding the noun which may be its *object* [italics added] or, less often, its object." Krebernik probably intended to contrast "subject" with "object." His footnote explained, "Clear examples of names containing a direct object of their verbal element are ab-ri -a-ḫu, ar-si -a-ḫa (and variant spellings), ar-šè -ti-lu, ù-da aḫ/a-ḫa." See Manfred Krebernik, "Prefixed Verbal Forms in Personal Names from Ebla," in *Eblaite Personal Names and Semitic Name-Giving*, ed. Alfonso Archi (Missione Archeologica Italiana in Siria, 1988), 86. The first-person form of the prefix conjugation indicates that the noun form is objective in function. Compare Giovanni Pettinato, *The Archives of Ebla* (Garden City: Doubleday & Company, 1981), 64.

[35]Payne, "שָׂרָה," *TWOT*, 2:883.

[36]Speiser, *Genesis*, 257.

[37]Driver, *Genesis*, 296-97.

[38]Nahum M. Sarna, *Understanding Genesis* (New York: Schocken Books, 1966), 206.

[39]The reference to the name change following Jacob's return to Bethel (Gen. 35:1-13) is recapitulation rather than recurrence. Compare Speiser, *Genesis*, 271.

[40]פְּנִיאֵל. The alternate form, פְּנוּאֵל, also means "Face of God."

6

At Sinai:
The Covenant of Holiness

*You will be for me a kingdom of priests
and a holy nation.*

Exodus 19:6

Three months after their supernatural deliverance from Egyptian bondage, the Israelites bivouacked at the base of a rugged mountain in the desert of Sinai (Ex. 19:1-2). The precise location of Mount Sinai[1] is unknown,[2] but the events which transpired there are of far greater importance than the question of site identification. At the "mountain of God" (Ex. 3:1) the patriarchal Deity entered into a formal covenant relationship with the descendants of Abraham, Isaac, and Jacob.

Covenant Analysis

As previously noted, Old Testament covenants may be evaluated from several different perspectives.[3] The covenant at Sinai[4] obviously established a specific connection between God and His people and constituted a formal treaty or pledge. Its elements included a historical introduction (Ex. 19:3-4),[5] stipulation(s) (Ex. 19:5a), blessings (Ex. 19:6), a formal agreement (Ex. 19:8; 24:3,7), and even regulations (Ex. 20:1—23:33). It also featured a ratification rite (Ex. 24:4-8), the erection of a memorial marker (Ex. 24:4), codification (Ex. 24:4,7), a possible reference to a solemn meal (Ex. 24:11), and the institution of a covenant sign (Ex. 31:16-17). Accordingly, the Sinai transaction contained classic covenant elements so that the record of the event fits nicely into its proposed ancient Near Eastern setting.

Of particular importance is the fact that the covenant included stipulation(s). The entire formula began with an explicit requirement introduced by a hypothetical particle translated "if."[6] The arrangement was, therefore, specifically conditional, which means that the covenant was obligatory in character, not promissory. Whatever one's understanding of the nature of the stipulation(s) may be, the fact that a condition of any kind was required indicates that the condition had not yet been satisfied. Obviously, then, ethnic ancestry was not an adequate qualification for the covenant. To be a physical descendant of the patriarchs was not enough. While the covenant offer was extended to the Hebrew tribes, just being Hebrew would not guarantee covenant participation.

Covenant Distinctions

"The covenant with Israel" or "the covenant with Moses" are interchangeable generic expressions which may be applied in a general sort of way to the overall religious situation in the Old Testament. Unfortunately, the labels lack precision. Even when applied to the Sinai transaction, they are not completely accurate. The ambiguity stems from the fact that three covenants with Israel are specified in the Old Testament as prior to Israel's initial entry into Canaan. Because of these multiple descriptions, the agreement at Sinai must be very clearly and carefully distinguished.

Covenant of Entry. An additional covenant reference, for example, is contained in Exodus 34:10, "I am making a covenant with you. Before all your people I will do wonders never before done in any nation in all the world." As Childs observed, the general context and similarity in content led Wellhausen and others to conclude that chapter 34 is a "parallel account to ch. 20 of the Sinai covenant."[7]

W. H. Gispen, on the other hand, has suggested that "this covenant was to be a renewal of the first covenant, which had been broken by the sin of the golden calf."[8] While Gispen's view avoids a slavish adherence to a notion of anonymous authors and phantom editors, it does not correlate well with the textual data. J. P. Hyatt noted, "There is nothing in the language which suggests a covenant renewal." He added further, "The present account tells nothing of a ceremony in which the people accept the covenant and its terms, as one finds in 24:3,7."[9]

Although Hyatt's opinion that the language avoids the notion of covenant renewal may be subject to debate, his statement about the absence of ratification ceremony is irrefutable. How, then, may one harmonize the divergent covenant descriptions?

The resolution is relatively simple and obvious. In the first place, these are not necessarily irreconcilable accounts of the same event. This premise requires the importation of considerable contextual and historical presupposition. Nothing in the text, as it stands, supports or even suggests this assumption. The apparent parallels between Exodus 20 and 34 are cosmetic, at best, while their distinctives are clear and positive. Moreover, as Hyatt indicated, specific references to renewal are totally absent. The conclusion, therefore, is that these are two different covenants and that they are distinguished on the basis of context and content.

The context of the covenant in Exodus 34 is made distinct by the fact that Israel had just violated her original covenant commitment in the "molten calf" episode.[10] The geographical setting for the developments in chapters 34 and 20 was the same, but the time and circumstances were dramatically different. A deposit and a withdrawal have much in common; they are both monetary transactions that occur in banks. Even if they occur on the same day and are negotiated by the same party in the same bank, they are definitely not the same transaction. Similarly, the two covenants in Exodus share common location and terminology but are radically different.

Still, the covenant God and the covenant people were certainly the same in both instances. Or were they? In Exodus

20, the Israelites were a freshly liberated people who stood on the threshold of a new relationship with the God of their ancestors. They were about to become a glorious new community "bound for the promised land," a land that had been divinely pledged to them as an "everlasting possession" (Gen. 17:8). In Exodus 34 they were a people who had flagrantly violated their newly negotiated covenant status and had seriously jeopardized their very existence.

In one terrible spasm of forsaking God, they shattered the dreams that had sustained their corporate life and hope for generations. They were the same people perhaps, but only to a point. Names and faces might have been identical, but the character and status of the people were profoundly altered.

Even the disposition of the covenant God had been modified by Israel's arrogant disobedience. Offended righteousness is reflected in YHWH's admonition to Moses, "Now leave me alone so that my anger may burn against them and that I may destroy them. Then I will make you into a great nation" (Ex. 32:10). The infidelity that would characterize later Hebrew covenant performance was already evident, and God was already offended. The situation in Exodus 34 was clouded and complicated by earthly betrayal and heavenly disappointment.

The covenant context in Exodus 34 explains the terse covenant content. When YHWH proposed to destroy Israel and replace the current generation with his descendants, Moses interceded for the people. While insisting that He would hold the people accountable for their sin (Ex. 32:33-35), YHWH did agree to direct Israel to Canaan in keeping with His pledge to Abraham (Ex. 33:1-3). Further, in response to Moses' anguished plea (Ex. 33:15), YHWH granted a muted disclosure of His awesome majesty and then initiated a new covenant guaranteeing Israel's entry into the land.

The new, second covenant was unilateral and promissory. The only requirement was lineage from Abraham, a condition that Israel had already fulfilled. No additional stipulations were required. The covenant benefit was also singular: a providential entrance into Canaan (Ex. 34:10-11). Then YHWH appended a solemn rejoinder to remind

Israel of its total covenant responsibility (Ex. 34:12-27). Although this addendum is similar to earlier provisions, it is basically summary in nature rather than repetitious.[11] We conclude, therefore, that this is neither a parallel description of the covenant at Mount Sinai nor a renewal of it. Instead, it is a second, distinct covenant that only promises Israel's entrance into the land. Consequently, it may be designated the Covenant of Entry.

Covenant of Possession. The covenant at Mount Sinai must also be distinguished from the transaction that is described in the Book of Deuteronomy. That confusion should cloud the distinction between these two covenants is strange in light of the explicit statement of the text:

"These are the terms of the covenant the LORD commanded Moses to make with the Israelites in Moab, in addition to the covenant he had made with them at Horeb" (Deut. 29:1).

Two visible surface features indicate the difference: (1) the covenants were negotiated at different places, and (2) they were instituted at different times. The two locales are clearly marked by the contrast between Moab and Horeb. The time differential is just as obvious. The event at Sinai occurred three months after Israel's exodus from Egypt (Ex. 19:1),[12] while the Moab matter took place just before the death of Moses (Deut. 31:2).[13] Accordingly, miles and years of desert wandering separated the two incidents as they are described in the Books of Exodus and Deuteronomy.

Lest some latter-day spectator of the text should confuse the two, the writer added a distinctive qualifier[14] which is reflected in the NIV translation, "in addition to." The expression may be used to distinguish something from a previous, similar item in order to discriminate one from the other.[15] It is so employed here. Gesenius construed the term as having "a purely adverbial meaning" and is the equivalent of *"taken by itself."*[16] Time, place, and terminology, therefore, combine to dictate that the two covenants be carefully recognized as separate and distinct from each other.

In addition, the Sinai and Moab contracts are different in total content as well as historical circumstance. Granted, the requirements appear to be similar if not identical. But,

as will be presently noted, the resemblance is just that—
and nothing more. A careful scrutiny of the text will reveal
a pivotal shift in the deuteronomic terminology which cannot be ignored.

The fundamental disparity between the two arrangements is demonstrated by the expanded catalogue of blessings and curses in the deuteronomic code (Deut. 28—30), a
list totally absent in the Sinai agreement. Moreover, notice the focal point of the agenda. All of the benefits and
warnings have to do with the land. Even when the LORD
projected Israel's banishment from Canaan (Deut. 28:36-
68), the land continued to be the frame of reference (Deut.
29:22-29). As might be expected, then, restoration to the
land is the key feature of the covenant's finale (Deut. 30:1-
20). From first to last in the Moab context, the emphasis is
on the land, Israel's promised inheritance.

In the bleak wilderness of Sinai, the land was but a distant dream, a fantasy inspired by an ancient promise and
sustained by four hundred years of misery. From the land
of Moab, on the banks of Jordan, Israel could "cast a wish-
ful eye / To Canaan's fair and happy land"[17] where their
dream of Utopia would become earthly reality. So, because
of its center of interest, as well as the geographical setting, the contract in Moab may be described as the Covenant of Possession.[18]

J. Wash Watts proposed that this covenant and the one
in Exodus 34[19] were "conditioned upon birth and circumcision," adding that the covenant of possession required "circumcision of the heart as well."[20] Something more than
birth or ritual was obviously demanded in the Covenant of
Possession, but the exact emphasis of its requirement is
best revealed in a contrast with that of the Sinai stipula-
tion(s). Suffice it to say at this point that YHWH con-
fronted Israel with three distinct covenant proposals
before their entrance into the land.

Covenant Condition(s)

The requirements specified in Exodus 19:5 and Deuteronomy 28:1 are so similar as to almost coincide. The affin-

ity is reflected in most translations, but the verb formulas translated in the NIV as "obey . . . fully" (Ex. 19:5) and "fully obey" (Deut. 28:1) are, essentially, exactly the same in the Hebrew text.[21] The solitary verb (שָׁמַע) is used extensively in the Old Testament to describe the reception of speech or sound.[22] Generally, it means "to hear" and nothing more, though occasionally it may include the notion of "listen to" or "obey."[23]

The construction employed in both of these instances, however, clearly indicates a stress or emphasis that transcends the routine. It is produced by the addition of the infinitive absolute before the finite (or conjugated) form of the verb. Grammarians are in general agreement that this syntactical formula was used by the biblical writers to denote emphasis.[24] Still, the exact meaning of the pattern, the intensification of the act of hearing, is not altogether clear. Since this formula is used in two different but equally strategic situations, one may logically assume that something important was intended. The assumption is reinforced by an examination of the construction in other contexts.

The pattern appears in at least six additional instances,[25] with a structure so rigid as to suggest idiom, i.e., "an expression whose meaning cannot be derived from the customary meaning of the component words."[26] If so, then the verbal phrase means more than a literal "if to hear, you hear" translation would allow. Moreover, its use by multiple authors would indicate an idiom of thought rather than style.[27] It is also worthwhile to note that in every case the idiom is introduced by a hypothetical particle (אִם) and constitutes the protasis of a conditional sentence.

In each circumstance, Israel was challenged to meet a certain standard. The benefits promised if they would meet the condition stipulated reveal the importance of the matter. They included exemption from the diseases which had plagued Egypt (Ex. 15:26), becoming YHWH's "treasured possession" (Ex. 19:5), protection and providence (Ex. 23:22-23), fruitfulness in the land (Deut. 11:13-14), the bountiful blessings of YHWH (Deut. 15:5-6), exaltation by YHWH (Deut. 28:1), preservation of the Davidic throne (Jer. 17:24-26), and participation in the rule of the

Priest-King (Zech. 6:11-15). The dazzling array of consequences to the conditional formula must surely call attention to its importance.

Obviously, the augmented form of the verb meant more than simply to hear or to listen. The idiom may therefore be a classic example of what Sawyer described as "metaphorical transference." In this case it moves from the concrete to the abstract,[28] in which response would exceed the mere reception of sound waves. The expression apparently designates a disposition of commitment and loyalty that would exhibit itself in unqualified obedient response to whatever the LORD might instruct. Watts offered this evaluation:

> "Obey my voice" is a description of faith rather than works.... It is distinguished from "Keep my covenant," which follows, so applies to the obedience of faith instead of the obedience of works.... Nevertheless, it is vital to our understanding of the teaching here to recognize that this expression makes faith to be the pivotal point in this covenant, as it is in every biblical offer of spiritual salvation.[29]

The context of Exodus 19:5 and the parallel uses of the pattern appear to support Watts's interpretation. Furthermore, examples of metaphorical transference abound in the Old Testament.[30] The prophets, especially, used literal terms to describe spiritual concepts (Isa. 35:1-10; Joel 2:23-27). So despite the fact that the verb is not conventionally acknowledged as soteriological in character,[31] the use of this particular idiom in multiple contexts strongly suggests a soteriological frame of reference.[32] Watts correlated the conditions and promises of the Exodus text in this conclusion:

> These promises are promises to spiritual Israel as surely as those to Christians in I Peter 2:9. The only essential difference is that those addressed in I Peter 2:9 are Christians, whose faith is assumed; while those addressed here are a mixture of believers and unbelievers, whose faith must be reckoned conditionally.[33]

Another feature of the stipulation (as translated) in Exodus 19:5 demands evaluation: the significance and force of "and keep my covenant."[34] As previously noted, the two conditional formulas in Exodus 19:5 and Deuteronomy 28:1 are almost identical; but the distinction between the two is a critical item. Indeed, the clarification of the pattern in Deuteronomy 28:1 provides a clue to the uniqueness of the parallel in Exodus 19:5. Both begin with the aforementioned idiom built on the verb שָׁמַע ("hear") followed by the same verb, שָׁמַר, which means "keep" or "guard."[35]

But the inflected forms of the second verb are different, with "keep" modified as an infinitive construct (לִשְׁמֹר) in Deuteronomy and complemented by a second infinitive construct (לַעֲשׂוֹת) based on עָשָׂה ("do"). This accounts for the difference in the translations "keep" (Ex. 19:5) and "carefully follow" (Deut. 28:1). The double-infinitive construct in Deuteronomy means literally (placed together and without context) "to keep to do."

The form of an infinitive construct is relatively easy to identify, but its syntactical performance can produce a rather bewildering assortment of options and possibilities. Waltke and O'Connor, for example, indicate that an infinitive construct may function as "a true infinitive, a verb and a noun." Because of its versatility, an infinitive construct may serve as either the subject or object of a verb, the construct of another noun, the predicate of a clause (for example, a temporal or purpose clause), and even as a verbal complement.[36]

As a result of the wide range of possibilities, a conclusive evaluation of the infinitives in Deuteronomy 28:1 may not be possible; but probably both should be construed as *"explanatory or epexegetical."*[37] If that equation can be applied to both infinitives, then each is explaining "the circumstances or nature of a preceding action."[38] In the case of "to do," it explains the meaning of the preceding "to keep," while "to keep" expands the thought of the preceding verbal idiom "fully obey." The syntactical flow might be diagrammed:

fully obey = to keep = to do.

In this text, then, the meaning of "fully obey" is clarified by the infinitive construct tandem.

Conditional Patterns. Before the two covenant paradigms can be fully distinguished, however, one must consider the design of conditional sentences in the Hebrew

Old Testament. As in English, conditional formations occur in a number of different formats which reflect, at least
theoretically, relative degrees of certainty in the mind of
the speaker or writer.[39] The crucial concern in evaluating
the covenants in Sinai and Moab, though, is not the level
of certainty in protasis and apodosis (condition and consequence), but precision in defining the transition from the
protasis to the apodosis. Using the equal sign (=) as a
guide to the transition zone from condition to consequence,
the following paradigms are possible:

$$\#1 \quad A = B$$
$$\#2 \quad A + B = C$$
$$\#3 \quad A = B + C$$
$$\#4 \quad A + AB + BC = D \ (+E)$$
$$\#5 \quad A^1 + A^2 = B \ (+C)$$

In model #1, a single condition produces a single result.
In model #2, a dual (or multiple) condition issues in a singular result. Model #3 has a single condition with a dual
(or multiple) result. Model #4 features a singular condition
(with explanation) that has a single (or multiple) result.
Model #5 has a single condition (with elaboration) that
has a single (or multiple) result.

Just as conditional sentences may or may not contain
distinctive introductory particles,[40] so the shift from condition to consequence is not always evident and may be
marked only "by the simple juxtaposition of two clauses."[41]
However, one peculiar pattern is generally recognized as
designating the shift from protasis to apodosis: the *vav* (ו)
followed by the perfect form of the verb.[42] This classic
function of the *vav* plus the perfect led Waltke and O'Connor to observe: "The proposed original function of the
weqatalti construction to signify the apodosis of a conditional clause shines through almost all of its uses in Biblical Hebrew."[43]

The *weqatalti* pattern, to use Waltke and O'Connor's
designation, is so clearly associated with the apodosis of a
conditional sentence that its presence should clearly sig-
nal the transition. When the syntactical principle is
evenly applied, it may, indeed, reduce the level of confusion. In the A = B situation (model #1), the application is

relatively simple, as in Genesis 18:26: "If I find . . . (then) I will spare."[44] However, as the conditions and consequences become complicated, difficulties may arise. A multiple protasis condition followed by a single result (model #2) is contained in Zechariah 3:7, although both NIV and KJV translate the verse as though it contained a dual condition and a triple result.[45]

Ignoring models #3 and #5 for the moment, notice that Deuteronomy 28:1-2 illustrates model #4. The protasis is marked by the idiom "If you fully obey" that is explained by the double infinitive construct. (This, of course, is A + AB + BC = D + E.) The full condition would be: "If you fully obey by carefully following all his commands." Two *weqatalti* forms then introduce the dual apodosis. They are (he) "will set you" and (they) "will come." Putting the two components together (with italics indicating the location of each transitional *vav*) produces this modified translation:

"And it shall be,[46] if you fully obey the LORD your God by carefully following all his commands I give you today, *then* the LORD your God will set you high above all the nations on earth, *and* all these blessings will come upon you."

Now consider the conditional formula in Exodus 19:5: "if you obey me fully and keep my covenant, then out of all nations you will be my treasured possession." The format would suggest a straightforward A + B = C paradigm. However, as an Deuteronomy 28:1 only the idiom "obey . . . fully" is tagged with the hypothetical particle (אִם). It is followed by two *weqatalti* verb forms; both "keep" and "be" feature the perfect conjugation with *vav*.

The question is, "Which perfect with *vav* introduces the apodosis?" Unfortunately, the answer is not always obvious. Evaluating a similar construction, S. R. Driver noted that "it is only the sense which shews" where the apodosis begins.[47] The uncertainty may be compounded when multiple *weqatalti* verbs string together. For example, Jacob's vow, "If God will be with me" is followed by four perfect verbs with *vav* (Gen. 28:20-21).[48] Only the force of the verbs in the immediate context provides a clue to the alteration from condition to result. In the light of the fact that the first three verbs appear to elaborate the meaning of the vague and ambiguous "be with me," the translations are likely correct in assigning the transition to the fourth *weqatalti* verb.[49]

I am convinced, however, that this pattern represents an enhancement of the condition rather than an expansion. Accordingly, I propose the paradigm $A^1 + A^2 = B$ of model #5 as opposed to the model #2 pattern (see Zech. 3:7 for model #2).

Exodus 19:5 presents a relatively simple format. The idiom in the protasis is followed by two *weqatalti* forms. The options are limited, and the context does not suggest or require that the transition from protasis to apodosis be shifted from the first *vav* with perfect to the second. Indeed, in all such situations (barring some critical contextual factor), the plausible assumption would be to construe the initial *weqatalti* as the first unit in the apodosis. The paradigm, then, would be $A = B + C$ of model #3. Following that pattern, we propose the translation (italics added): "Now if you obey me fully, *then* you will keep my covenant *and* you will be my treasured possession out of all nations."[50]

The implications of the foregoing analysis are worth noting. First, observe that the conditional paradigms represent the application of independent syntactical principles. Although the applications may not always be evenly applied, still the connection between the principle and the application may be pursued in either direction.

Second, if the idiom "obey fully" is actually a concrete definition of saving, biblical faith, then the Sinai covenant hinged on faith rather than ancestry or ritual. Consequently, Watts's designation of the arrangement as the "Covenant of Holiness" [51] is on target. Moreover, this perception of salvation associated with Sinai is remarkably compatible with Paul's insistence that "by observing the law no one will be justified" (Gal. 2:16).

Third, if saving faith is so defined, then it is faith alone that ensures covenant status. However, faith is not defined as mere intellectual assent. Rather, it is characterized as a commitment to the LORD and intentional, deliberate compliance with His covenant. Quality of performance might be one thing; but the agreement extended no alternative to obedience. "If you obey me fully, then you *will* keep my covenant" (italics added; see Jas. 2:18).

Covenant Benefits

The second *weqatalti* form guaranteed, "you will be my treasured possession."[52] Just as acceptance of the covenant offer included a concomitant obligation to "keep his covenant," it also guaranteed a special status. Behind the expression "treasured possession" stands the single Hebrew word *sĕgullāh*.[53] The word occurs eight times in the Hebrew Old Testament,[54] with the locations in Exodus, Deuteronomy, and Psalms all referring to Israel's singular covenant relationship to YHWH. The verse in Chronicles explains *sĕgullāh* in terms of "gold and silver," while in Ecclesiastes it includes the wealth of "kings and provinces." In Malachi 3:17, YHWH Himself projected the time when His "treasured possession" would be complete by the inclusion of all who "feared the LORD and honored his name" (Mal. 3:16).[55] Evidently, then, the term denotes a special treasure of great value and importance and, in the covenant context, connotes a unique status or relationship.

Covenant Deity

The caricature image that portrays the God of the Old Testament as an angry, vindictive deity finds at least some inspiration in the data incorporated in the Sinai covenant. This distortion is actually the result of blurred perception in two areas. First, it ignores the concise, explicit instruction about the benevolent nature and character of YHWH that is contained elsewhere in the Book of Exodus. Exodus 3:14-15, for example, demonstrates the durability and dependability of the God who would enact a covenant with Israel.

Furthermore, in the tragic, post-molten calf setting, the LORD's own exegesis of His name in Exodus 34:6-7 exhibits something of the magnitude and depth of His unfathomable being. In a hallmark definition of His character that would be cited and recited in later biblical texts,[56] the LORD described Himself as compassionate (רַחוּם), gracious (חַנּוּן), patient (אֶרֶךְ אַפַּיִם),[57] faithful (חֶסֶד),[58] and just.[59] Embedded in this remarkable elaboration is an extraordinary word about the divine resolution of the human sin problem, a resolution that will epitomize ultimate mercy. Reluctantly, we postpone an examination of the divine remedy until the nature and consequences of the sin problem are explored in the next chapter.

Second, exegetical myopia overlooks the gleams of heavenly mercy that shine from the core of the Sinai covenant. Some, for example, have appealed to Exodus 20:4-6 as a basis for the view that the God of the "Old Covenant" was mean and vicious, scarcely able to control His furious anger.[60] One might, indeed, draw such a conclusion from a casual reading of the second commandment:

"You shall not make for yourself an idol in the form of anything in heaven above or on the earth beneath or in the waters below. You shall not bow down to them or worship them; for I, the LORD your God, am a jealous God, punishing the children for the sin of the fathers to the third and fourth generation of those who hate me, but showing love to a thousand generations of those who love me and keep my commandments" (Ex. 20:4-6).

However, a cautious probing of the text offers some intriguing results. Quite evidently, the edict prohibited the production of all idols or icons, regardless of their respective associations.[61] The basis for this ban is attributed to the fact that YHWH is a "jealous God." At first glance, the adjective "jealous" would seem to indicate childish petulance on the part of the LORD. The impression is strengthened by an examination of the verb that stands behind the adjective. Leonard J. Coppes provides this clarification:

> This verb expresses a very strong emotion whereby some quality or possession of the object is desired by the subject. . . .
> It may prove helpful to think of "zeal" as the original sense from which derived the notions "zeal for another's property" = "envy" and "zeal for one's own property" = "jealousy."[62]

While the verb may have either a positive or negative connotation, it is worthwhile to note that this particular adjective "is used solely for God and in the context of idolatry" and "occurs only in the Pentateuch (five times)."[63] In the context of potential paganism, the term tags the urgent zeal with which the LORD resisted Israel's disposition to turn to other gods. His opposition did not stem from a juvenile inability to encounter competition. Rather, it resulted from His knowledge that there was no competition. Keenly aware that apart from Himself there was no other god or deliverer (Isa. 45:22), and sensitive to the fact that Israel's apostasy would be total and meaningless futility (Jer. 2:11-13), YHWH vigorously resisted the Hebrews' penchant for idolatry. The zeal of YHWH, therefore, stipulated the protective concern that the LORD felt for His own.

Furthermore, the language of verse 5 would imply punishment of the innocent or at least the transference of guilt from one generation to the next. Before drawing that conclusion, though, the student of the text should observe that the "common causal conjunctions" that customarily denote cause and effect relationships are totally absent from the verse.[64] Accordingly, the text does not specifically affirm that the children were to be punished because of the sins of their fathers. Such a construction of these words is inconsistent with the general biblical view of individual responsibility and explicitly contradicts other statements about accountability (Ezek. 18:1-4).

The phenomenon targeted, therefore, may be nothing more ominous than the expanding influence of parental example. The principle, condensed in the adage "like father, like son," is here applied to the insidious and expanding evil influence that one generation may exert over another. Wonderful contradictions to the pattern might occur; but, once more, the exception only confirms the rule. The interpreter does not necessarily, therefore, need to charge the covenant deity with random or irresponsible viciousness.

Is such a rosy, positive interpretation consistent with the general flow of the context, or have we simply imposed an alien flavor on this stern commandment? How, indeed, may one extrapolate a positive message from a totally negative statement? If the Second Commandment were to conclude at the end of verse 5, an optimistic evaluation would be difficult, if not impossible, to defend. However, despite the disruptive interruption created by division into verses, the commandment does *not* stop with verse 5. Rather, verses 5-6 are linked together by a coordinating form of the conjunction that decisively links the two to-gether.[65] Verse 6 constitutes both the conclusion and the climax to the total command contained in the two preceding verses. One must, therefore, interpret verses 4 and 5 in light of verse 6.

This calls attention to the presence of another idiom in verse 5, the expression translated "third and fourth generation." In some English editions, the idiom is signaled by italic print for the word "generation." The editorial device is employed to alert the English reader to the fact that the word in italics is not specifically present in the Hebrew text.[66] In this case, the Hebrew word "generation"[67] is absent in verse 5 (and verse 6 as well). The two numerals (שְׁלֵשִׁים and רִבֵּעִים) are actually plural forms of their respective ordinals and literally mean "thirds" and "fourths." This explanation is not to contest the suitability of using "generations"; the formula is a perfectly acceptable Hebrew idiom that evidently denotes "generation" (Gen. 50:23).

If, however, "generation" is appropriate in verse 5, then (as in NIV) it is mandatory in verse 6. Accordingly, the climactic conclusion in verse 6 provides a comparison between YHWH's pledge to punish sin with His eagerness to exhibit "love"[68] by contrasting "thirds and fourths" with "thousands." The emphasis is not on wrath but on mercy. The "mountain" of His desire to lavish goodness and compassion is compared with the "molehill" of His determination to visit sin. Bottom line—the tenor of the commandment concentrates on divine charity rather than on bloodthirsty retaliation.[69]

I conclude, therefore, that the covenant ratified at Mount Sinai may be appropriately designated as the Covenant of Holiness. It was offered to corporate Israel, but participation was based on individual faith and commitment. Its regulations were never intended to provide a basis for personal or national justification. Rather, they were given as a guide to performance that would be consistent with the nature of the covenant Deity.

Their provisions were so lofty and noble, however, that they only illustrated the glaring moral discrepancy between the God of the covenant and the people of the covenant. If acceptance and maintenance in the covenant were to be experienced, it must be on the basis of a willingness to obey rather than on impeccable performance. Thus, by the unattainable requirements of the Law that were both protective and prohibitive, they were "shut up unto faith."[70]

Notes

[1]Also known as Horeb (Ex. 3:1; 33:6).

[2]For a discussion of possible options, see Aviram Perevolotsky and Israel Finkelstein, "The Southern Sinai Exodus Route in Ecological Perspective," BAR 11, no. 4 (July–August 1985): 26-41 and Emmanuel Anati, "Has Mt. Sinai Been Found?" BAR 11, no. 4 (July–August 1985): 42-57.

[3]See the preceding Excursus.

[4]Core covenant material is contained in Exodus 19—24.

[5]The first eighteen chapters of the book ("the Exodus tradition") may be construed as the historical prologue. See George E. Mendenhall, *Law and Covenant in Israel and the Ancient Near East* (Pittsburgh: The Presbyterian Board of Colportage of Western Pennsylvania, 1955), 37 and Philip B. Harner, "Exodus, Sinai, and Hittite Prologues," *JBL* 85, no. 2 (June 1966): 233-36.

[6]BDB, see under "אִם," 49. For a discussion of the significance of the conditional formula, see John I. Durham, *Exodus*, vol. 3 of *Word Biblical Commentary*, ed. David A. Hubbard and Glenn W. Barker (Waco: Word Books, Publisher, 1987), 262.

[7]Brevard S. Childs, *The Book of Exodus*, 3rd ed. (Philadelphia: The Westminster Press, 1976), 605. Following Wellhausen, who assigned chapter 34 to J and 20 to E, Childs concluded, "The present shape of the Sinai tradition in Exodus bears the decisive shaping of a redactor who combined J and E" (*Exodus*, 608).

[8]W. H. Gispen, *Exodus*, trans. Ed Vandermaas (Grand Rapids: Zondervan Publishing House, 1982), 314.

[9]J. P. Hyatt, *Exodus*, in *The New Century Bible Commentary*, ed. Ronald E. Clements and Matthew Black (Grand Rapids: William B. Eerdmans Publishing Company, 1971), 323.

[10]Compare Exodus 20:4-5 with 24:7; 32:4.

[11]Note parallels to chapters 20, 23.

[12]Moses would have been over eighty years of age at that time (see Acts 7:23-30).

[13]See A. D. H. Mayes, *Deuteronomy*, in *The New Century Bible Commentary*, ed. Ronald E. Clements and Matthew Black (Grand Rapids: William B. Eerdmans Publishing Company, 1979), 360.

[14]For examples of the use and force of the term, מִלְּבַד, see BDB, 94 and Hans-Jürgen Zobel, "בָּדַד," *TDOT*, 1:473-79.

[15]See Genesis 26:1; Leviticus 23:38; Numbers 6:21.

[16]GKC, 378.

[17]Samuel Stennett, PROMISED LAND, 1787.

[18]Watts, *Teaching*, 118.

[19]Which he labeled "a covenant of settlement" (*Teaching*, 118). Watts construed Exodus 34:10-27 as an "alteration" or "renewal" of the original covenant. See J. Wash Watts, *A Distinctive Translation of Exodus with an Interpretative Outline* (South Pasadena: Jameson Press, 1977), 134-35, 151. His premise that the alteration was based on "pardon" (Ex. 34:9), not "forgiveness," may be tenable in light of the use of סָלַח in the Book of Leviticus (Lev. 4:20,26,31, where ceremonial cleansing is emphasized) but is contradicted by its use in Isaiah 55:7 and Jeremiah 31:34; 33:8; 50:20. Moreover, as Watts acknowledged, the syntactical transition between Exodus 34:9 and 34:10 could be either "logical result" or "logical contrast" (*Syntax*, 97-100).

[20]Watts, *Teaching*, 118.

[21]The conditional formula is אִם־שָׁמוֹעַ תִּשְׁמְעוּ (with second masculine plural in the conjugated imperfect) in Exodus 19:5 and אִם־שָׁמוֹעַ תִּשְׁמַע (second masculine singular) in Deuteronomy 28:1.

[22]For example, Genesis 27:6 and 1 Kings 1:41. For a full listing of uses, see BDB, 1033-34 and KB, 4:1452-55.

[23]See BDB, 1034 and KB, 4:1453.

[24]J. Weingreen, *A Practical Grammar for Classical Hebrew* (Oxford: Clarendon Press, 1952), 79; Thomas O. Lambdin, *Hebrew*, 158; Ronald J. Williams, *Hebrew Syntax: An Outline*, 2nd ed. (Toronto: University of Toronto Press, 1980), 37-38; Waltke and O'Connor, *Syntax*, 581.

[25]Exodus 15:26; 23:22; Deuteronomy 11:13; 15:5; Jeremiah 17:24; Zechariah 6:15.

[26]Richard N. Soulen, *Handbook of Biblical Criticism* (Atlanta: John Knox Press, 1978), 82.

[27]See Elliot E. Johnson, *Expository Hermeneutics: An Introduction* (Grand Rapids: Zondervan Publishing House, 1990), 187.

[28]John F. A. Sawyer, *Semantics in Biblical Research* (Naperville, IL: Alec R. Allenson, 1972), 53-54.

[29]Watts, *Teaching*, 79-80.

[30]Sawyer, *Semantics*, 53-54.

[31]Note Sawyer's discussion of the "associative field" and "lexical group" affiliated with *HOŠIA* (*Semantics*, 29-48, 61-72).

[32]For a discussion on the importance of context, see Moises Silva, *Biblical Words and Their Meaning* (Grand Rapids: Zondervan Publishing House, 1983), 138-43.

[33]Watts, *Teaching*, 80.

[34]Note Watts's description "obedience of works" (*Teaching*, 79).

[35]BDB, 1036. Even "AWOL" Hebrew students will probably recognize the familiar שָׁמַר used in verb paradigm models because of the strong nature of its individual consonants.

[36]Waltke and O'Connor, *Syntax*, 598-610; Ronald J. Williams, *Syntax*, 35-37; Lambdin, *Hebrew*, 128-29; Watts, *Syntax*, 65-70.

[37]Waltke and O'Connor, *Syntax*, 608. Their evaluation corresponds to Watts's "specific nature of the verbal state" (*Syntax*, 67).

[38]Waltke and O'Connor, *Syntax*, 608.

[39]For discussions of the question of certainty, see GKC, 493-98; Watts, *Syntax*, 111-16; Henry Ferguson, "An Examination of the Use of the Tenses in Conditional Sentences in Hebrew," *Journal of the Society of Biblical Literature and Exegesis* 2 (1882): 40-63; S. R. Driver, *A Treatise on the Use of the Tenses in Hebrew*, 3rd ed. (Oxford: Clarendon Press, 1969), 174-94; Michael R. Spradlin, *An Investigation of Conditional Sentences in the Hebrew Text of Isaiah*, diss. (Mid-America Baptist Theological Seminary, 1991).

[40]GKC, 493. Lambdin observed, "Conditional sentences in Hebrew may be virtually unmarked" (*Hebrew*, 276).

[41]GKC, 493.

[42]Driver described the formula as a *vav* "consecutive and the perfect" (*Tenses*, 174); Williams labeled the *vav* as "resumptive" (*Syntax*, 85); Davidson used "*vav* conv. perf. . . . in apod"; see A. B. Davidson, *Hebrew Syntax* (Edinburgh: T & T Clark, 1894), 176.

[43]Waltke and O'Connor, *Syntax*, 525.

[44]The transitional *vav* is reflected by (then). As will be noted later, even this basic formula may be ambiguous.

[45]This is surprising since the particle גַּם is not a recognized transitional particle (see James E. Smith, "גמם," *TWOT*, 1:167, BDB, 168-69, and KB, see under "גַּם," 1:187-88) while the *weqatalti* form definitely is. We propose the translation, "If you will walk in my ways and if you will keep my requirements and also govern my house and have charge of my courts, then I will give you a place among these standing here."

[46]NIV ignores the presence of וְהָיָה.

[47]Driver, *Tenses*, 174. His remark is based on the observation of Genesis 32:9.

[48]For a parallel, see Exodus 3:13.

[49]See NIV and KJV.

[50]Again, the italicized words represent the transitional *vav*.

[51]Watts, *Teaching*, 118.

[52]The affirmation in verse 6, "You will be for me a kingdom of priests and a holy nation," is introduced by means of a "progressive imperfect" (see Watts, *Syntax*, 36-38). Compare Waltke and O'Connor's "*incipient present non-perfective*" (*Syntax*, 505-506). A development emerging from the "treasured possession" status, the prospect of Israel's becoming a "holy nation" inspires and justifies the descriptive title, "Covenant of Holiness." See Watts, *Teaching*, 118.

[53]The word סְגֻלָּה is related to the Akkadian terms *sakalu* ("acquire property") and *sikiltum* ("personal property"). See R. D. Patterson, "סגל," *TWOT*, 2:617. KB cites association with akk. *sug/kullu* (herd [of cattle]), see under "סְגֻלָּה," 3:701. Sarna also observed that *sikiltum* "is used in the titles of the monarch in parallel with 'servant' and 'beloved' of a god," Nahum M. Sarna, *Exploring Exodus* (New York: Schocken Books, 1986), 131. Durham commented, "The image presented is that of

118

Mighty to Save

the unique and exclusive possession, and that image is expanded by what appears to be an addition ('for to me belongs the whole earth') to suggest the 'crown jewel' of a large collection, the masterwork, the one-of-a-kind piece." See John I. Durham, *Exodus*, vol. 3 of *Word Biblical Commentary*, ed. David A. Hubbard and Glenn W. Barker (Waco: Word Books, Publisher, 1987), 262.

[54]Exodus 19:5; Deuteronomy 7:6; 14:2; 26:18; Ecclesiastes 2:8; 1 Chronicles 29:3; Psalm 135:4; Malachi 3:17.

[55]Note also KJV's beautiful line, "when I make up my jewels" (in Mal. 3:17).

[56]For example, see Numbers 14:18; Nehemiah 9:17.

[57]On this Hebrew idiom, Elsie Johnson commented, "Thus the double meaning of *'aph* as "nose" and "anger" appears evidently only in Hebrew. It is interesting that in the OT the nose plays a certain role in the description of anger: Ezk. 38:18, 'my anger will rise up in my nose'.... Moreover, there is a clear connection between anger and snorting, e.g., in Ex. 15:8; Ps. 18:16(15); Job 4:9." See Elsie Johnson, "אַף," *TDOT*, 1:351. Hence, YHWH is "longsuffering (*'erekh 'appayim*) and does not become angry easily" (Johnson, "אַף," *TDOT*, 1:360).

[58]In comparing חֶסֶד to "*chen*" (grace), Norman H. Snaith concluded, "*Chesed*, by contrast, presupposes a covenant, and has from first to last a strong suggestion of fixedness, steadfastness, determined loyalty." See Norman H. Snaith, *The Distinctive Ideas of the Old Testament* (New York: Schocken Books, 1964), 130. Compare Nelson Glueck, *Hesed in the Bible*, ed. Elias L. Epstein, trans. Alfred Gottschalk (Cincinnati: The Hebrew Union College Press, 1967).

[59]I construe "just" as a workable "end result" meaning for the expression נַקֵּה לֹא יְנַקֶּה. KB proposes that the formula means "to leave unpunished" (*ungestraft lassen*) or "declare innocent" (*straffrei erklären*); see under "נקה," 3:680. Fisher and Waltke observed, "The root *nāqâ* with the meaning 'to be clean, pure, spotless' is found in Akkadian, Arabic, and Aramaic.... The derived juridical notion 'to be acquitted,' 'to go unpunished' is found only in Hebrew." See Milton C. Fisher and Bruce K. Waltke, "נָקַה," *TWOT*, 2:596.

[60]One anonymous commentator, in a brief newspaper essay, summarized these verses in a one-facet conclusion, "Yes, The God of The Old Testament is a jealous God. Says so Himself in this Commandment!" See *Why Do the Heathen Rage?* (Mt. Juliet, TN: n.d.), 103. So much for exegesis.

[61]The edict would exclude even representations of YHWH (Ex. 32:1-5).

[62]Leonard J. Coppes, "קָנָא," *TWOT*, 2:802. Compare A. Murtonen, *Hebrew in Its West Semitic Setting* (New York: E. J. Brill, 1989), 1Bb:379.

[63]Coppes, "קָנָא," *TWOT*, 2:803.

[64]GKC, 492. Note the use of עֵקֶב in Genesis 22:18 and יַעַן כִּי in Isaiah 3:16-17.

[65]See Watts, *Syntax*, 90-97.

[66]Or Greek text in the New Testament.

[67]The Hebrew term דּוֹר.

At Sinai: The Covenant of Holiness

[68]Actually, the Hebrew word is חֶסֶד, which is a more comprehensive term than "love." See Snaith, *Distinctive Ideas*, 94-130. Because of the nature of the term's association with covenant, I prefer the translation "covenant-loyalty."

[69]Compare Deuteronomy 7:9. Childs noted that "in contrast to this stern judgment the mercy of God continues for a thousand generations." See Childs, *Exodus*, 406.

[70]See Galatians 3:23 in KJV.

7

The Sin Problem: Critical Nomenclature

... forgiving wickedness, rebellion and sin.

Exodus 34:7

What's in a name? that which we call a rose
By any other name would smell as sweet.[1]

The well-known line from Stratford-upon-Avon's famous bard reminds us that name labels are, at best, superficial tags that derive rather than impart meaning. The rich color and haunting fragrance of a lovely blossom, any blossom, are not determined by an assigned name. Each flower's fragile beauty is the product of its essence, its being, not the consequence of the term attached to it. In like fashion, other items, concepts, and experiences transcend the words that designate them. In a more somber vein, one could paraphrase Shakespeare's words with the axiom, "Poison by any other name is just as dangerous." In the framework of biblical hamartiology and human experience, one could affirm, "Sin by any name is just as deadly and destructive."

Exodus 34:6-7 records YHWH's own memorable exegesis of His name. The three primary terms used in the Old Testament to describe the human sin problem appear in verse 7 (עָוֹן, פֶּשַׁע, and חַטָּאָה). The circumstantial "packaging" of the terms bespeak their importance. Although labels and names are only superficial, the magnitude of mankind's moral estate defined by these three words makes a clear perception of their meaning vital.

An anxious patient hangs on every word of an examining physician in order to hear, in words easily understood, the precise diagnosis of the physical illness. Similarly, earth's weary and troubled pilgrim sometimes searches the pages of the Holy Book in quest of an accurate and understandable definition of the sinful heart's condition. These three words, used by God Himself, provide that spiritual profile. Apparently each individual term incorporates a separate nuance. If each does not have a distinctive shade of meaning, if they are identical synonyms, then why would God bother to use all three? They must surely be more than hollow theological abstraction or redundant religious jargon. Accordingly, each expression merits careful analysis.

Terminology and Substance

A number of helpful volumes have been published in recent years that offer advice and assistance to the Old Testament exegete.[2] The writers, by and large, have made a valuable contribution to the potential quality of Old Testament research in general and the excellence of preaching from the Hebrew Old Testament in particular. They have warned against haphazard handling of the sacred text and have directed attention to the danger of an undisciplined approach to the language of either Testament.

Moises Silva cautioned against "an exaggerated estimate of etymological studies," the danger of an "illegitimate totality of transfer" of meaning from one text to another, the failure to discern the possible differences of meaning in a given word, the failure to study "semantically related words," and "confusing the word for the reality."[3] D. A. Carson offered a fifteen-point warning list in his discussion of "word-study fallacies," a treatment worthy of careful examination.[4] The subtitle to John F. A. Sawyer's work, "New Methods of Defining Hebrew Words for Salvation," provides a clue to the methodology of his monograph (*Semantics in Biblical Research*). In essence, he documented a meticulous study of the Hebrew word for *salvation* in the Old Testament. His detailed research provides a challenging example of thorough investigation.

By admonition and example, then, these writers have encouraged responsible technique in handling the primary languages of the biblical text, a valuable contribution indeed. This emphasis serves to remind us that the inaccurate assignment of meaning to individual components of the text can only lead to muddled exegesis, which, in turn, sharply reduces the prospect of correct interpretation.

Context. The evaluation of individual word-meaning can be a rather tricky procedure if one is honestly searching for all that the writer was trying to communicate. The level of "semantic motivation" of a given expression may range from "transparent" to "opaque" and all points in between.[5] Accordingly, the clarity and value of the meaning of isolated terms can fluctuate wildly depending on their relative level of transparency. Sometimes, to assign a precise sense to key terms, even to some that are used frequently, may prove to be a difficult task.

Another item of concern is the matter of context. Sawyer addressed that issue with this admonition:

> What is quite inadmissible, and the deserving target of so much criticism since Barr's *Semantics*, is the assumption that because a word has a particular meaning in one context, it automatically has the same meaning in another quite different context a couple of thousand years earlier.[6]

Silva endorsed this stress on the importance of word environment:

> Accordingly, one should treat with healthy skepticism discussions of biblical synonyms that fail to indicate the specific contexts in which the supposed similarities and differences among the words occur.[7]

On a reassuring note, he added that "context almost always excludes irrelevant meanings."[8] A point well taken! However, to assign a *"determinative* function to context" and conclude that "context does not merely help us understand meaning—it virtually *makes* meaning"[9] undoubtedly carries a legitimate emphasis too far—if by context, one means singular, isolated context. The scrutiny of a term in *all* of its occurrences would perhaps justify the foregoing evaluation, but that would mean the analysis of "total context," which is actually the study of usage. This, in effect, constitutes the examination of an "isolated context" in its "total context," that is, the meaning and performance of a given term in all of its known uses.

While, as Sawyer warned, semantic luggage cannot be randomly imported from one context to another, the individual use of a term in a solitary context is not necessarily an accurate guide to meaning. In some instances, the study of a term's total context may be a relatively limited project. In others, it may be a massive undertaking, if not an impossible task. Still, while the datum of an isolated context is important, without the data of total context, it may prove to be indecisive.

An oft-quoted paragraph from The Declaration of Independence provides an appropriate illustration of the limitations of word transparency and context:

> We hold these truths to be self-evident, that all men are created equal, that they are endowed by their Creator with certain unalienable Rights, that among these are Life, Liberty and the pursuit of Happiness.[10]

Certain terms in this brief excerpt are obviously of monumental importance. An understanding of words such as "truths," "created," "equal," "Creator," "Rights," "Life," "Liberty," and "Happiness" is absolutely essential if one is to grasp the significance of this profound statement. Yet, in terms of "transparency," all of these would have to be described as opaque. They are abstract terms rather than concrete, their meanings not decisively self-evident. Moreover, while the importance of the context is evident from the character of the total document, the context contributes little to the semantic value of the individual expressions. On the other hand, it is the meaning of these individual words that imparts value and worth to the context.

How, then, might foreign students in the process of learning English ascertain the precise sense of these key terms? They might consult an appropriate bilingual dictionary in much the same manner that students of Greek and Hebrew scrutinize lexica. A second way might be to examine "mother-tongue" translations of texts (if available) that contain the words under study. Or they could examine all of the known English texts (total context) in which these words occur and compare their individual significance. They could try to explore the etymology of the words; for example, they might note the Latin background of "liberty."[11] Finally, they might evaluate the semantic cluster to which an individual word is related. For example, in the case of "Life," they could inspect the performance of the verb "live" that is associated with the noun, including its gerundive ("living") and idiomatic uses (for example, "live down"). The students might also evaluate the adjectives "live" (an example of polysemy) and "livable," the adverb "lively," derived terms such as "livelihood," even antonyms such as "lifeless" or "dead."

This would prove to be a considerable undertaking for the new learner, of course. But the "total context" and "semantic cluster" research is essentially what the adult native speaker of English brings to a reading of the Declaration.

Concept. Occasionally, the study of an idea is more revealing than the evaluation of nomenclature. In studying the concept of sin in the New Testament, for example, Silva cautioned:

> It must be clear in our minds whether we want to know all that the Bible teaches concerning the doctrine of sin (the "concept") or the range of meaning covered by the specific word. . . . If we are studying *words*, then the most important tool is Bauer's *Lexicon*, but if we are interested in *ideas* . . . it is not reasonable to base our study primarily on words.[12]

Word study, in isolation, may ignore the illustration of a principle in a given context simply because a key term is missing, with unfortunate results. A description or an example of bravery can be more revealing than a definition, but it does not follow that words are devoid of meaning. Some software programs for the modern computer have "search" capabilities in which symbols such as *, ?, or \% may substitute for random or unknown letters or combinations. The individual terms in the biblical text, however, are not anonymous symbols or meaningless abstractions; they do have specific value. It is on this basis that Sawyer could define the "semantic fields" of Hebrew words in terms of "associative fields" and "lexical groups."[13] Perhaps, short of specific definition, the ideal situation develops when both the key term under investigation and an example occur in the same context.[14] Unfortunately, such instances are rare.

An Analysis of the Sin Problem

With these considerations in mind, we now address the nature of the sin problem as reflected in the three critical terms in Exodus 34:7. Kaiser proposed that a term may be construed as significant if it meets one of these criteria:

> (1) it plays a key role in the passage being exegeted;
> (2) it has occurred frequently in previous contexts; or
> (3) it is important in the history of salvation as revealed up to this point.[15]

On the basis of Kaiser's guidelines, one may confidently conclude that all three of these words meet all three of his criteria.[16] Although we do not propose to conduct a serious exegesis of the passage, the words are surely critical to such a project. Their importance to the history of salvation at any point is self-evident.

Because of the general scope of our investigation, we will not be able to examine every use of each term (in its "total context"), though the reader may find such a project challenging and enlightening. We will attempt to probe the semantic value of each term in some specific ways. We will undertake to relate each word to its semantic or "root" cluster (more about that later), with special regard to the importance of the verbal notion behind the noun. And we will evaluate the level of metaphorical transference associated with each.

Semantic Clusters. James Barr, in his provocative *Semantics of Biblical Language*, seriously challenged "etymologizing"[17] and criticized what he called "the root fallacy." In so doing, he conceded:

> It is of course true that in Hebrew words, especially those of the common triconsonantal pattern, there is a fairly characteristic stability of the consonant series along with variation of the vocalism for different forms, so that it becomes possible for practical purposes to speak of the consonant sequence as the "root."[18]

He then cautioned that "'parts of speech' are very distinct in Semitic" and that the notion of the "root" verb must not be allowed to usurp the value of nominal forms.[19] He added further:

> A moment's thought, however, should indicate that the "meaning" of a "root" is not necessarily part of the meaning of a derived form. Still less can it be assumed that two words having the same root suggest or evoke one another.[20]

He then cited the example of the Hebrew words for "bread" (לֶחֶם) and "war" (מִלְחָמָה)[21] as an illustration of the precariousness of linking verb and associated noun together in the same semantic package. He further warned that "the 'root' may not be extant at all, or extant not in Hebrew but in cognate languages, or not extant in the 'simple form.' "[22]

Barr's critique cannot be ignored, but his evaluations are not as decisive as they might appear. In the first place, as Barr acknowledged, Hebrew words are indeed structured around a triconsonantal core; and that phenomenon has provided the traditional structure for many Hebrew lexica.[23] Seow expressed it this way:

> The Hebrew root defines a word inasmuch as it gives the basic semantic field within which words with that root fall. The basic nuances of a root are so important that some standard lexica list words according to their roots, rather than their final forms.[24]

Eduard Y. Kutscher wrote:

> The consonants are carriers of the primary semantic distinctions, at least in the verb and in nouns derived from the verb. The vowels play the role of modifiers indicating grammatical and secondary semantic meanings.[25]

Waltke and O'Connor observed, "Most words in Hebrew include a *root*, a sequence of consonants associated with a meaning or group of meanings,"[26] adding that the "root and affix system is the heart of Hebrew morphology."[27] In addition, they apparently endorsed G. B. Caird's statement, "If we know the meaning of a root and rules of inflexion and morphology . . . it is usually possible to work out for ourselves the meaning of cognate forms [that is, forms from the same root]."[28]

Barr's citation of the semantic divergence between "bread" and "war" constitutes an appeal to an exception rather than a pattern. While anomalies exist, random occurrences only prove the rule. For every discrepancy noted, scores of examples of triconsonantal root clusters with a shared semantic value could be offered.[29] Even though some "verbal roots" are not present in the Hebrew Old Testament, the principle still obtains. Associations may not always be clear (or exist at all), but a "core aura" of meaning is usually affiliated with a given triconsonantal root.[30] "The semantic connexion between a word and its root may be virtually snapped"[31] or totally nonexistent, but the pattern cannot be ignored.

In exploring these consonantal clusters, the search is not for some hypothetical "original meaning" or even the earliest attested use of a word. "Original" and "earliest" may prove to be highly elusive terms themselves, since both concepts are subject to debate in many instances.[32] Besides, even if an original meaning could be unequivocally determined, that meaning might not necessarily prevail in all situations. Moreover, the earliest meaning might not extend into subsequent usage. We will attempt, however, to ascertain the semantic aura of the terms under consideration by examining what appear to be the more primitive forms of the root and comparing those with later patterns. In so doing, we will concentrate on what Sawyer labels a "lexical group" rather than his "associative field."[33]

Verb Priority. A significant feature of biblical Hebrew is the intimate association between verbs and nouns. Infinitives and participles may function as nouns, and many nouns are actually built on participial formations. As a result, it is sometimes difficult to determine if a given participle has completed the transition into a noun.[34] As the progression, verb > participle > noun, would suggest, nouns are generally derived from verbs.[35] To be sure, some verbs appear to have developed from nouns;[36] but in most instances, nouns were inspired by verbs.

This hierarchy of development suggests that the core flavor of the verb will generally influence the meaning of the noun rather than vice versa. Caution must be exercised lest too much verbal meaning be superimposed on the noun, but early uses of the verb provide potential insight into the nuances of derived nouns. Accordingly, we will examine the performance of the verbs behind the key nouns of the text.

Metaphorical Transference. Another important consideration is the connection between the specific and the general or "metaphorical transference." Robert Gordis wrote:

> We should like to call attention to two positive and constructive principles that are intimately related: *the importance of semantic change* and *the ubiquity of psychological association as a basic component of the human mentality.*[37]

Gordis called attention to the fact that words do change in meaning. He also noted that semantic modification usually "makes sense," even if it goes "beyond the dictates of formal logic or coherence."[38] He further added:

> Thus it remains true, Barr's doubts to the contrary notwithstanding, that the original sense of words is generally concrete and that the abstract meaning is secondary. . . .
> Failure to recognize this principle of semantic change from the concrete to the abstract leads at times to radically unsound procedures in exegesis and textual criticism.[39]

Sawyer's comment supports Gordis's evaluation, "Metaphorical transference from concrete to abstract is more common than the opposite type."[40] Accordingly, the pursuit of primitive meaning will reverse the pattern of developed or extended meaning and try to "retrace the footsteps" of metaphorical transference.

Yet another issue lies beyond the "concret-to-abstract" flow sequence—namely, the correlation between the secular and the sacred. Just as semantic change drifts from item to concept, so mundane meanings expand to incorporate religious flavor. The three words of our text are theologically motivated; but they, or their verbs, also appear in nontheological contexts. We conclude that, in all probability, inhabitants of the religious environment appropriated secular terminology for sacred use. Regardless of the priority, the question is, "Why was this word chosen for sacred (or secular) vocabulary, and in what way is its meaning significant to the religious (or profane) audience?" Accordingly, we will attempt to observe levels of meaning by tracing the noun to the verb, the abstract to the concrete, and the sacred to the secular.

Definition of Key Terminology

The three key words in the text are the primary terms that describe the moral aberration of mankind in the Old Testament. Frequently used and quoted in religious circles, their precise meaning is often obscure, even to the religious, even in English. Some regular churchgoers, for example, might have difficulty defining "iniquity" (KJV, "wickedness" in NIV) and be unable to use the word apart from the expression "dens of." (An effort to handle "wickedness" might not fare much better.)

God's Word condemns it, but what does "wickedness" (iniquity) mean? More specifically, what did the key Hebrew words for the sin problem mean to the ancient Old Testament audience? What application, if any, does that have to our situation?

Wickedness. Nouns in Hebrew may be fashioned from verbs by vowel change, gemination or reduplication of radicals, and by the addition of prefixes, infixes, or suffixes.[41] The noun behind the translation "wickedness" (עָוֹן) is a sample of the latter type. It is probably derived from the verb *'avah* (עָוָה),[42] which occurs just eight times in the Old Testament.[43]

Used in the *Niph'al*, *Pi'el*, and *Hiph'il* stems, it alternately modifies "mind," "paths," "ways," "right," and a "rebellious woman." It is translated as "warped" (Prov. 12:8), "made crooked" (Lam. 3:9), "perverted" (Job 33:27; Jer. 3:21) and "perverse" (1 Sam. 20:30). In Isaiah 21:3, the verb action is prompted by "what I hear" (in a context of distress) and is translated "am staggered." In Psalm 38:6(7) it is parallel to a verb meaning to "bow down" (שַׁחֹתִי).[44] In a setting of climactic judgment (Isa. 24:1), NIV translates *'ivvah* (עָוָה) with the verb "ruin."[45]

The fascinating thing about these uses of the verb is the fact that, with the possible exception of the Samuel reference, none seem to reflect any specific moral connotation.

Despite the notion of wickedness associated with the noun, the verb does not represent the concept of doing or performing wickedness. In what way, then, does the noun depict an aspect of human depravity?

The basic idea common to all the uses of the verb seems to be that of "bending," "twisting," "perverting," or "distorting." This perception led Carl Schultz to conclude, "The derivative noun 'āwōn occurs with only the derived, abstract theological notion of the root: 'infraction, crooked behavior, perversion, iniquity, etc.'"[46]

Accordingly, in the light of the core flavor of the verbal root, we concur with Schultz that "wickedness" is to be understood in terms of "distortion" or "perversion," recognizing that the latter term is not restricted to sexual aberration only. In formulating this conclusion, we have tried to analyze the term by considering the uses of the verb with which it is associated and giving priority to concrete and secular occurrences (no problem in this case). If an appropriate illustration of the concept could be isolated, a clear example of moral "distortion" as a hamartiological norm, our confidence in this definition of the meaning of "wickedness" would be strengthened.

A review of the Eden scenario provides such a model. There the deadly mixture of curiosity, doubt, and pride prompted Adam and Eve to commit a defiant act of disobedience. How and in what way did the innocuous act of eating "fruit from the tree" constitute disobedience? Eating, in and of itself, can scarcely be considered a major moral error. God created mankind with the innate capacity and need to eat. To be sure that food would be ingested regularly, He added a recurrent desire or craving for food, called appetite.

The external deed also included an internal, less obvious dimension. In and through the performance of eating, the first man and woman were making history's initial ethical decision. Again, the exercise of moral choice does not necessarily produce unacceptable conduct. Just as God created people with a physical appetite, He also endowed them, uniquely, with the capacity for moral evaluation. All creatures in the animal world eat, but only the human animal distinguishes good from evil. Only people are free moral agents. How, then, did the independent exercise of this God-given capacity constitute an unsuitable deed?

In both instances, history's first couple was exercising legitimate capabilities, the ability to eat and the capacity for moral decision. The problem centered, however, not in the use of these faculties, but rather in their *misuse*. In the garden, man and woman abused innate privileges by "bending" or "perverting" them so that the capacity for good became the occasion for evil. As then, so now, one facet of mankind's sin problem is the persistent perversion of God-given appetites and chronic misappropriation of perfectly acceptable functions. "Wickedness," therefore, stipulates more than wild, unbridled degeneracy. It also applies to the abuse (or misuse) of any and all abilities, even those that are not necessarily evil in and of themselves.

Rebellion. The fundamental force of the term פֶּשַׁע is more transparent. Translated in the KJV as "transgression," the noun is derived from a verb that is more political or even military in character than religious. In 1 Kings 12:19, for example, the verb describes the insurrection of the northern ten tribes against the rule of Rehoboam. In 2 Kings 1:1 it marked Moab's revolt against Israel following the death of Ahab. It clearly means to "revolt" or "rebel."

This basic notion was amplified and applied to Israel's relationship to YHWH by the Old Testament writers. In Isaiah 59:13 it appears in a context replete with expressions such as "treachery" (כַּחֵשׁ), "turning our backs" (נָסוֹג), "oppression" (עֹשֶׁק), and "revolt" (סָרָה). YHWH Himself employed the term to characterize Israel's apostasy, using it in parallel with yet another word for rebellion (מָרְדוּ, Ezek. 2:3). The noun therefore, even in the religious sense, retains an inevitable vestige of "insurrection."

Again the garden tragedy furnishes an historical object lesson or application. The "defiant act of disobedience" did not involve an organized plot against Eden's divine government. Man and woman did not perpetrate deliberate, grandiose anarchy, perhaps, but the results of their revolt were as calamitous as if they had. In any time or circumstance, only a radical few would dare to initiate a calculated, intentional insurrection against heaven. Willful or not, refusal to submit to His supervision and control is tantamount to rebellion. What an appropriate word, then, to characterize our inveterate insistence on "doing it my way." "Rebellion" captures beautifully the disposition attributed to the fallen angel of *Paradise Lost* by Milton's memorable line, "Better to reign in hell than serve in heaven."[47]

Sin. The third and final term for the sin problem is an expression with which the average reader of the Old Testament is probably more familiar. It is associated with a verb used extensively in the Old Testament. In most instances, both the verb and noun are employed in a religious sense. In a rare example of secular application, the verb describes the remarkable proficiency of a Benjamite squadron of left-handed slingshot specialists. According to the report, this unusual group of "southpaws" could "sling a stone at a hair and not *miss*" (Judg. 20:16, italics added).[48] Of course, the verb usually translated "commit sin" is here designated "miss."

On the evidence of the primitive and nonreligious use of the verb, the noun has been described as "missing the mark." The noun in Exodus 34:7 is actually a rare form that occurs only here and in Isaiah 5:18,[49] but the meaning is the same as the more customary terminology. What is involved, though, in the adoption of this particular concept to define the sin problem? How is the notion of "missing the mark" or "failure to hit the mark"[50] appropriate in the arena of abstract religious ideas?

In the first place, what is the mark or target that mankind is said to have missed? Unfortunately, the immediate context of our verse offers no answer to that question. The total Old Testament frame of reference does suggest a tantalizing hint or two. Norman H. Snaith, in a chapter on the righteousness of God, made this evaluation: "We take therefore the original significance of the root *ts-d-q* to have been 'to be straight.'" He added further, "It stands for that norm in the affairs of the world to which men and things should conform, and by which they can be measured."[51]

The equation "righteousness = straightness" or "straightness = righteousness"[52] is appealing, especially in light of the fact that "righteous" was used to describe the accuracy or honesty of weights (Deut. 25:15), scales, and the *ephah* (Lev. 19:36). Snaith's conclusion, then, is persuasive:

"*Tsedeq*, with its kindred words, signifies that standard which God maintains in this world. It is the norm by which all must be judged."[53]

It is at least possible that the target which mankind has universally missed is the absolute moral straightness (accuracy) of God. If this is true, then let us be done with the vain attempt to vindicate our feeble piety by comparing ourselves with ourselves. The standard is not my neighbor's integrity; it is the impeccable flawlessness of God. Any deviation, subtle or severe, from the absolute straightness of the divine moral perfection constitutes missing the mark—sin. "For all have sinned and fall short of the glory of God" (Rom. 3:23).

As appealing as the foregoing may be, it is not precisely demonstrated in the Eden profile. The garden offers quite another option. There, in the only sinless environment of history, man and woman experienced direct and unbroken fellowship with their Creator. God designed "the flower of creation" with the marvelous capability to commune with Himself, the eternal Lord of Glory. That, in fact, was the very purpose for mankind's existence. However, when the earthlings rebelled against the Maker, they not only shattered the tranquility of the earthly Paradise; they also perpetrated the supreme malfunction of the ages.

Simultaneous with the first moment of sin, man and woman's capacity for intimate, cordial fellowship with God was destroyed. From the standpoint of the divine strategy, they lost the very reason for living. They missed the mark of knowing God directly and personally. The crowning zenith of God's creative strategy failed to perform according to design specifications. The original pair were history's first "misfits." Mankind was out of step with the universe and eternity.

All succeeding generations have walked in the ethical steps of the first two. So whatever the target missed or the goal unattained, the term "sin" eloquently connotes mankind's tragic disqualification.

The Scope of the Sin Problem

Our text offers nothing specific about the total extent of the sin problem. The collective performance of the Hebrew tribes, however, would strongly suggest that a sinful mind-set had totally permeated their ranks.[54] Despite eager pledges of faithfulness (Ex. 24:7), the fledgling "holy nation" quickly abandoned its covenant responsibility and eagerly violated covenant sanctions. Even among the spiritual elite within Israel, sin exerted its damnable influence. The princely Moses was not exempt from its impact (Num. 20:7-12).

One might readily suspect that sin was a common denominator both within and beyond Israel. The surmise is decisively confirmed throughout the Old Testament record. Few flawless "saints" are depicted in the Old Covenant environment.[55] The account accurately, and sometimes painfully, reports the misconduct that marred the record of Israel's most valiant. The man after God's own heart (1 Sam. 13:14) is dutifully described as an adulterer and "assassin by remote control" (2 Sam. 11:1-27, author's paraphrase). No whitewash, no cover-up!

The Old Testament also traces evidence of the sin problem among Israel's neighbors.[56] The international environment of the ancient Near East was certainly no better than the spiritual circumstance within the covenant community. If anything, it was worse. Far and near, sin did abound.

The record not only describes the universality of the sin difficulty; it also speaks directly to the magnitude of the problem:

"There is no one who does not sin" (1 Kings 8:46).

"Everyone has turned away, / they have together become corrupt; / there is no one who does good, / not even one" (Ps. 53:3).

"Who can say, 'I have kept my heart pure; / I am clean and without sin'"? (Prov. 20:9).

"We all, like sheep, have gone astray, / each of us has turned to his own way" (Isa. 53:6).

"All of us have become like one who is unclean, / and all our righteous acts are like filthy rags" (Isa. 64:6).

Accordingly, the sin problem was not just extensive. It was universal and absolute. Its devastating and destructive influence demanded attention—divine attention.

The Remedy for the Sin Problem

The text provides an insight into the nature of the divine attention to the sin dilemma. On the surface of the text, though, the divine response appears to be ambivalent and indecisive. How is one to understand the apparent paradox between the pledge to "forgive" sin on one hand and the insistence that the guilty not go "unpunished" on the other?[57] Can the two features be reconciled?

The verb behind the translation "forgive" (נָשָׂא) is another critical word with wide flexibility of meaning. In its literal or concrete sense, it is basically an action verb that pictures physical performance. It described the work of the floodwaters as "they *lifted* the ark high above the earth" (Gen. 7:17, italics added) and the activity of the pagan seamen who "*took* Jonah" (Jonah 1:15, italics added)[58] in order to cast him overboard. The verb literally means to "lift," "lift up," "carry," or "bear."[59]

As might be expected, the term was also employed in a figurative or metaphorical sense. For example, Cain complained, "My punishment is more than I can *bear*" (Gen. 4:13, italics added), referring to his intangible burden of guilt and penalty.[60] The core flavor of "lift up" or "bear" also extended to nominal forms, including "chief" (נָשִׂיא, Ex. 22:27; verse 28 in English)[61] and "burden" or "oracle" (מַשָּׂא, Isa. 13:1).[62]

However, as the translation "forgive" indicates, the verb assumed a deeper symbolic significance.[63] It is classically associated with the resolution of the sin problem. While in some instances the notion of forgiveness or pardon is dominant, the aura of "lift up" lingers.[64] In addition, something about the strategic use of the term suggests that the gap between "bear" and "forgive" is too wide to be bridged so casually. Furthermore, the tension of Exodus 34:7 is not resolved by a nonchalant definition of "forgive."

In the description of the moving Day of Atonement ceremony נָשָׂא was used in connection with the disposition of the scapegoat that would "carry on itself all their [Israel's] sins" (Lev. 16:22). It was used in the prophet's haunting projection of the rejected man of sorrows, "Surely he *took up* our infirmities" (Isa. 53:4, italics added). One can only speculate, to be sure, but the Hebrew verb נָשָׂא might have been on the lips of the Baptizer when he announced, "Look, the Lamb of God who *takes away* the sin of the world" (John 1:29, italics added).

As Schultz noted in his discussion of the word for wickedness, "it denotes both the deed and its consequences, the misdeed and its punishment."[65] A similar perception applies to the other two expressions as well.[66] Accordingly, the clause may be translated, "bearing the punishment (guilt) of wickedness, rebellion, and sin." The conclusion that "sin can be forgiven and forgotten, because it is taken up and carried away"[67] is not quite adequate. YHWH's forgiveness, to be sure, does involve the removal of sin's guilt; but He does not arbitrarily cancel guilt and nullify responsibility. Sin's removal and His forgiveness are predicated on His voluntary pledge to bear the full penalty of the sin problem Himself. "He himself bore our sins in his body on the tree" (1 Pet. 2:24).

Notes

[1] William Shakespeare, *Romeo and Juliet*, act 2, scene ii, lines 43-44.

[2] For example, James Barr, *The Semantics of Biblical Language* (Oxford: University Press, 1961); John F. A. Sawyer, *Semantics in Biblical Research* (Naperville, IL: Alec R. Allenson, 1972); D. A. Carson, *Exegetical Fallacies* (Grand Rapids: Baker Book House, 1984); Moises Silva, *Biblical Words and Their Meaning: An Introduction to Lexical Semantics* (Grand Rapids: Zondervan Publishing House, 1983) and *God, Language and Scripture* (Grand Rapids: Zondervan Publishing House, 1990).

[3] Silva, *Biblical Words*, 25-26. See also Barr's critique of "popular etymology," James Barr, "Etymology and the Old Testament," in *Language and Meaning* (Leiden: E. J. Brill, 1974), 4.

[4] D. A. Carson, *Exegetical Fallacies* (Grand Rapids: Baker Book House, 1984), 25-66.

[5] Sawyer, *Semantics*, 49-50. As Sawyer noted, "transparent" motivation may include phonetic, morphological, and transferred (analogy) motivation. His observation that Chinese "represents an extreme form of opaqueness" is not uniformly accurate. Since many of the written symbols in Chinese (and Japanese) were originally pictographic and ideographic in nature, examples of morphological and analogical motivation abound; see Oreste and Enko Vaccari, *Pictoral Chinese-Japanese Characters, VII*, 4th ed. (Tokyo: Vaccari's Language Institute, 1961). The characters for *tree, mountain, river,* and *rain*, for example, clearly

reflect their association with the phenomena of nature. At least in Japanese, many words that are associated with emotion of any sort include an abbreviated form of the symbol for heart as an individual component of a "Logical Aggregate" character.

[6]Sawyer, *Semantics*, 9.

[7]Silva, *God*, 91.

[8]Ibid., 94.

[9]Silva, *Biblical Words*, 139. A perspective assigned by Silva to "linguists."

[10]Thomas Jefferson et al., "The Declaration of Independence," 1776.

[11]This procedure would correspond to Barr's Etymology E.: Use of a Cognate Language to Discover the Sense in Hebrew" category. See James Barr, "Etymology and the Old Testament," in *Language and Meaning: Studies in Hebrew Language and Biblical Exegesis* (Leiden: E. J. Brill, 1974), 15-16.

[12]Silva, *Biblical Words*, 26-27.

[13]See Sawyer, *Semantics*, 28-59.

[14]For example, see David's demonstration of חֶסֶד, along with the explicit use of the term, in his treatment of Mephibosheth (2 Sam. 9:1-13).

[15]Walter C. Kaiser, Jr., *Toward an Exegetical Theology* (Grand Rapids: Baker Book House, 1981), 143.

[16]With the possible exception of חַטָּאָה, which occurs only twice in the Old Testament (BDB, see under "חָטָא," 306-308). Since this word simply features an alternate "spelling" of the more common (alternate) form, the question is moot. Besides, "frequently" is hardly precise.

[17]Defined as "giving excessive weight to the origin of word as against its actual semantic value," Barr, *Semantics*, 103.

[18]Ibid., 100.

[19]Ibid., 101.

[20]Ibid., 102.

[21]Both BDB (535-37) and KB (2:500) list the words under different roots (an example of homonymy).

[22]Barr, *Semantics*, 102-103.

[23]With nouns being listed under their assumed verbal roots rather than being listed alphabetically. See BDB for an example of this procedure.

[24]C. L. Seow, *A Grammar for Biblical Hebrew* (Nashville: Abingdon Press, 1987), 21.

[25]E. Y. Kutscher, *A History of the Hebrew Language*, ed. Raphael Kutscher (Jerusalem: Magnes Press, Hebrew University, 1982), 5.

[26]Waltke and O'Connor, *Syntax*, 83.

[27]Ibid., 84.

[28]Ibid., 84-85.

[29]For example, consider the semantic aura associated with the root אָכַל. (See BDB, 37-38 and KB, 1:44-46.) Barr later characterized this kind of correlation as "generative" rather than "historical." See Barr, "Etymology," 13.

[30]Exceptions include instances in which different meanings share the same form. For עָנָה, both BDB and KB list four separate roots (BDB,

772-77; KB, 3:805-808). On the other hand, multiple roots may share identical or similar meaning. For example, עוּר (listed as a second root in BDB, 735) and עָרָה (BDB, 788) are defined as "be bare" ("naked"), while עָרַר means "strip oneself" (BDB, 792, second root).

[31]Sawyer, *Semantics*, 50.

[32]See Barr's discussion of *etymon* and *origins*, Barr, "Etymology," 19-23.

[33]Sawyer, *Semantics*, 30. He described "associative field" as including "all the words associated in any way with a particular term." A "lexical group," on the other hand, "consists only of words very closely related to one another." We have confined "very closely related" to the consonantal root.

[34]For example, the word for "shepherd," רֹעֶה. KB lists the form as both **qal** participle and noun. See KB, 4:1174-75.

[35]Compare GKC's extended discussion of "verbal nouns" (226-39) and Kutscher's reference to "nouns derived from the verb" (*History*, 5). Note also that lexical groupings are built on verb roots, for the most part.

[36]Compare the verb עָקַב with the noun עָקֵב (BDB, 784). See also GKC's discussion of "denominative nouns" (239-41).

[37]Robert Gordis, *The Word and the Book* (New York: KTAV Publishing House, Inc., 1976), 16.

[38]Ibid.

[39]Ibid., 16-17.

[40]Sawyer, *Semantics*, 54.

[41]See Sabatino Moscati, et al., *An Introduction to the Comparative Grammar of the Semitic Languages* (Wiesbaden: O. Harrassowitz, 1980), 77-84.

[42]Though BDB posits a second root (730), "commit wickedness." See the redundant proposal for נָבָא, 611.

[43]Job 33:27; Psalm 38:6-7; Proverbs 12:8; 1 Samuel 20:30; Isaiah 21:3; 24:1; Jeremiah 3:21; and Lamentations 3:9.

[44]See BDB, 1005. NIV translates (נַעֲוֵיתִי, *Niph'al*) as "bowed down" with (שַׁחֹתִי) as "brought very low."

[45]Showing correlation with a related noun עַוָּה (Ezek. 21:32).

[46]Carl Schultz, "עָוָה," *TWOT*, 2:650. KB's definition of עָוֹן ("Vergehen, Sünde," "durch Sünde bewirkte Schuld," KB, 3:756) reflects the religious use of the term in the Old Testament and ignores a possible relationship to עוה (under **nif**, "gebeugt, verstört," KB, 3:752-53).

[47]Milton, *Paradise Lost*, book 1, line 263. *pš'* also occurs in Ugaritic (in parallel to "pride"). See G. R. Driver, *Canaanite Myths and Legends* (Edinburgh: T. & T. Clark, 1956), 54 (Aqhat II, vi, 42-43).

[48]See also Proverbs 8:36; 19:2.

[49]For other spellings or modifications see BDB, 308-309.

[50]See G. Herbert Livingston, "חָטָא," *TWOT*, 1:278. Compare K. Koch, "חטא," *TDOT*, 4:309-319.

[51]Snaith, *Distinctive Ideas*, 73.

[52]In the interest of time and space, I ignore the question of the direction of transference and the fact that this verb is probably denominative (see BDB, 842).

[53]Snaith, *Distinctive Ideas*, 77.

[54]See Exodus 32:1-6.

[55]Joseph might be construed as a rare exception, but the omission of misconduct in the Joseph story does not dictate an assumption of sinlessness.

[56]See Isaiah 13—23.

[57]The concept behind the pattern נַקֵּה לֹא יְנַקֶּה seems to connote "acquittal." See KB's note, "**ungestraft lassen**" (KB, 3:680).

[58]Literally, they "took up" Jonah.

[59]Consult BDB (see under "נָשָׂא," 668-71) and KB (see under "נשא," 3:683-86).

[60]For more esoteric uses, see Psalm 89:23 (English verse 22) and Genesis 39:7. In these instances "beguile" and "covet" would seem to apply.

[61]In other words, "one elevated." For a possible connection between this term and Egyptian *nsw* and Sumerian *ensí*, see Giovanni Pettinato, *The Archives of Ebla*, Afterword by Mitchell Dahood (Garden City: Doubleday, 1981), 278-79.

[62]BDB distinguishes two nouns (BD, 672).

[63]Note Walter C. Kaiser's three categories of meaning (Kaiser, "נָשָׂא," *TWOT*, 2:600-601).

[64]See the unforgettable intercession of Moses (Ex. 32:32).

[65]Schultz, "עָוָה," *TWOT*, 2:650.

[66]See BDB, 833; 307-309.

[67]Kaiser, "נָשָׂא," *TWOT*, 2:601.

8

Covenant and Sacrifice: Day of Atonement

The life ... is in the blood.

Leviticus 17:11

The pageantry of the atonement drama was fraught with symbolism and allusion. The high priest clothed in white, the stifled moan of dying animals, the thick, sweet aroma of smoke-blended incense, the dark brilliance of fresh blood, and the unseen Holy Presence that brooded somewhere within the sacrosanct recesses of the portable sanctuary—all these strange sights, smells, sounds, and shadows must have made a deep, sobering impact on the ancient Hebrew spectators of Yom Kippur.

Yom Kippur[1] (Day of Atonement) has been labeled "the holiest Jewish holiday."[2] Although the historical significance of the Passover might challenge the prominence of Yom Kippur, none of the other Jewish festivals[3] compared with the "holy" atmosphere that pervaded the moving ritual of the Day of Atonement. Unquestionably associated with Israel's chronic sin quandary, the strange and bizarre elements of the ceremony undoubtedly contributed something vital to YHWH's expanding message of salvation.

Ceremony

The description of the assorted ritual features contained in Leviticus 16 seems a bit complex, if not convoluted.

Accordingly, efforts to disentangle the divergent threads of the account vary; and students of the text may offer rather dissimilar analyses. As a case in point, we share two perspectives of the ceremony. The two do not exhaust all of the options, but they do illustrate major possibilities.

Locus-Event Analysis. The nineteenth-century German scholar Johann Heinrich Kurtz attempted to outline the atonement procedures by focusing on events and locations. He proposed that the total drama included three fundamental "stages," but his detailed evaluation suggests this outline:

Preparation Lev. 16:1-4
Ritual in Most Holy Place   Lev. 16:5-15
Ritual in Holy Place Lev. 16:16-17
Ritual in Fore-Court Lev. 16:18-19
Ritual After Atonement Lev. 16:20-34[4]

Kurtz's guideline is certainly faithful to the sequence of details provided in the text. Still, his analysis does not resolve the ambiguity about the relationship between event and place.

Literary Analysis. Gordon J. Wenham, in his commentary on the Book of Leviticus, approached the chapter with a sensitivity to a literary pattern of configuration that was relatively common in the ancient Near East. The style of composition featured a propensity to sketch a general overview and then provide the details of the account. In much the same way that a camera long shot establishes the scene in modern movie and TV production, the ancient writers would first outline the totality of the item to be described. Then, as the camera zooms in for following close-ups that detail the visual narrative, they would spell out the specifics of their journal.[5] K. A. Kitchen described the approach as "a general summary-outline plus a more detailed account of one (or more) major aspect(s)" and commented that the technique "is commonplace enough in Ancient Oriental texts."[6]

Working from a literary perspective, Wenham offered this detailed outline of Leviticus 16:

1–2   Introduction
3–5   Animals and priestly dress needed for the ceremonies
6–10   Outline of the ceremonies

11–28 Detailed description of the ceremonies
      11–19 the blood-sprinkling rites
      20–22 the scapegoat
      23–28 cleansing of the participants
29–34 The people's duty[7]

Outlines may modify written records; but, in this case, the record itself documented a conglomerate of "happenings." The happenings undoubtedly involved an uninterrupted, independent yet overlapping flow of multiple activities. A summary of those individual occurrences, like the formulation of outlines, is subject to one's perspective. May I propose, however, that the total ceremony consisted of the following basic actions by the high priest. Removing the customary regalia of his noble office and donning immaculate white linen, Aaron:

(1) slaughtered a bullock, entered the Holy of Holies (carrying a censer of burning incense), and sprinkled its blood on the "mercy seat" to make atonement for himself and his household;

(2) slaughtered the goat of the sin offering and sprinkled its blood on the "mercy seat" to make atonement for the people;

(3) placed his hands on the head of the second goat (the scapegoat) and symbolically transferred the sins of the people to the animal;

(4) and sent the scapegoat away into the wilderness.[8]

Semantics

The actors, sets, props, scenario, and action of Yom Kippur abounded with types, symbols, and subtle imagery.[9] As in the exegesis of the divine Name (Ex. 34:6-7),[10] the key terminology attached to the activity report is of crucial importance. Unfortunately, some critical components of the written message are all but lost in a code of religious nomenclature. The NIV has reduced the translational haze; however, obscurities linger. Following the procedures used in the preceding chapter, let us evaluate some of the pivotal terms in the account and search for further clarification.

kipper. This term (כִּפֶּר) is not a misspelling of *kippur.* Instead, it represents the verb that is connected with the noun *kippur(īm).*[11] This form of the verb[12] occurs in Leviticus 16[13] and is translated "make atonement." An extremely significant term that denotes a profound theological concept, *kipper* was used extensively to describe a facet of covenant-related liturgy in the Old Testament. The antiquity of this technical and highly stylized use of the term as sacred vocabulary is clearly attested in the biblical record and beyond.[14] The precise meaning of "make atonement" and its symbolic ramifications, however, are not altogether self-evident and clear.

Someone has said that to decipher the meaning of "atonement," simply divide the English word into its respective components: at-one-ment. The device is remarkably simple, with a rather amazing result. Moreover, the at-one-ment paradigm reflects a biblical term and captures a biblical concept. Sadly, the connection has nothing to do with atonement in the Old Testament. Instead, the at-one-ment notion is more compatible with the New Testament idea of reconciliation.[15]

What, then, does "make atonement" actually mean? What are its semantic parameters? What does it imply? The evidence is somewhat indecisive, if not contradictory. A conclusive definition is probably not possible. Nevertheless, what is the evidence? What are the options?

A widely accepted view is the position that *kipper* means to "wipe clean" or "purify." In discussing the symbolism of the burnt offering Wenham observed:

> In those rituals where *kipper* means "to wipe clean" or "to cleanse" it is clear that the blood is the cleansing agent that has to be applied carefully to the polluted object, e.g., the horns of the altar (4:25) or the mercy seat (6:14).[16]

Allen P. Ross insisted that the usage of the term demonstrates that it means "expiate, pacify, atone."[17] In the context of ceremonial protocol as proscribed in the Levitical ritual, the idea of cleansing or purification does indeed seem to be a dominant tone in *kipper*. Moreover, the emphasis accords well with the general use of the equivalent term in Akkadian, a verb that has been defined as meaning "to wipe off," "to clean objects," or "to purify magically."[18] The data seem to be convincing if not conclusive.

Before considering other options, one should examine the evidence for "cleansing" as the primary idea in *kipper*.

In the first place, Wenham's argument is jeopardized by his suggestion that the mercy seat was a "polluted object."[19] This equation hardly seems to be compatible with the designation of the area between the two cherubim (in other words, the "mercy seat") as YHWH's unique dwelling place.[20] Furthermore, the opinion that *kipper* meant "the cleansing of polluted objects" focuses on things and ritual rather than people and relationships. We are convinced, however, that the atonement process described in Leviticus did not have to do primarily with the ritual purification of ceremonial artifacts. Rather, *kipper* symbolically addressed the core of the human sin problem.

In addition, the religious use of the term in the Old Testament, as well as in many Akkadian texts, seems to represent verb performance that has already experienced metaphorical transference. If this is true, the liturgical association is a derived usage. A more primitive meaning of the verb will not necessarily override its later semantic function; but if an earlier meaning can be established, then it may help to clarify the developed sense of *kipper*. As always, however, context will be crucial to a correct understanding. Suffice it to say at this point that the notion of cleansing as the meaning for *kipper*, even if correct, represents a later, restricted use of the term.

Another recommendation for the meaning of *kipper* is "to pay a ransom." In addition to the concept of cleansing, Wenham proposed:

> Alternatively *kipper*, "to make atonement," may be derived from the Hebrew word *kōper*, meaning "ransom price." A *kōper* is the money a man condemned to death can pay to escape the death penalty (Exod. 21:30; Prov. 6:35). *Kipper*, "to make atonement," could then be literally translated, "to pay a ransom (for one's life)."[21]

This suggestion is quite tenable. The noun *kōper* is clearly attested, and *Pi'el* verbs are frequently denominative in character. In explaining the meaning of *kipper*, R. Laird Harris observed, "These intensive stems often indicate not emphasis, but merely that the verb is derived from a noun whose meaning is more basic to the root idea."[22] Then, under the heading *"kōper,"* Harris concluded: "From the meaning of *kōper* 'ransom,' the meaning of *kāpar* can be better understood. It means 'to atone by offering a substitute.'"[23] While the transition from "ransom" to "substitute" is a rather precarious modification for *kōper*, the opinion should be noted.

A rather dramatic modification of this view is provided by the late Mitchell Dahood's Afterword in Pettinato's *The Archives of Ebla*. Regarding those who relate *kipper* to *kōper*, he wrote that they:

> . . . .will surely find new ammunition in the bilingual vocabulary where URUDU, "copper," is reproduced by Eblaite *kà-pá-lu = kà-pá-ru*.[21] In Akkadian lists Sumerian URUDU is translated *erû*, "copper." Here, then, is another lexical argument for distinguishing Eblaite from Akkadian. Hence biblical *kōper* could originally have meant "copper," and since the settling of differences between Israelites themselves or between Israelites and God involved the transfer of something of value (a person, an animal or commutation of such in the form of commodity or currency), this etymology would accord with the subsequent development of this institution. It also sheds light on *kappôret*, a slab of gold placed on top of the ark of the testimony. This slab may have been of copper but coated with gold.[24]

The equation is fascinating, but Dahood has suggested a semantic shift similar to that of Harris; only he proposes that "ransom" and "copper" are connected under the consonantal umbrella of *k-p-r*.

Another opinion is possible. In a footnote Wenham conceded, "A third meaning 'to cover,' from Arabic *kappara*, was once favored by many scholars. This has little to commend it."[25] Harris also rejected the notion of "cover" in the root *kāpar* with this explanation:

> There is an equivalent Arabic root meaning "cover," or "conceal." On the strength of this connection it has been supposed that the Hebrew word means "to cover over sin" and thus pacify the deity, making an atonement (so BDB). It has been suggested that the OT ritual symbolized a covering over of sin until it was dealt with in fact by the atonement of Christ. There is, however, very little evidence for this view.[26]

Does this rejection of "cover" as a core aura of meaning for the consonant cluster *k-p-r* agree with all the significant data? Several questions need to be addressed: (1) What, precisely, does "cover" mean? (2) Is there a general (or primitive) meaning that might explain extended

meanings? (3) What is the connection between the verb
forms and the nouns that share the *k-p-r* consonant root?
(4) Is there a concrete secular meaning that might anticipate abstract religious meanings? (5) What meaning best
accords with the total context of Leviticus 16?

Ross expressed his dissatisfaction with the "cover" identification by this statement: "We do not do justice to the
OT to say that sins were merely covered over and not removed."[27] If *kipper* means "cover over," "cover up," or, as in
the case of the Arabic equivalent "conceal," then we would
agree with Ross's disclaimer. Furthermore, Ross was correct to insist that the biblical view of atonement includes
removal of sin. However, "hide," "seclude," or "camouflage"
are not necessarily what was communicated by *kipper*.
The "cover" aspect does not cancel the purification phase
of atonement. The exact focus of "cover" in *kipper* may be
best illustrated by the context, a bit later. For the moment, though, we reject the idea that *kipper* simply means
"cover up" in the sense of conceal.

The primitive meaning of the verbal root, at least in this
particular case, is connected to the question of correlation
between verb, noun, and stem. Harris reported that the
root *kāpar* "is never used in the simple or Qal stem, but
only in the derived intensive stem."[28] That appraisal is
correct, but only if one posits a second root for *k-p-r*. BDB
displays *kōper* as representing two nouns (meaning "ransom" and "pitch" respectively) and lists two verbs: *kipper*
(*Pi'el* stem, "cover over," "pacify," "make propitiation") and
kāpar (*Qal* stem, "pitch"). All four notices share the same
consonantal root.[29]

The situation is complicated by the fact that the noun
and verb which are translated "pitch" only occur one time
in the Old Testament (Gen. 6:14). NIV translated the "cognate verb" construction[30] of the verse as *"coat it with
pitch."*[31] Despite the limited use, I suggest that *kipper*
("make atonement") is not derived from *kōper* ("ransom")
but that it is the "D stem" adaptation of the *Qal kāpar*
("coat," i.e., "pitch" or "cover").

Explaining the meaning and association of stems in the
Hebrew verb system, GKC recorded:

> Verbal stems are either original or derived. They are
> usually divided into—
> (a) Verbal stems proper (*primitive verbs*), which exhibit
> the stem without any addition . . .
> (b) *Verbal derivatives*, i.e., *secondary* verbal stems,
> derived from the pure stem.[32]

Waltke and O'Connor wrote, "The most commonly used verbal stem is the *Qal* or 'light' stem, also known as the G (*Grundstamm*) or B (Basic) stem."[33] In describing the correlation between *Qal* and *Pi'el* stems (of the same verb), they added, "With *Qal* transitive verbs the *Piel* is resultative: it designates the bringing about of the outcome of the action designated by the base root."[34]

If *kipper* is the D stem of *kāpar*, as I propose, then *kipper* would designate the "result" of covering and would be almost causative in force, i.e., "provide a covering."[35]

The evidence from Akkadian[36] does not seem to confirm this proposition, however, at least on the face of it. If "cover" does represent a primary meaning for *k-p-r*, some indication of that in Akkadian might be expected. As in biblical Hebrew, however, the Akkadian cognate *kapāru* meant "to wipe off." While that does, indeed, reflect the prevalent meaning of the verb according to *CAD*, a secondary definition includes "to smear on (a paint or liquid)"; and the illustration cited describes an application of bitumen."[37] So while the Akkadian does not convincingly confirm "cover over" as a dominate meaning for *k-p-r*, neither does it contradict that possibility. Additional evidence is needed.

A secular use of *kipper* (*k-p-r* in the D stem) in the Hebrew Old Testament provides additional insight into the concrete, nonreligious function of "make atonement." As Jacob approached Canaan on his return trip from Paddan Aram, he recalled the circumstances that had led to his hasty departure years before. Uncertain about his reception at the hands of his aggrieved brother, Esau, and never one to leave a situation to "blind chance," Jacob sent a delegation of his servants in advance with an impressive herd of animals as a "gift" for his brother (Gen. 32:13-16).[38]

The rationale for the generous present is provided by the statement, "I will pacify him with these gifts I am sending on ahead" (Gen. 32:20[21]).[39] The circumstance is, of course, "nonritual," so NIV has translated *kipper* as "pacify." Actually, the expression literally affirms, "I am determined (cohortative form of the verb) to *kipper* his face." *k-p-r* occurs in the D stem, exactly as in Leviticus 16, followed by "his face" as the direct object of the verbal action.

The religious meaning, "make atonement," makes no sense at all in this context. Moreover, "cleanse" or "wipe clean" (his face) does not fit the circumstance either. "Pay a ransom" might apply, in the light of the elaborate "gift"; but that notion is not compatible with the designation of "his face" as direct object.

However, the translation "I am determined to *cover* his face" will accommodate to the verb-direct object situation and also makes sense in the context. Jacob's intent was to provide a gift that would intervene in his behalf, so that the advancing Esau would see his younger brother, as it were, through a token of compensation and an evidence of remorse. In other words, Jacob was attempting to "cover" his brother's face with a present that would appease the offended Esau.

kappōret. Another factor in deciphering the force of "make atonement" is the significance of the allied term, *kappōret* (כַּפֹּרֶת), traditionally labeled "mercy seat." The *kappōret* figured prominently in the Yom Kippur ceremony, and its mention in Leviticus is of considerable importance. As a glance at the terms confirms, *kipper* (כִּפֶּר) and *kappōret* (כַּפֹּרֶת) are morphologically similar; and they are probably semantically related as well. In all likelihood, the KJV translation "mercy seat" reflects "*Gnadensthul*" of Luther's German translation of the Hebrew expression.[40]

Identified with the space between the two cherubim atop the ark of the covenant and intimately associated with the radiant presence of YHWH (Ex. 25:22), the *kappōret* was both a tangible item of the tabernacle furnishings and a crucial feature in the atonement ritual. Instructions for the production of the *kappōret* indicate that it had only two dimensions, length and width (Ex. 25:17). Although the expression "mercy seat" may suggest a three-dimensional object, the *kappōret* was unmistakably flat. NIV's translation "atonement cover" conveys the two-dimensional nature of *kappōret* and implies that, in addition to its liturgical function, it also served as a "lid" to the ark.

I suggest, however, that "cover" (as "atonement cover" implies) designates more than "lid" or "top." *kappōret* was not only the cover to the ark of the covenant that contained the book of the Law (Deut. 31:26),[41] but it was also the place where the ritual act of "providing a cover" took place. It was the location where blood was sprinkled to "make a cover" for the sins of the people. The character of the "blood covering" is clarified further by the correlation between the Law (located in the ark) and the symbolism of blood.

The book of the Law was a record of the righteous demands of Israel's holy covenant God. The demands included moral, social, and religious provisions that were designed to guide and guard the covenant people. Unfortunately, they were provisions that Israel systematically and consistently violated. The noble demands only underscored the human frailty and sinfulness of Israel. The requirements of the Law confirmed that "all have sinned." What, then, were the consequences of sin, violation of the Law?

The banishment of Adam and Eve from the Garden of Eden indicated something of the nature and magnitude of sin's penalty. They were separated from God and denied access to the Tree of Life (Gen. 3:23-24). That double-level forfeiture represented mankind's loss of the God-quality and God-quantity of life—in other words, death. As the following stanzas of the Genesis record confirm, death quickly became an expanding and catastrophic component of human existence.

Among the flickering scenes of Yom Kippur, perhaps no feature was as somber and arresting as the slaughter of animals: the bull for the high priest and his family, the goat for the congregation of the people. The basis? The reason for their deaths? In a word: sin! The struggling death throes of these lowly creatures, their warm blood, the crimson-splattered garments and utensils of worship, the solemn warning to the high priest that he abide by correct procedures "so that he will not die" (Lev. 16:13)— all these sobering elements combined to communicate the truth that the cost of sin is death. Later, but still in the Old Covenant reference, the lethal connection was explained, "The soul who sins . . . will die" (Ezek. 18:4). The equation is explicit: sin produces death.

At this point, the larger context provides a significant insight into the atonement concept. YHWH Himself explained the economy of blood sacrifice:

"For the life of a creature is in the blood, and I have given it to you to make atonement for yourselves on the altar: it is the blood that makes atonement for one's life" (Lev. 17:11).

The clause "the life of a creature is in the blood" encapsulates a fundamental physiological fact. A human or animal does not have to be stricken by some dread disease or terminal illness to die. He (she, it, they) does not have to sustain a bone-shattering injury, be shot, swallow poison, drown, get electrocuted, hang, inhale carbon monoxide, overdose on drugs, or experience other such extreme measures in order to die. All of the above are certainly deadly enough, but they are not necessary to induce death. Simply prick a small vein (not even an artery is required) and slowly extract the dark red fluid called blood. As blood is withdrawn, life seeps away.

Blood, in essence, is the "life support system" for all animals, including mankind. Without its vitalizing energy flowing in our cardiovascular system, we soon perish. "The life of a creature is in the blood." The shedding of blood, therefore, was synonymous with the "pouring out" of life—in other words, death. So blood was a symbol of death as the consequence of sin—the violation of God's holy law.

The essential interpretive factors have been considered, and I submit the following considerations. The atonement terminology did not involve the idea of cleansing per se. Nor did it have to do with the offer of a ransom. The core flavor of the consonantal root *k-p-r* was "cover" (but not in the sense of conceal or hide). This semantic emphasis would explain extended or transferred meanings and also suggests a logical connection between concrete secular meanings and abstract religious meanings. Furthermore, it provides a semantic context for all forms of *k-p-r* that occur, without having to resort to hypothetical roots. In addition, I am convinced that this fundamental meaning best accords with the total context of Leviticus 16.

The nuance "provide a cover" suggests an atonement scenario that involves the application of blood as a symbol of death, not a camouflage device. The blood was sprinkled on the "place of covering"[42] where YHWH dwelt between the cherubim atop the ark of the covenant. The austere holiness of the covenant God was suggested by the designation of the sacred cubicle behind the mysterious veil (most holy place) where the ark was deposited. There, YHWH figuratively looked out upon Israel from the receptacle that contained the book of the Law and surveyed a nation of lawbreakers. One and all, they transgressed His Law, broke His covenant, violated His holiness.

Once a year, in the Yom Kippur ritual, YHWH gazed at His people through the crimson haze of sprinkled blood. In that annual ceremony He symbolically accepted the blood (of an innocent substitute) as a token of death for the penalty of sin. Sin was not hidden; it was not forgotten; it was not ignored. In a figure, not substance, it was punished by the death of a blameless replacement. The imagery of atonement then calls to mind the line of the hymn writer, "He, to rescue me from danger, / Interposed his precious blood."[43]

Symbolism

How exactly did the Hebrew worshipers understand all of this? Were they sensitive to the subtle hints of redemptive strategy, or was it just mechanical formality? Well, who can say? For that matter, what degree of national character does a tourist sense when visiting the Washington Monument or Lincoln Memorial in the nation's capital? Does one feel both the pain and dignity of the nation's past? Appreciate the worth of its present or the challenge of its future? Or does the tourist only see structures?

For that matter, who can gauge the casual church member's insight while reading the fifty-third chapter of Isaiah? What spiritual truth does one comprehend? How much does one perceive? And the typical individual on the street! What does the average person understand or care about the Golgotha incident? We can only surmise. We must remember, however, that the message of God's Word and its integrity may not be a matter of popular discernment. Current fad and eternal truth are not necessarily one and the same.

Whatever the comprehension of the Israelite congregation during Yom Kippur, certain cardinal lessons may be derived from its content. The setting, characters, and events combined to communicate much.

The Holiness of YHWH. The august, sacred nature of the LORD was conveyed eloquently by word and situation. As previously noted, the very identification "most holy place" disclosed something of the sacred nature of Israel's covenant Deity. The small chamber that sheltered the ark was totally inaccessible to anyone other than the high priest, and even the high priest was permitted to enter its sacred confines only once a year. Moreover, that noble dignitary was sternly warned that he must put incense on a censer of burning coals to generate smoke that would obscure the "atonement covering" in order to avoid death. The terminology, verbal warning, limited access, and uncommon procedures reflected the transcendent righteousness of YHWH.

The Magnitude of Sin. Death, even that of animals, is a sober and sobering spectacle to behold. The severity of mankind's sin problem was abundantly illustrated in the fate of the animals that were used in the *kipper* rites. Though less demanding gifts might be offered in other tabernacle worship, only the shedding of blood would suffice in Yom Kippur. The price of sin was high. Death was its inevitable and unavoidable consequence.

The High Priestly Office. The venerable high priest (first Aaron, then his successors) performed a vital role in the Yom Kippur drama, and his function actually constituted a significant didactic symbol. His very position (not necessarily his individual character) in the Levitical worship system indicated something of the singular importance of his office. As he performed his ceremonial assignments in the atonement ritual, new dimensions of the high priestly station were disclosed. The permission to enter the most holy place demonstrated his sacramental privilege of accession into the very presence of hallowed deity. His conveying the burning incense past the veil and application of blood on the "atonement cover" represented his mediatorial and intercessory capacities. Thus the figure of the high priest represented a distinctive component in the imagery of atonement protocol.

Vicarious Sacrifice. Another element of the salvation message demonstrated through Yom Kippur was the principle of the death of an innocent substitute for the guilty. Some readers of the Old Testament have found this idea abhorrent. For example, one interpreter wrote:

> The most common mis-interpretation of sacrifice in the Old Testament is that which is associated with the view of penal substitution. With regard to atoning sacrifices in the Old Testament, this is the view which assumes that there is a transfer of guilt from the worshipper to the sacrificial victim, that the innocent animal is punished in the place of the worshipper, and that the worshipper is thus delivered from the punishment which he deserves because of his sin.[44]

The perception of penal substitution, as described above, is correct; but the interpreter's rejection of the concept as "misinterpretation" is based on misinterpretation. One aspect of misinterpretation is the failure to discriminate the ritual procedures of Yom Kippur from other Levitical offerings. They have similarities, to be sure, but they must be differentiated. To do otherwise leads to convoluted argument and a comparison of "apples and oranges."

Second, although the Day of Atonement needs to be distinguished from other worship patterns, the unity of its unique ceremony must not be fragmented. Specifically, the symbolism of the two goats (the sin-offering and the scapegoat) is essentially singular. They do not represent two independent features of atonement but two indivisible facets of a single truth.

In referring to the scapegoat ritual, Robert H. Culpepper acknowledged, "Here the idea of the transference of guilt is clearly expressed." He insisted, though, that the fate of the animal "is not to be interpreted in terms of penal substitution."[45] However, rather than observe the correlation between the two animals within the framework of Yom Kippur, he then cited the pattern in Leviticus 1:4. Even that appeal led to this concession: "What the worshipper's laying his hands upon the head of the victim in the ritual of sacrifice did mean is not so easy to determine."[46]

Granted, it is not easy to determine if one has already ruled out its meaning on the basis of presupposition. Without that obstacle the force of its symbolism is otherwise evident. The laying of hands on the head of the animal did represent the "transference of guilt," and its sacrifice did symbolize vicarious punishment. In the earlier setting (in Leviticus), one animal depicted this dual concept. During the Day of Atonement ceremony, however, two animals were utilized to reveal clearly the double aspect of the ritual.

In Yom Kippur, without the figurative transmission of guilt (as in Lev. 1:4; 3:2; 4:4), the sin-offering creature was slain and its blood applied on the "atonement cover" to make a "covering" for the sins of the people. That procedure represented the death of an innocent for the guilty— in other words, penal substitution. The proposal that blood represents life rather than death with the translation, "it is the blood that makes atonement, by reason of the life"[47] ignores a fundamental feature. The blood must be shed before its efficacy could be operative. It was not *just* blood, still coursing in the veins; it was blood spilled that provided atonement.

Life was represented by the blood, yes; but it was life poured out as a symbol of death. If that were not so, then the death of the ceremonial animals was not only senseless and totally devoid of meaning. It was savage and inhumane.

Another misinterpretation is the suggestion that penal sacrifice involves the appeasement of the wrath of God. The argument insists:

> . . . .that the wrath of God is not analogous to the wrath of man, and that the Hebrew idea of sacrifice is not analogous to the crude pagan ideas in which the angry deity is bought off and his wrath appeased by the blood of the sacrificial victim.[48]

The foregoing is an example of "straw man" argumentation. To picture the Yom Kippur ceremony in terms of the mollification of a vindictive heavenly tyrant by the death of a helpless victim is caricature at its worst (or best)!

To be sure, God is angry with sinners, not just sin in the abstract. Sin is only a theological speculation apart from a sinner. It may be committed, cussed, or discussed, but it cannot be weighed, photographed, or heated over a Bunsen burner. Without a perpetrator there is no "sin deed," except in theory. While God is unhappy with sin, He is angry with the sinner (John 3:36). "But how can God love us if he is angry with us?" Only those without children would raise such a question.

The issue at stake was (is) not God's rage or anger. It was and is His unparalleled holiness. YHWH did not indulge in some annual celestial temper tantrum that demanded the bleating death of some bleeding victim. The sprinkling of the blood was not designed to soothe uncontrolled fury and somehow stimulate indulgent favor. Rather, it was designed to satisfy a perfect holiness in the divine nature that can neither condone nor tolerate the utter abhorrence of sin.

The perspective that views the consequence of sin as a trivial or negotiable item fails to comprehend the exalted rightness of God. "The wages of sin" (any sin, every sin, all sin) "is death" (Rom. 6:23). Sin must be punished—by death. God's wrath does not demand it. God's holiness cannot avoid it. Yom Kippur with all of its symbolism was not designed to induce divine favor; its ceremonies (that anticipated a subsequent complete and adequate sacrifice) were instituted because there *was* divine favor.

Penal substitution in the Yom Kippur sin-offering is vindicated by the fact that the animal slain was only a symbol of a later, perfect sacrifice. The "later, perfect sacrifice" would ultimately be provided by YHWH Himself, at a painful cost beyond human comprehension. Accordingly, the death of an innocent substitute did not display brutal viciousness on the part of the covenant Deity. Rather, it projected something of the magnitude of His incalculable grace.

The Scapegoat. The instruction about the scapegoat[49] procedure was precise and explicit:

"When Aaron has finished making atonement for the Most Holy Place, the Tent of Meeting and the altar, he shall bring forward the live goat. He is to lay both hands on the head of the live goat and confess over it all the wickedness and rebellion of the Israelites—all their sins— and put them on the goat's head. He shall send the goat away into the desert in the care of a man appointed for the task. The goat will carry on itself all their sins to a solitary place; and the man shall release it in the desert" (Lev. 16:20-22).

The exact destiny of the "sin-bearing" animal was not specified,[50] but its significance was unequivocal. The guilt of the people was figuratively transferred to the animal, and the creature then carried that "burden" away into the desert. The imagery is clearly "removal" of guilt—in other words, cleansing. This goat was the one that symbolized the purging aspect of the atonement. The blood of the sin-offering animal provided the penalty (*kipper*) portion of the atonement process; the scapegoat (*azāzēl*) foreshadowed the purification dimension.

Repentance. The concluding instructions for Yom Kippur required a period of what might be described as "soul searching." The clause "you must deny yourselves (Lev. 16:29,31)" literally says "you shall afflict your souls."[51] Wenham noted that the expression "is rare," and added, "In Isaiah (58:3) it is associated with fasting. Psalm 35 suggests a wide range of penitential practices were involved, including self-examination and prayer."[52] This instruction implied that, while the resolution of the sin problem symbolized in Yom Kippur was an occasion for rejoicing, serious reflection on the tremendous cost of sin was a time for remorse and repentance.

Summary

Three critical features or functions of Yom Kippur need to be remembered. First, the sin-offering animal symbolized the death of an innocent substitute for the guilty sinner. Second, the scapegoat symbolized the role of a "sin-bearer" who would remove the sinner's guilt. Third, the temporary (and sinful) high priest represented the intercessory and mediatorial work of the eternal (and perfect)

High Priest in behalf of sinners. All three of these components are essential to a correct appraisal of the meaning of the Day of Atonement. They are also indispensable to a full biblical doctrine of atonement.

However, all of those procedures were only symbols or types. In other words, they possessed no literal cleansing or atoning energy in and of themselves. In fact, none of the sacrifices in Jewish liturgy—not one drop of blood sprinkled on the atonement cover—none of the blood shed on Israel's altars—secured the purging or forgiving of one sin. Not in that age or any other age. No, all of the blood sacrifices in ancient Israel were anticipatory—looking forward to the one acceptable sacrifice—a symbol of the blood shed by the true "Lamb of God," whose blood alone has the power to cleanse and redeem.

Surely the spectator-participants of Yom Kippur in the ancient tabernacle-temple setting sensed that the atonement drama portrayed something awesome and magnificent. The crimson-flecked scenario must have etched a deep consciousness of personal sin in every sensitive heart. Who could have failed to grasp something of the vicious monstrosity of sin? Sin exacted an inevitable penalty—death! In the solemn Yom Kippur rites, it was the death of a substitute—the innocent for the guilty. Still, the audiovisual montage was reenacted again and again and again. The recurrence of ritual suggested that something about it was incomplete, inadequate.

Was it possible? Amid the ceremony's bizarre mixture of sights, scenes, and sounds, did the worshiper perceive the lengthening shadow of a cross?

Notes

[1]Literally, יוֹם הַכִּפֻּרִים (Lev. 23:27; 25:9) and יוֹם כִּפֻּרִים (Lev. 23:28).

[2]*The American Heritage Dictionary of the English Language*, new college ed., see under "Yom Kippur."

[3]J. P. Lewis, "Feasts," *The Zondervan Pictorial Encyclopedia of the Bible*, vol. 2, 2nd printing, ed. Merrill C. Tenney (Grand Rapids: Zondervan Publishing House, 1977), 521-26; Larry Walker, "Festivals," *Holman Bible Dictionary*, ed. Trent C. Butler (Nashville: Holman Bible Publishers, 1991), 484-90.

[4]Based on J. H. Kurtz, *Sacrificial Worship of the Old Testament*, trans. James Martin (reprint, Grand Rapids: Baker Book House, 1980), 385–96.

[5]Compare Genesis 1:26-30 and 2:7-25 for an illustration of parallelism and expansion.

[6]K. A. Kitchen, *Ancient Orient and Old Testament* (Chicago: Inter-Varsity Press, 1966), 117. Kitchen cited texts from Egypt and Urartu as illustrations of the literary device.

[7]Gordon J. Wenham, *The Book of Leviticus*, *The New International Commentary on the Old Testament*, ed. R. K. Harrison (Grand Rapids: William B. Eerdmans Publishing Company, 1979), 228.

[8]For a more detailed summary, compare C. L. Feinberg, "Atonement, Day of" in *The Zondervan Pictorial Encyclopedia of the Bible*, vol. 1, 2nd printing, ed. Merrill C. Tenney (Grand Rapids: Zondervan Publishing House, 1977), 413-16.

[9]See Milton S. Terry, *Biblical Hermeneutics*, 9th printing (Grand Rapids: Zondervan Publishing House, 1981), 334-79 for a discussion of types, symbols, and symbolico-typical actions.

[10]See chapter 7 of this book.

[11]Remember that only the plural form of the noun is actually present in Leviticus.

[12]In the *Pi'el* stem.

[13]And elsewhere. See BDB, 497-98.

[14]See KB, 2:470 for an indication of the range of occurrence of the term.

[15]The Greek term καταλλαγή (from καταλλάσσω).

[16]Wenham, *Leviticus*, 59.

[17]Allen P. Ross, "The Biblical Method of Salvation: A Case for Discontinuity," in *Continuity and Discontinuity*, ed. John S. Feinberg (Westchester, IL: Crossway Books, 1988), 175.

[18]See "Kapāru," vol. 8 in *The Assyrian Dictionary of the Oriental Institute of the University of Chicago*, ed. A. Leo Oppenheim (Chicago: Oriental Institute, 1978), 178 (work hereafter cited as *CAD*).

[19]For that matter, I question the propriety of describing the altar as "polluted."

[20]For example, see Exodus 25:22; Numbers 7:89; Psalm 99:1.

[21]Wenham, *Leviticus*, 28.

[22]R. Laird Harris, "כָּפַר," *TWOT*, 1:453.

[23]Ibid.

[24]Mitchell Dahood in *The Archives of Ebla*, 282-83. We will comment later on the connection between the rite of atonement and the mercy seat.

[25]Wenham, *Leviticus*, 59.

[26]Harris, "כָּפַר," *TWOT*, 1:452.

[27]Alan P. Ross, "Discontinuity," 356.

[28]Harris, "כָּפַר," *TWOT*, 1:453. The description "intensive" stem is really misleading and gradually being replaced by "D stem." See Waltke and O'Connor, *Syntax*, 396-400. C. L. Seow labeled the stem as "D bin-

Covenant and Sacrifice: Day of Atonement

yān" (conjugation), C. L. Seow, *A Grammar for Biblical Hebrew* (Nashville: Abingdon Press, 1987), 111.

[29]BDB, see under "I. כפר," 497-98. Compare KB, see under "I כפר," 2:470-71.

[30]See R. W. Pence and D. W. Emery, *A Grammar of Present-Day English*, 2nd ed. (New York: Macmillan Publishing Company, 1963), 57.

[31]The text (בַּכֹּפֶר . . . וְכָפַרְתָּ) literally means "cover over" with a "covering."

[32]GKC, 114. An illustration of the "secondary verbal stems" is קִדַּשׁ (the *Pi'el* stem of קָדַשׁ).

[33]Waltke and O'Connor, *Syntax*, 362.

[34]Ibid., 400.

[35]For an example of causation in the *Pi'el* stem, see Ibid.

[36]"Akkadian is the oldest attested Semitic language"; see Kasper Klaus Riemschneider, *An Akkadian Grammar*, 3rd ed., ed. Thomas A. Caldwell, John N. Oswalt and John F. X. Sheehan (Milwaukee: Marquette University Press, 1977), 1. A general term that includes both Babylonian and Assyrian dialects, Akkadian was written with cuneiform signs.

[37]"*kapāru*," *CAD*, 179. Note the similarity to Genesis 6:14, *ištu šaplānu adi eliš itt'm ka-pi-ir elēnu kupram ka-pi-ir* ("from the base upward it is . . . smeared with *ittû*-bitumen, the upper part is smeared with *kupru*-bitumen"). The application of "various medications" is used with the D-stem example *eli šinnēšu ta-kap-pár*.

[38]More than five hundred in number, the animals were actually divided into droves or herds.

[39]אֲכַפְּרָה פָנָיו הַמִּנְחָה.

[40]For a full discussion, consult S. J. Schultz, "Mercy Seat," in *The Zondervan Pictoral Encyclopedia of the Bible*, vol. 4, 2nd printing, ed. Merrill C. Tenney (Grand Rapids: Zondervan Publishing House, 1977), 190.

[41]Note the addition of "an omer of manna" (Ex. 16:33) and Aaron's rod (Num. 17:10).

[42]Note the use of the preposition עַל ("upon") following כִּפֶּר (Lev. 16:16,18).

[43]Robert Robinson, NETTLETON, 1758.

[44]Robert H. Culpepper, *Interpreting the Atonement* (Grand Rapids: William B. Eerdmans Publishing Company, 1966), 24-25.

[45]Ibid., 25-26.

[46]Ibid., 26.

[47]Ibid., 27.

[48]Ibid.

[49]The Hebrew term for "scapegoat" is עֲזָאזֵל (Lev. 16:10). For a discussion of possible meanings, see Wenham, *Leviticus*, 233-35.

[50]Wenham's discussion explores the possibilities. See Ibid.

[51]The expression is עִנִּיתֶם אֶת-נַפְשֹׁתֵיכֶם.

[52]Wenham, *Leviticus*, 236.

9

In the Land of Uz

I know that my Redeemer lives.

Job 19:25

"Evil! Does it exist—or do bad things just happen?" The dark, provocative cover to a nationwide news magazine posed this haunting question, and the publication's lead article was entitled "Essay: Does Evil Exist?"[1] Despite the rosy optimism of earlier generations and remarkable and positive latter-day developments, the writer ruefully commented, "Utopia, this century has learned the hard way, usually bears a resemblance to hell. An evil chemistry turns the dream of salvation into damnation."[2] Regardless of inclination or conclusions, that a nonreligious journal would address the profound issue of good and evil betrays the fact that the secular world, too, is concerned with moral and spiritual values. Like it or not, people of all types find themselves struggling with the tension between salvation and damnation, whatever the terms may mean to them individually.

Interest in the topic may also unmask a growing anxiety about the results of a dominantly humanistic approach to history, society, mankind, and life. This practical atheism has sired strange offspring. Leaving God, biblical morals, and traditional values out of the classroom, we have taught our children that they are the ultimate stage in evolutionary progression. We have assured them that since they have emerged from animals, they are only animals, nothing more, with no religious or ethical absolutes. Now the graying generation is astounded and disturbed when the young behave like animals. Where does it all lead?

The evidence of concern about the nature of evil also highlights an awareness that the conflict between good and evil involves more than philosophical conjecture. If spiritual warfare does rage, then its battleground is earth, and its theater of operations is human experience. The ordinary individual is caught in its deadly crossfire. The wounds of combat are not all reserved for a distant eschatalogical battle. People are hurt, suffer, and die—now! Salvation and damnation are both immediate and ultimate. Sin exacts its excruciating toll of pain now as well as later. In similar fashion, the healing balm of the LORD's salvation provides both temporal and eternal therapy. The timeless now presents a strange and somewhat contradictory mixture of salvation and damnation—an earthly blend of oil and water, as it were.

The people of faith, in varying degrees, have always been subject to the pain and distress generated by the conflict between good and evil. The spiritual warriors of the Old Testament were no exception. The writer of Hebrews reviewed their combat record with this appraisal:

"Some faced jeers and flogging, while still others were chained and put in prison. They were stoned; they were sawed in two; they were put to death by the sword. They went about in sheepskins and goatskins, destitute, persecuted and mistreated" (Heb. 11:36-37).

An outstanding figure in that ancient battle brigade was, of course, Job. His experience still provides a classic profile of pain. Job's example constitutes more than just a model of patience. Through the crucible of pain, it provides an amazing insight into the soteriological design of the ages.

Lance Morrow summarized the prose prologue to Job:

> An eerie scene at the beginning of the *Book of Job*, that splendid treatise on the mysteries of evil, has God and Satan talking to each other like sardonic gentlemen gamblers who have met by chance at the racetrack at Saratoga. God

seems to squint warily at Satan, and ask, in effect, So Satan,
what have you been doing with yourself? And Satan with a
knowing swagger replies, in effect, I've been around the
world, here and there, checking it out. Then God and Satan
make a chillingly cynical bet on just how much pain Job can
endure before he cracks and curses God.[3]

Is that really all there is to it? Is the welfare of the
godly individual simply subject to the capricious and calloused whims of two celestial gamblers who are more concerned with their wager than the fate of the afflicted? If
one buys that proposition, pessimistic cynicism is almost
sure to follow. Such cynicism quickly leads to hollow, fu-
tile despair.

Without a sense of ultimate right and wrong, and with
blurred moral vision that could no longer discern between
good and evil (Isa. 5:20), the skeptics of Isaiah's day declared, "Let us eat and drink; for tomorrow we shall die"
(Isa. 22:13, KJV). If God is not good, if Satan is not evil, if
good is not really good and evil is not really evil, then
that's all there is. Wonder of wonders, Job, the paragon of
pain, categorically rejects that bleak, sterile nihilism!

The Sin-Suffering-Death Syndrome

The experience of Job provides a timeless paradigm for
the study of the tension between good and evil, success
and calamity. It probes the subtle connection between sin
and consequence, the origin and nature of evil, and the
baffling mystery of suffering. The mystifying calamity in
the life of Job also impinges on the study of salvation in
the Old Testament. The ancient poem built around Job's
ordeal does not describe how he became a saint of YHWH,
but it does provide insight into what the salvation-rela-
tionship with the Lord might include. In brief, it not only
analyzes the puzzle of the suffering of the innocent; it also
scrutinizes the problem of the suffering of the saints. In so
doing, it raises some correlative issues.

Retribution: Fiction or Fact? In attempting to discern
some rhyme or reason in the bewildering fate of Job, Eliphaz, one of Job's "friends," made this pious judgment: "As
I have observed, those who plow evil and those who sow

trouble reap it. At the breath of God they are destroyed; at the blast of his anger they perish" (Job 4:8-9). The Eliphaz equation does more than tie sin and calamity in a tight cause-effect bundle. It also attributes the effect directly to God. That, in turn, raises two questions: (1) Is a specific calamity the immediate and inevitable penalty of a specific sin? (2) Is God the initiator of every penalty?

On the surface, the biblical answer to both questions would seem to be an unequivocal yes. The New Testament explicitly confirms Eliphaz's dictum in the warning:

"Do not be deceived: God cannot be mocked. A man reaps what he sows. The one who sows to please his sinful nature, from that nature will reap destruction; the one who sows to please the Spirit, from the Spirit will reap eternal life" (Gal. 6:7-8).

The principle is clear: sin does produce destructive consequences, and God is involved personally and directly in the process. If this is true, then divine retribution is a biblical, theological, and experiential fact.

Klaus Koch, however, raised the question in print, "Is There a Doctrine of Retribution in the Old Testament?" and concluded that "actions have built in consequences."[4] He acknowledged that YHWH supervised the scene but insisted that it was dominated by the principle of the "Sin-Disaster-Connection on the one hand and the Good Action-Blessings-Connection on the other."[5] Koch construed the moral cause-effect relationship to be so mechanical as to reject the deduction that God really personally intervened in the process at all, at least in the Old Testament.

Significantly, Koch based his conclusion primarily on data contained in Proverbs, Hosea, Qohelet (Ecclesiastes), and Job. In my opinion, his thesis cannot be sustained, even in those books. It is seriously challenged by other passages that underscore the LORD's active administration of judgment. (See Deut. 28—29; Amos 1—2; Isa. 63:1-3.)

The matter is really a question of emphasis. There is indeed a cause-effect relationship between sin and consequence. The biblical record and human experience confirm the devastating association. In some situations, the connection is intimate and immediate. Anger and hatred, for example, may erupt in an act of murder or violence with instant, tragic, and irrevocable results.[6] In such instances, the cause-effect relationship may be, for all practical purposes, a mechanical operation.

It does not follow, however, that God is an "absentee landlord" in the moral supervision of history. The Old Testament affirms that God does hold persons accountable for their actions and attitudes. Moreover, God may work both within and beyond the conventional patterns of cause and effect. In other words, divine retribution, based on the holy and gracious nature of YHWH and human moral responsibility, is a fact.

According to the Old Testament, YHWH directly executed retribution against isolated objects of judgment (Amos 1:3—2:3). From time to time, He even personally intervened in the lives of His saints to impose direct penalty (Num. 20:7-12; 2 Sam. 12:11). The biblical evidence, then, indicates that sin may produce immediate, automatic consequences. It also confirms that, while God may work in and through the natural process of cause and result, He may choose to go beyond those parameters. Eliphaz's observation was essentially correct. Sin does produce its own damnable results, and God does supervise the process. Eliphaz made two subtle mistakes. He failed to recognize that (1) not every calamity is the immediate result of a specific sin, and (2) occasionally, a superior economy is in force.

In the case of Job, the nice, neat "Sin-Disaster-Connection" was not applicable. Despite the withering denunciation of his friends (Job 8:6; 11:5-6), Job was not the perpetrator of some dark, foul deed that he refused to acknowledge (Job 15:5; 22:5,7,9). His distress did not represent punishment commensurate with an unidentified, hidden crime.

Eliphaz and his two associates were unaware that, in the person of Job, the sin-suffering syndrome had been canceled by executive decree. The three critics were completely ignorant of the heavenly council confrontations (Job 1:6-12; 2:1-6) and, consequently, misread the meaning of Job's tragedy altogether. Job himself was oblivious to the dialogue between God and Satan. Had he been privy to those negotiations, his miserable circumstance might have been more endurable. However, an important principle can be derived from the welter of Job's pain and confusion: even the godly suffer!

Sometimes we read the Bible through the rose-colored lenses of fantasy, focusing exclusively on the ideal while ignoring the real. We project larger-than-life champions of heroic proportions and neglect the real-life flaws and limitations of the flesh-and-blood people who walk through the pages of Scripture and who were subject to all of the restrictions of mortality as we are. The people of faith in the Old Covenant administration were just that—people. Even so, the grief of Job was streaked with genuine tears; his pain of heart and body burned with all of the searing intensity of the noonday sun. Job did not dwell at the "end of the yellow brick road." The land was Uz—not Oz!

Theodicy or Anthropodicy? An intriguing issue in biblical and theological studies is labeled "theodicy." According to the back cover of the volume, *Theodicy in the Old Testament*, "Theodicy is the attempt to explain the problem of evil while maintaining the belief that God is a moral creator who loves his people." To some writers that attempt seems to be a challenging, if not impossible, assignment. For example, James L. Crenshaw (the editor of *Theodicy in the Old Testament*) wrote, "We may thus define theodicy loosely as the attempt to pronounce a verdict of "Not Guilty" over God for whatever seems to destroy the order of society and the universe."[7]

It should be noted, in appreciation, that Crenshaw endeavored to provide some interpretive grid that would satisfactorily explain the enigma of undeserved suffering. In *Theodicy in the Old Testament*, he proposed that this brand of suffering might be perceived as: (1) retributive, (2) disciplinary, (3) revelational, (4) probative, (5) illusory, (6) transitory, and/or (7) mysterious.[8] In a subsequent volume, *A Whirlpool of Torment*, however, his modified analysis offered the following perspectives: (1) moral, (2) disciplinary, (3) eschatological, (4) metaphysical/psychological, (5) redemptive, (6) divine presence, and/or (7) skeptical.[9] He concluded this second list with the comment, "In the end, an antitheodicy emerges, one that focuses on divine freedom and human limits."[10]

Both sets of criteria contain legitimate considerations, but the complexity of suffering is as bewildering as the intricacy of human personality. No single factor is likely to be adequate to explain every situation. For Crenshaw, lamentably, to salvage God's honor is to sacrifice human integrity. He offered no definition of an "anthropodicy," but apparently he is persuaded that human integrity can only be maintained by holding God accountable for all evil. That supposition, of course, provides a latent affirmative answer to Eliphaz's question, "Can a mortal be more righteous than God? / Can a man be more pure than his Maker?" (Job 4:17).

No simplistic, single-facet answer to the problem of evil is ever likely. Questions about the cause, nature, responsibility, and results of evil are so perplexing and solutions so tenuous that Morrow opined, "almost all theodicies have about them a pathetic quality and seem sometimes undignified exertions of the mind."[11] That rather pompous criticism is tainted with irony by Morrow's concluding paragraphs in which he speculated about the possible "replicating" of the human body in the "better container" of a "robotic personoid."

In projecting the tantalizing possibility of sterilizing the mortal "container," Morrow struggled with the concept of filtering evil from the human soul. Pondering the result of leaving "the inheritance of Cain" in the abandoned "useless flesh," his final paragraph is composed of five sentences. Four of them are questions:

> ... will grace and love, evil's enemies wither too? The question goes back to the Garden. Does the good become meaningless in a world without evil? Do the angels depart along with the devils? If the stainless canister knows nothing of evil, will Mozart sound the same as gunfire?[12]

Disinterested or Prejudicial Piety? For Job, the enigma posed by the suffering of the saints was far more than an idle academic or theological exercise. It was a puzzle wrapped in the tattered shreds of a life that had been ripped apart by monstrous and insane circumstances, a reversal of fortune beyond the most neurotic imagination. His personal calamity involved physical loss that targeted both bountiful possessions and personal health. In the equivalent of a monumental market collapse, his vast holdings were suddenly snatched away, leaving him destitute. His body was attacked by a scourge of painful, itching, loathsome sores that made rest impossible and life almost intolerable. Still, the material distress was only the tip of the iceberg. The real ferment raged beneath the surface. The most devastating impact was internal rather than external.

The physical distress of Job's circumstance paled beside the psyche-shattering emotional jolt that he sustained. The loss of any loved one brings an excruciating psychological trauma at best, but perhaps there is no grief to strike the human spirit like that of the death of one's child. If that is only close to the truth, then imagine how Job must have felt when he received the horrifying news that all of his children had perished in the same unreasonable catastrophe. What a crushing weight of sorrow! What a paralyzing surge of anguish! Poor, heartbroken Job!

In this bleak context of darkest gloom, the admonition of Job's wife is more than a little puzzling. "Are you still holding on to your integrity? Curse God and die!" (Job 2:9). Her somewhat ambiguous words appear to be basically negative in tone, if not overtly blasphemous.[13] Samuel Terrien offered this evaluation:

> The woman's question and advice may be interpreted in two ways: (a) "Do you still pretend to be a perfect man? Do you not see that such a fantastic succession of calamities proves beyond doubt that you are a sinner? Bid God farewell and die!" Or (b) "Do you still ridiculously believe that your perfection is recognized by a righteous God? Let blasphemy bring its certain and immediate consequence. Curse God and die."[14]

Whatever meaning or intent one may ascribe to Job's wife, his reply makes it clear that he was both surprised and disappointed by her advice (Job 2:10). In some way, it would seem, his most intimate companion of the years had abandoned him in his moment of greatest need for encouragement and understanding.

To complete the picture of total gloom, Job's three friends came to "console and comfort." Despite their formal expression of compassion in "the approved ritual of mourning for the dead,"[15] they compounded his distress with their unfounded charges of guilt. In their self-righteous presumption, his colleagues became his antagonists. His friends were his accusers.

As demoralizing as all of these factors might have been, Job hurt at a deeper level. When Eliphaz first raised the "sin-disaster-connection" issue, evidently Job agreed with the stated principle. His request, "Teach me, and I will be quiet; / show me where I have been wrong" (Job 6:24), was not an effort to defend himself but an earnest attempt to understand what he had done to justify such calamity. Much of Job's emotional and psychological agony stemmed from his complete bafflement at the incomprehensible mystery of his distress. For him, the question of the innocent suffering was constricted to the matter of the righteous suffering, with the suffering of the righteous reduced to the scope of one.

The ultimate riddle for Job and the source of his deepest pain, however, was the bewildering mystery of divine silence.[16] Some have ascribed to Job a "disinterested virtue and piety,"[17] implying that he was virtuous for the sheer sake of virtue. While the notion of disinterested piety may be quite attractive, it comes perilously close to suggesting that "happiness is different things to different people." One might even assume that Job was religious because that was just his "thing." Had that been indeed the case, then Job would surely have found it easy to recant his misplaced faith and priorities. No, it was something deeper, more profound than superficial religious calisthenics.

For Job, God was not some "strange deity"[18] whose mysterious providences were beyond comprehension. Job had evidently known God in terms of a charitable abiding Presence and as a loving, benevolent Benefactor. His devotion, therefore, was not totally impartial. Rather, it was a sincere, grateful response to the overwhelming goodness of God in his life. Accordingly, Crenshaw came much closer to the core of Job's distress when he posed the question, "How can God turn against faithful servants and submit them to tests that propel them headlong into a whirlpool of torment?"[19]

Some modification of that particular question must surely have echoed again and again in the heart of Job. The real issue, then, was the apparent betrayal of his most trusted Friend, compounded by a terrible divine silence in the face of pain, death, and unanswered prayer.

The Arbitrator-Witness-Redeemer Connection

A new, ethereal character does emerge in the Book of Job, a figure associated with the production of Job's frustration. Helplessly enmeshed in the throes of contradiction, Job yearned for someone to intercede in his behalf, someone who could bridge the yawning chasm between God and himself. He lamented: "He (God) is not a man like me that I might answer him, / that we might confront each other in court. / If only there were someone to arbitrate between us, / to lay his hands upon us both" (Job 9:32-33).

The beleaguered saint thus longed for an illusory individual who would be qualified to make an accurate and acceptable "judgment call"[20] on Job's case. In his shattered circumstance, slandered and maligned by "friends," Job felt the need for an impartial and fair umpire, one who could and would arbitrate in his behalf. He desired a mediator.

As his distress deepened and the debate with his accusers intensified, Job affirmed his confidence in a heavenly witness who would testify "for the defense" before the divine tribunal. He bravely insisted, "Even now my witness is in heaven; / my advocate is on high" (Job 16:19). Job envisioned, in effect, a celestial advocate who would plead his case, defend his innocence, and vindicate his cause. Marvin H. Pope characterized the witness as "an intermediary, an intercessor who will testify on Job's behalf and plead for him with God as a man pleads for his friend."[21] What a beautiful dream!

Job's expanding conception of a heavenly ally reached its zenith in his breathtaking pledge of faith: "I know that my Redeemer lives, / and that in the end he will stand upon the earth. / And after my skin has been destroyed, / yet in my flesh I will see God; / I myself will see him / with my own eyes—I, and not another. / How my heart yearns within me!" (Job 19:25-27).

The term for "Redeemer" is the Hebrew word *gō'ēl* (גֹּאֵל).
Robert Gordis described the somewhat technical application of the term:

> A human *gō'ēl* is a kinsman; hence an active defender of
> one's interests, redeeming one from bondage (Lev. 25:48,
> 49), repurchasing a field (Lev. 25:26, 33; Ruth 4:4, 6) and
> marrying a childless widow (Ruth 3:4, 6, 13) . . . The *gō'ēl* is,
> above all, the blood avenger (Nu. 35:19; Deut. 19:6, 12: Jos.
> 20:3; II Sam. 14:11).[22]

This emblem does not represent, as Gordis noted, some
"unknown 'third party' "[23] but is the third manifestation of a
single figure. Pope concluded, "This witness for the defense
is to serve a purpose similar to that of the umpire of ix 33
and the vindicator of xix 25."[24] So Job's longing and faith introduced more than three distinct but anonymous characters. Instead, his vision projected a single, transcendent
personality who would champion Job's cause in a threefold
capacity. Appropriately, then, Job's manifesto of trust
anticipated a triple-level benefit: (1) mediation, (2) vindication, and (3) restoration—all of this long before the
incarnation.

The Faith Affirmation

Job's magnificent dream of a coming umpire-advocate-
redeemer is awesome when one remembers that the Old
Testament saint, so far as we know, possessed not one
page of biblical revelation. He certainly was a stranger to
the marvelous disclosures of the New Testament; yet the
content of his faith rings with a faint but unmistakable
gospel reverberation.

A Living Redeemer. Job's hope and trust focused on a
living Redeemer. In the first chill of adversity, Job had
vented his unspeakable anguish in a melancholy "death
wish." Regretting the day of his birth (Job 3:3) and the
fact that he had not died in infancy (Job 3:11), he longed
for a death that eluded him (Job 3:21). A bit later, as Job
pondered his dismal fate, he rebuked his "comforters":

"Are not my few days almost over? / Turn away from me
so I can have a moment's joy / before I go to the place of no

return, / to the land of gloom and deep shadow, / to the land of deepest night, / of deep shadow and disorder, / where even the light is like darkness" (Job 10:20-22).

As Job peered deeper into the dark monitor of gloom, however, he began to entertain illusions of hope: "If only you would hide me in the grave / and conceal me till your anger has passed! / If only you would set me a time / and then remember me!" (Job 14:13).

Then he raised the haunting, fascinating question, "If a man dies, will he live again?" (Job 14:14).

Thus, ascending from the utter depths of despair, culminating in a dazzling leap of faith, Job declared his confidence in a living "kinsman-redeemer" who would ultimately come to his rescue. Since Job's sons were dead, leaving him without an appropriate kinsman to function as redeemer, Job did indeed pin his hope "upon the existence of a heavenly being who would survive his own untimely death and bring about the miracle of a divine-human confrontation."[25] In the choking stench of death and amid the smoking ashes of life's sweetest dreams, Job announced triumphantly, "As for me, I do know (that) my redeemer is alive!" (author's translation of Job 19:25).

A Coming Redeemer. A startling addendum to Job's faith affirmation was the anticipation that his kinsman-redeemer "in the end . . . will stand upon the earth." The temporal modifier "in the end"[26] may only designate sequential development. The term is distinctly eschatological in flavor, however, and the context definitely accentuates that emphasis.[27] While the exact force of verse 26 is debatable,[28] the general sense seems to reflect Job's anticipation of some kind of vindication beyond death and the grave. That perspective, of course, is indisputably eschatological in orientation.

Job's earlier question and this somewhat ambiguous statement hardly provide the basis for a firm doctrine of resurrection. They do confirm that Job had a lucid belief in an afterlife. Moreover, link the concept of a "living Redeemer" with the context of His eschatological appearance "upon the earth"; add the prospect of a confrontation after the decay of the flesh; and the thought of resurrection is difficult to ignore.

A Sympathetic Redeemer. The precise nuance of "I myself will see him with my own eyes—I, and not another" (v. 27) is as difficult to determine as the statement in verse 26. The expression behind NIV's translation "and not another" (וְלֹא־זָר) invokes the notion of "strange" or "foreign."[29] A comparison of translations will disclose the ambiguity of the term.

Whatever force is attributed to the words, though, the general meaning of the total sentence seems quite obvious. Job anticipated that his ultimate encounter with the kinsman-redeemer would disclose a sympathetic, understanding friend, not a harsh, critical adversary. Despite the bewildering pain and disappointment of the unending moment, Job caught a fleeting glimpse of the splendor that lay beyond the vale of tears, a splendor that included final reconciliation with his Grand Champion of eternity.

Summary

What evaluations may be drawn from this limited analysis of Job's experience? For one thing, his ordeal demonstrated with almost brutal clarity that the saints of God are subject to all of the calamities that infest human existence. Godly devotion does not innoculate against distress, disturbance, heartache, suffering, or death. The "gospel according to Pollyanna" that promises "health, wealth, and prosperity" is completely contradicted by Job's tragedy. Moreover, the cheap opportunism that invites persons to serve the Lord in order to secure the blessings and "fringe benefits" of godliness is categorically refuted by the stubborn, persistent, and sorely tested faithfulness of Job (Job 13:15).

A second feature of importance in the Job episode is the emerging, still shadowy figure of a coming Redeemer. The triadic redemptive symbolism in the Day of Atonement ceremony has now been reinforced by the threefold role of a future "Vindicator." This, of course, would suggest that the soteriological message in the Book of Job transcended the temporal and liturgical limitations of the Old Covenant. That does not imply, however, that its salvation message, which blended hope in an afterlife with an expanding messianic consciousness, had no meaning in its original setting. Indeed, Job's very survival depended on its sustaining strength.

I reject, then, Terrien's proposal that "Job is in no way alluding to a Messiah," but I heartily concur with his contradictory concession, "Christian interpreters—as well as the innumerable hearers of Handel's oratorio, *Messiah*—have a right to find in this passage a prefiguration of the Christian experience of salvation."[30]

In addition, the log of Job's tormented voyage has provided spiritual and emotional "ballast" for many a lonely pilgrim in subsequent storms at sea. What saint has not turned in desperation to the chronicle of Job, only to find his own misery mirrored in the great man "of the East" (Job 1:3)? How many of God's people, in all ages, have found strength to endure because of the example of Job?

Finally, Job has helped those in the furnace of pain to appreciate the purifying value of anguish. His profound assessment still challenges: "But he knows the way that I take; / when he has tested me, I will come forth as gold" (Job 23:10). Job demonstrated in the laboratory of his suffering the refining, distilling benefit of adversity. Accordingly, the heat-tested gold of his faithfulness continues to challenge and inspire.

Moreover, although the battered, beleaguered saint came perilously close to abandoning his faith, he managed to cling tenaciously to his trust in the LORD. In so doing, he eloquently refuted Satan's sarcastic question, "Does Job fear God for nothing?" and the taunting charge, "But stretch out your hand and strike his flesh and bones, and he will surely curse you to your face" (Job 1:9; 2:5). With rugged, determined persistence, the man from Uz demonstrated the character of genuine faith and faithfulness. His example has left an abiding illustration of the true meaning of commitment.

A subtle reminder lingers from the pathos of Job's torment:

> The fact that suffering is woven into the very fabric of our universe and that it may be instrumental in bringing about God's gracious purpose for his people, reaches its ultimate manifestation in the Cross of Calvary.[31]

Notes

[1]Lance Morrow, "Evil," *TIME* (June 10, 1991): 48-53.

[2]Ibid., 51.

[3]Ibid., 52.

[4]Klaus Koch, "Is There a Doctrine of Retribution in the Old Testament?" in *Theodicy in the Old Testament*, ed. James L. Crenshaw (Philadelphia: Fortress Press, 1983), 66.

[5]Ibid., 62.

[6]For a biblical example, consider 2 Samuel 11:14–17.

[7]James L. Crenshaw, "Introduction: The Shift from Theodicy to Anthropodicy," in *Theodicy in the Old Testament*, ed. James L. Crenshaw (Philadelphia: Fortress Press, 1983), 1.

[8]Ibid., 4.

[9]James L. Crenshaw, *A Whirlpool of Torment* (Philadelphia: Fortress Press, 1984), 114.

[10]Ibid.

[11]Morrow, "Evil," 52.

[12]Ibid., 53.

[13]See Pope's comments, Marvin H. Pope, *Job*, vol. 15 of *The Anchor Bible*, 3rd ed., ed. William Foxwell Albright and David Noel Freedman (Garden City: Doubleday & Company, 1983), 21-22. Note especially the Septuagint's expansion of the remarks of Job's wife.

[14]Samuel Terrien, *The Book of Job: Introduction and Exegesis*, vol. 3 of *The Interpreter's Bible*, ed. George Arthur Buttrick (New York: Abingdon-Cokesbury Press, 1951-57), 921.

[15]Terrien, *Job*, 923. See 1 Samuel 31:13.

[16]Despite Crenshaw's disclaimer; see Crenshaw, *Whirlpool*, 119.

[17]Pope, *Job*, LXXIV; also see Ronald J. Williams, "Theodicy in the Ancient Near East," in *Theodicy in the Old Testament*, ed. James L. Crenshaw (Philadelphia: Fortress Press, 1983), 52.

[18]Crenshaw, *Whirlpool*, 118.

[19]Ibid., 119.

[20]Job used the participial noun, מוֹכִיחַ, based on the *hiph'il* stem of יָכַח. KB proposes that the *hiph'il* form of this verb includes the idea **zurechtweisen** ("to set right") and **entscheiden** ("decide," "arbitrate," "give judgment"), KB, 2:392. See also BDB, 406-407.

[21]Pope, *Job*, 125.

[22]Robert Gordis, *The Book of Job* (New York: The Jewish Theological Seminary of America, 1978), 205-206. Note the parallel to Watt's delineation of the *gō'ēl*'s function as redeeming a kinsman's freedom, homestead, name, and/or righteous satisfaction (*Teaching*, 128-30).

[23]Ibid., 527.

[24]Pope, *Job*, 125.

[25]Terrien, *Job*, 1053.

[26]The single Hebrew word אַחֲרוֹן.

[27]See BDB, 30-31.

[28]Compare the translations of Terrien (*Job*, 1054), Pope (*Job*, 139), and Gordis (*Job*, 198). The expression מִבְּשָׂרִי may mean "from my flesh," "apart from my flesh," or possibly even "after my flesh."

[29]See BDB, 266. Compare KB, 1:256.

[30]Terrien, *Job*, 1053.

[31]Ronald J. Williams, "Theodicy in the Ancient Near East," in *Theodicy in the Old Testament*, ed. James L. Crenshaw (Philadelphia: Fortress Press, 1983), 55.

10

The Fall of Jericho: A Study of the Principles of Penal Judgment

See, I have delivered Jericho into your hands.

Joshua 6:2

> Joshua fought the battle of Jericho,
>   Jericho, Jericho
> Joshua fought the battle of Jericho,
> And the walls came tumbling down.

Immortalized in the powerful words of the old spiritual, the report of the conquest of Jericho remains one of the most bizarre accounts in the annals of military history. Not only do the highly irregular assault tactics set the Jericho campaign apart from other battle plans; also, the lopsided margin of Israelite victory may be without comparison until the overwhelming conquest by coalition forces in "Operation Desert Storm."

However, the destruction of the ancient Canaanite stronghold did not result from superior Israelite numbers, weaponry, or strategy. Jericho was delivered into the hands of Israel by the "commander of the army of the LORD" (Josh. 5:14). Consequently, and perhaps surprisingly, the noise and confusion of that primitive warfare provide an important contribution to the expanding disclosure of YHWH's salvation design.

Perspectives

As in the study of almost any literary document or narrative account, the siege and fall of Jericho may be examined from several different perspectives. The unique and strange content of the report in the Book of Joshua accentuates the importance of understanding the data correctly, but it also adds to the difficulty of analysis. Consequently, viewpoints and opinions about the destruction of Jericho and its meaning may differ radically.

Historical. Inevitably, the story of Jericho's collapse must be evaluated from the viewpoint of its authenticity. Some reject the historicity of Jericho's conquest on the basis of the strong supernatural element in the report. Whether or not one believes that the events recorded actually occurred, "the fall of Jericho, as described in Joshua 2—6, was a siege culminating in a 'miraculous' destruction of the walls."[1] That appraisal is right on target. The Book of Joshua does describe the demise of Jericho as an event beyond the conventional laws of nature. One who cannot accommodate the "miraculous" will have difficulty accepting the credibility of the Joshua account.

Another factor to be considered is the highly selective nature of biblical narrative. William G. Dever's evaluation addresses that issue and is worthy of consideration:

> For them (the Biblical writers) and for their original readers, the Bible is "his story," rather than "history," the interpretation of certain happenings as seen through the eyes of faith. To be sure, the Bible is historical in the sense that it contains an account of particular peoples and occurrences at particular places and times, and in this respect it contrasts sharply with some of the mythological literatures of other ancient religions. But concrete events are important in the Bible only as they illustrate God's actions and their consequences for people here and now. The modern notion of a disinterested secular history would have been inconceivable to Biblical writers.[2]

The point is well taken. Also, the suggestion that, in essence, the biblical writers exercised a theological economy in the organization of selected historical information will be of particular value in the study of Jericho's fall. At any rate, Joshua 2—6 reports an event that constitutes a crucial historical link between Israel's entry into Canaan and the subsequent establishment of a Hebrew monarchy in the land.

Archaeological. The story of the archaeological excavations at Tell es-Sultan, the modern name of the site of ancient Jericho, is almost as spellbinding as that of the city's destruction by Joshua. While preliminary explorations of the region were conducted as early as the eighteenth century,[3] "the first major excavation at Jericho was conducted by an Austro-German expedition under the direction of Ernst Sellin and Carl Watzinger from 1907 to 1909."[4]

The two most prominent names associated with the archaeology of Jericho are John Garstang and Kathleen Kenyon. Garstang, a British archaeologist, excavated from 1930 to 1936 and concluded that the city was destroyed around 1400 B.C., evidently by the invading Israelites.[5] Kenyon, who excavated from 1952 to 1958, challenged Garstang's evidence and evaluations, however, concluding that the city was actually destroyed around 1550 B.C. and that the site was basically unoccupied during the Late Bronze Age.[6] That would have meant that there was no fortified Jericho in existence in 1400 B.C. for Joshua to conquer.[7] Her interpretation of the archaeological data has been widely accepted, influencing many to doubt the accuracy of the Joshua account. For example, John R. Bartlett, a colleague of Kenyon, reported:

> It is now clear that there is no archaeological evidence to support the idea that the town of Jericho collapsed about the date usually assigned to Joshua, in the thirteenth century BC, and it is also clear from scholarly examination of the biblical account that Joshua 6 cannot be interpreted as a simple chronicle based on eye-witness report.[8]

In recent years, however, Kenyon's appraisal has been vigorously contested.[9] In particular, Bryant G. Wood has challenged her methodology and questioned her conclusions. Wood's own examination of the evidence has led him to disagree sharply with Kenyon. He discovered what he believes to be remarkable correspondence between the archaeological evidence at Jericho and the biblical account. He summarized his findings in this statement:

> All this evidence converges to demonstrate that City IV was destroyed in about 1400 B.C.E., *not* 1550 B.C.E. as Kenyon maintained.

> If the Hyksos did not destroy Jericho and the Egyptians did not destroy Jericho, then who did? The only written record to survive concerning the history of Jericho in the Late Bronze Age is that found in the Hebrew Bible.
> When we compare the archaeological evidence at Jericho with the Biblical narrative describing the Israelite destruction of Jericho, we find a quite remarkable agreement.[10]

In the light of his training, field experience, and expertise,[11] Wood's findings cannot be summarily ignored. Any future research in the area must include a consideration of his evaluations.

Military. A vital part of the Hebrew conquest of Canaan, the Jericho episode almost demands some kind of military critique. As a matter of fact, qualified analysts have studied the battle tactics of Israel's invading army in the context of ancient military strategy. The venerable archaeologist Yigael Yadin, former chief of staff of the Israel Defense Forces, and Jewish historian Abraham Malamat have examined the Hebrew incursion into the land and reported their evaluations.[12]

In describing the fall of Jericho, Malamat observed that "militarily the attack depended on expert intelligence and infiltration into the city with the help of Rahab the harlot."[13] He also commented, "The repeated encircling of Jericho on six successive days . . . has sometimes been regarded as a psychological device to lower the enemy's guard, preparing the way for a breach into the city."[14]

Erika Bleibtreu, research assistant at the Oriental Institute of Vienna University, suggested that the ancient Assyrians employed five basic techniques in conquering an enemy city. Based on her analysis of Assyrian palace reliefs, she concluded that an invading army might: (1) scale the walls of the city, (2) batter through its walls or gate, (3) tunnel under the city's wall, (4) maintain a seige (blockade), or (5) cut off the city's water supply. Bleibtreu prefaced her list by noting that "a combination of two or more of these methods can usually be observed at each site of attack."[15]

Perhaps because of the Assyrian orientation to her analysis, Bleibtreu overlooked Malamat's consideration of the role of military intelligence and psychological warfare in the Jericho campaign. These two options might be added to her list. One additional method might be allowed in the case of Jericho: "trumpet assault."

Theological. Garstang, director of the first significant excavation at Jericho, called attention to the importance of Joshua 5:13-14 in this comment:

> Firstly, it reminds us appropriately at this stage of the essential fact that, although the earliest documents, quoted in our Introductory Section, contain a connected and reasonably coherent narrative of events, they, no less than the Bible as a whole, were conceived from first to last as the records of a religious movement, written down, arranged, and later annotated, by men who were inspired and guided by the very religion which it was their purpose to perpetuate. We should fail then to grasp the full meaning of the text, or to gauge the historical value even of those oldest documents, if we ignored altogether the spiritual element which pervades these writings. Secondly, it forms the prelude to an unparalleled episode, in which the sacrifice of Jericho with its living population is performed as a sacramental act; and so to some extent it prepares the reader to find the military incidents and material aspect of the occasion almost lost to view behind the details of the religious ceremonial that solemnised the event.[16]

Thus, before the words were written, Garstang applied Dever's perception that the Bible features "the interpretation of certain happenings as seen through the eyes of faith" to the strange military victory at Jericho. Garstang, thereby, highlighted the importance of priority. The theological significance of Jericho's fall must not be lost in the debris analysis of excavational artifacts, the critique of military strategy, and speculation about historical authenticity. Indeed, the *meaning* of the destruction of Jericho is as important as the fact of it.

Scenario

Before the message of Jericho's fall can be fully validated, some specific details of the episode need clarification. Moreover, some rationale for religious or theological evaluation needs to be certified.

Strategy. Somewhat surprisingly, students of the assault are not unanimous in their understanding of the particulars of the attack. Garstang, for example, proposed, "The word translated 'compass,' it should be noted, has nowhere in the historical books of the O.T. the sense of 'march round': the rendering 'surround' or 'encircle' would be more exact."[17] Garstang appealed to the Septuagint version's "do thou set around about it (in a circle) the men of war"[18] as support for his proposal.

This interpretation is appealing. And, while the Hebrew verb (סָבַב) may mean either "go round" or "surround,"[19] its use in describing the transportation of the ark (Josh. 6:11)[20] hardly corresponds to "surround." Besides, the command to "march around" the city "seven times" (Josh. 6:4,15)[21] is not consistent with the idea of simple encirclement. Accordingly, we conclude that the Hebrew battle plan did involve marching around the circumference of the city, once a day for six days and seven times on the last.

Wall Demolition. Garstang found what he believed to be evidence of a collapse of the walls of Jericho. While observing that their destruction "is not attributed by the Bible narrative to a physical agency," he cautioned that "we should not overlook in this connexion the possible effect of earthquakes, which in themselves would doubtless have been regarded at the time as direct manifestations of Jehovah's powers."[22] Wood concurred with Garstang's assessment:

> The collapse of the city wall may well have been the result of an earthquake, since there is ample evidence for earthquake activity at the end of the life of City IV. Again, geophysicist Amos Nur:
> "This combination, the destruction of Jericho and the stoppage of the Jordan, is so typical of earthquakes in this region that only little doubt can be left as to the reality of such events in Joshua's time."[23]

Garstang concluded, "As to the main fact, then, there remains no doubt: the walls fell outwards so completely that the attackers would be able to clamber up and over their ruins in the city."[24] So, by whatever means and in whatever time period, the ruins of Jericho confirm that a massive demolition of the city did occur and that it included a monumental collapse of city walls.

Considerations

Prior to our addressing the meaning of the Jericho report, two other items require attention. One has to do with the meaning and implication of a word (or concept) in the text. The other has to do with the application of the total narrative. The two matters, then, are exegetical and hermeneutical in nature.

Cherem. Because of the nature of Hebrew guttural letters, no one system of transliteration enjoys universal acceptance. Accordingly, the English reproduction of the key term *ḥērem*[25] may vary, but the meaning of the concept will not be affected by that. Snaith proposed:

> In Hebrew the word *cherem* came to refer . . . to that which has been *qodesh* to a god other than Jehovah, and which therefore, whenever possible, was 'devoted' to Jehovah by being utterly, completely, and ruthlessly destroyed. . . . One god's *qodesh* was another god's *cherem*. The devotees of one god therefore destroyed all they could capture of the other god's property, whether it was animate or inanimate.[26]

Leon J. Wood noted that "this word is used regarding almost all the cities which Joshua's troops destroyed (e.g., Jericho, Josh. 6:21 . . .), thus indicating the rationale for their destruction."[27]

Marten H. Woudstra made this observation:

> The symbolical nature of Jericho's fall, historical though it be, should not escape the reader. The very first city of the promised land was to be Israel's by a mere shout raised at the command of Joshua, the Lord's servant. The symbolical nature of this event is also expressed by the fact that the *curse* applied to Jericho and its inhabitants is to be most severe. This curse (Heb. *ḥerem*) meant that something or someone was absolutely and irrevocably consecrated so that it could not be redeemed (Lev. 27:28-29). It also meant that the object (person) was sentenced to utter destruction.[28]

Trent C. Butler called attention to the unique economy of the term in the Joshua setting: "חרם in 6:17 is the only instance in the OT where men and goods are included. Everywhere else the verb, not the noun, is used in reference to men."[29] Accordingly, one may conclude that the term usually designated people (not just things) who were beyond redemption and subject to judgment.

Moreover, as Robert G. Boling pointed out, the word and activity were not restricted to Israel alone. "It is not a uniquely Israelite word or practice. The ninth-century Moabite king Mesha speaks thus of 'devoting' the Israelites to his god Chemosh."[30] The invoking of ḥērem at Jericho, then, not only explains the scope and magnitude of the city's destruction. It also helps to clarify the economy of such radical measures.

"Principlization." Walter C. Kaiser, Jr. has persuasively maintained that authorial intent is the key to correct biblical interpretation. He insisted:

> A literary work like the Bible can have one and only one correct interpretation and that meaning must be determined by the human author's truth-intention; otherwise, all alleged meanings would be accorded the same degree of seriousness, plausibility, and correctness with no one meaning being more valid or true than the others.[31]

Thus, while rejecting "moralizing, allegorizing, psychologizing, spiritualizing, or subjectively editorializing on a selected Biblical text,"[32] he has advocated "principlization." He defined "principlization" as stating "the author's propositions, arguments, narrations, and illustrations in timeless abiding truths, with special focus on the application of those truths to the current needs of the church."[33]

Applying Kaiser's concept of principlization to the Jericho narrative (at least tentatively) would support the position that there was (and is) a message in and beyond the battlefield report. Is there really a lesson to be learned from the ancient destruction? If so, what?

Theological Analysis

Beyond the enigmatic battle plan, the somewhat cryptic description of events, the supernatural demolition of Jericho's walls, the frightening annihilation of her populace—what did this report of ancient warfare actually mean? True, it meant the total devastation of the Bronze Age Canaanite stronghold; but what was the significance of that? Why was so much space and attention given to the Jericho account?[34]

Since Jericho's destruction involved *hērem*, the event must be construed as an historical act of judgment. That being the case, the principle involved must surely relate to matters of judgment. But how, and in what way?

I suggest that YHWH's divine judgment actually operates at several different levels. First, there is what may be described as "natural judgment." Koch defined that sphere of judgment as the "Sin-Disaster-Connection."[35] In other words, sin frequently produces its own inherent consequences, and that painful correlation is a part of the judgment process. Second, the LORD supervises and directs a "continuing historical judgment." This aspect of judgment is reflected in specific acts of divine retribution that transcend the routine processes of nature and may be expressed in corporate or individual applications.[36] Third, in my opinion, a "judgment of the nations" is predicted as a distinct and historical event.[37] Fourth, the New Testament distinguishes an eschatological "judgment of believers" that involves an end-time evaluation of the saints (2 Cor. 5:10). Fifth, there is a "penal judgment" that is associated with the "great white throne" scenario projected in the Revelation (Rev. 20:11-15).

The extermination of Jericho would certainly qualify as an illustration of the second category in the proposed list, a "continuing historical judgment." For that matter, all of the cities destroyed in the conquest of Canaan would fit that "judgment slot." However, the inordinate amount of attention devoted to the Jericho campaign, the prominence of *hērem* in the destruction "rites," and the climactic, terminal nature of the event combine to suggest that more may be involved in the incident. Garstang cautioned, "There is no record of a determination comparable with this, the solemn sacrifice of an entire town."[38]

Accordingly, while hoping to avoid the "spiritualizing" criticized by Kaiser, I propose that the fall of Jericho not only fits our second judgment classification. It also constitutes a classic model of the fifth category, "penal judgment." I will attempt, therefore, to analyze the Joshua narrative from that perspective and offer principles which may derive from the fall of Jericho as a "sacramental act"[39] of penal judgment. Furthermore, in isolating the appropriate lessons or guidelines, I will try to correlate the resulting evaluations with the total teaching of the Bible.

The Certainty of Judgment. The liquidation of Jericho typifies final, penal judgment in the fact that its destruction was settled and determined before the actual event. Garstang called attention to the importance of the confrontation between Joshua and "the commander of the LORD'S army" on the eve of battle.[40] In that "campaign briefing," the field commander assured Joshua, "See, I have delivered Jericho into your hands" (Josh. 6:2). What an amazing disclosure! Without a "shot being fired," before the assault tactics were explained, without the deployment of a single military unit, the result of the battle was already determined.

Whatever the precise historical context, the righteous retribution of YHWH's judgment is settled prior to its implementation. Consider the Lord's chilling announcement to Zedekiah, Judah's final king:

"Do not deceive yourselves, thinking, 'The Babylonians will surely leave us.' They will not! Even if you were to defeat the entire Babylonian army that is attacking you and only wounded men were left in their tents, they would come out and burn this city down" (Jer. 37:9-10).

Within and beyond history, when YHWH finally rises to execute punitive judgment, the issue is settled, established in advance. This predetermined aspect of Jericho's visitation reflects an awesome truth about the "last judgment." Strictly speaking, it is not, exclusively, some dim, distant eschatological event or a vague and speculative addendum to history. Rather, it is a present condition, awaiting a pending but certain development.

Consonant with the Jericho scenario, the New Testament warns of the immediate, existential aspect of penal judgment. "Whoever believes in him is not condemned, but whoever does not believe *stands condemned already* because he has not believed in the name of God's one and only Son" (John 3:18, italics added).[41] John added, "Whoever rejects the Son will not see life, for God's wrath *remains* on him" (John 3:36, italics added).[42] The intimate association between present guilt and ultimate penalty was also emphasized by Simon Peter. "The Lord knows

how to rescue godly men from trials and to hold the un-
righteous for the day of judgment, while continuing their
punishment" (2 Pet. 2:9).

These statements indicate that the verdict of guilty has
already been pronounced against the ungodly. All that remains is the actual execution of punishment. Like the en-
circled and doomed defenders of Jericho, the final fate of
unbelievers is determined before the fact.

When the soldiers of Jericho gazed down upon the
strange band of Hebrew warriors from the desert, they
probably felt safe and secure behind the massive, impreg-
nable walls that protected them. They could scarcely have
anticipated that their defensive fortifications would be
reduced to mounds of rubble in a moment. Neither re-
vetment and parapet walls[43] nor military expertise could
spare Jericho from her unavoidable destiny. Like someone
trying to hide from the force of a hydrogen bomb in a card-
board box at ground-zero, the Jerichoites sought protection behind stone barricades—in vain!

"Then the kings of the earth, the princes, the generals,
the rich, the mighty, and every slave and every free man
hid in caves and among the rocks of the mountains. They
called to the mountains and the rocks. "Fall on us and
hide us from the face of him who sits on the throne and
from the wrath of the Lamb! For the great day of their
wrath has come, and who can stand?" (Rev. 6:15-17).

Who, indeed!

The Source of Judgment. Again, the "Commanding
Officer" declared, "*I have delivered Jericho.*" Though He
would use the leadership of Joshua and the battle skills of
the Israelite soldiers, the actual initiator of Jericho's doom
was none other than YHWH Himself. What a formidable
prospect, that the Lord of glory will personally supervise
the execution of penal judgment! However, that strategy,
in Scripture, is not restricted to events in the Jordan valley so long ago. Throughout the Old Testament, YHWH is
depicted as the supreme agent of judgment and salvation
alike. As the "red-stained warrior" in Isaiah's theophanic
vision affirmed, the one "Mighty to Save" will ultimately
implement final judgment, "trampling in anger" and
"treading in wrath" (see Isa. 63:1-4).

The tension provoked by YHWH's dual role in redemption and judgment does not denote some internal, divine contradiction. His supervision of punishment in no way precludes His commitment to deliverance. In fact, since judgment and salvation are, in essence, "front and back" of the same coin, His involvement in one includes commensurate participation in the other (Isa. 61:1-2). Nor is divine dedication to retribution an exclusive Old Testament perspective.

Paul, the consummate New Testament theologian, endorsed the salvation-judgment paradigm and added a specific Christological flavor. He concluded his memorable sermon before the Court of the Areopagus with this revealing announcement:

"Therefore since we are God's offspring, we should not think that the divine being is like gold or silver or stone. . . . For he has set a day when he will judge the world with justice by the man he has appointed. He has given proof of this to all men by raising him from the dead" (Acts 17:29,31).

Just as Isaiah's theophanic figure would engage in both redemptive and retributive activity, the one risen from the dead (Christ the Redeemer) will be God's agent to judge the world. Is this curious blend of grace and wrath truly consistent with the claim that "God is love" (1 John 4:8)? How would John, who formulated that magnificent dictum, respond to the insistence that God, in the person of His Son, will punish sinners? How would the apostle who felt so totally bathed in the tender affection of his Master that he referred to himself as "the disciple whom Jesus loved"[44]—how would *that* John react to such a stern doctrine of "righteous vengeance?"

As a matter of fact, he did speak to the question. In a phenomenal, apocalyptic glimpse of history's grand finale, John observed an incredible "invasion from outer space" and logged this report in Revelation 19:11-16:

"I saw heaven standing open and there before me was a white horse, whose rider is called Faithful and True. With justice he judges and makes war. His eyes are like blazing fire, and on his head are many crowns. He has a name written on him that no one knows but he himself. He is dressed in a robe dipped in blood, and his name is the Word of God.

The armies of heaven were following him, riding on white horses and dressed in fine linen, white and clean. Out of his mouth comes a sharp sword with which to strike down the nations. 'He will rule them with an iron scepter.' He treads the winepress of the fury of the wrath of God Almighty. On his robe and on his thigh he has this name written:

King of Kings and Lord of Lords."

The imagery and terminology between the visions of Isaiah and John are so obvious as to eliminate the need for belabored comparison. Moreover, it is also possible that any similarity between the Battle Commander at Jericho and Revelation's Field Marshal of the heavenly armies may not be altogether incidental.

The Scope of Judgment. Another striking feature of Jericho's ruin was the totality of its devastation. "They devoted the city to the Lord and destroyed with the sword every living thing in it—men and women, young and old, cattle, sheep and donkeys" (Josh. 6:21). The troops of Joshua not only effectively demolished the fortifications and buildings of Jericho; but, with one striking exception, they also completely eradicated its populace. No one escaped the sword of YHWH's decisive visitation. Jericho's destruction was complete and absolute.

This fact corresponds to descriptions of penal judgment elsewhere in the Bible. Amos, for example, portrayed final retribution's inescapable fate in this sinister vignette: "Woe to you who long / for the day of the Lord! / Why do you long for the day of the Lord? / That day will be darkness, not light. / It will be as though a man fled from a lion / only to meet a bear, / as though he entered his house / and rested his hand on the wall / only to have a snake bite him" (Amos 5:18-20).

And remember the totality of judgment depicted in the Apocalypse: "But the cowardly, the unbelieving, the vile, the murderers, the sexually immoral, those who practice magic arts, the idolaters and all liars—their place will be in the fiery lake of burning sulfur. This is the second death" (Rev. 21:8).

As at Jericho, when the Lord rises up in judgment, the results will be complete, total, and effective. There will be no enclaves of rebellion, no lingering pockets of resistance. All opposition to the heavenly rule will be absolutely and eternally eradicated.

The Delay of Judgment. As harsh and severe as the penalty imposed on Jericho may seem, it was not the result of some random, unreasonable outburst of divine anger. Nor was it a hasty, precipitous act. To the contrary, it was an event that the righteous Judge had postponed for a long, long time. The delay factor is not explicit in the context of Joshua 2—6, but it was a vital part of the Jericho operation nonetheless.

As stated elsewhere in this study,[45] YHWH's explanation to Abraham about the extended delay of his seed's possession of Canaan included the justification, "for the sin of the Amorites has not yet reached its full measure" (Gen. 15:16). While the term Amorite might designate a specific national or ethnic group, it was also the generic term for all of Canaan's population.[46] As a matter of fact, "Amorite" is used in that broader sense in Joshua 5:1. Consequently, the visitation on Jericho and the other cities of Canaan was an act of divine retribution that had been suspended for *four hundred years* (Gen. 15:13). It could hardly be construed as a hasty act.

This delay factor at Jericho also corresponds well with other biblical data about God's deferral of penal judgment. The definitive New Testament statement, of course, is Peter's solemn admonition, "The Lord is not slow in keeping his promise, as some understand slowness. He is patient with you, not wanting anyone to perish, but everyone to come to repentance" (2 Pet. 3:9). Accordingly, rather than illustrating divine propensity for retribution, Jericho provides a beautiful historical example of the LORD's mercy and reluctance to punish. Just so, God, in apparent infinite patience and compassion, postpones, delays the punishment of the wicked.

The Swiftness of Judgment. Speed of punishment scarcely seems to be compatible with the feature of delay. Still, the time of an event can be distinguished from its rate or duration. Accordingly, although the destruction of Jericho was a development that had been long delayed, its actual fall was swift and sudden. Granted, the repeated circling of the city walls consumed seven days; but those tactics were only preliminary to the main event. Note the terse, succinct account, "When the trumpets sounded, the people shouted, and at the sound of the trumpet, when the people gave a loud shout, the wall collapsed" (Josh. 6:20). The length of the brief, savage battle that followed is not specified, but the issue was decided "at the sound of the trumpet."

This aspect of Jericho's judgment is also validated elsewhere in the Bible. That would appear to be the emphasis of the warning, "A man who remains stiff-necked after many rebukes / will suddenly be destroyed— / without remedy" (Prov. 29:1). The principle is also reflected in the somber declaration to a certain rich man, "You fool! This very night your life will be demanded from you. Then who will get what you have prepared for yourself?" (Luke 12:20). Penal judgment, whether at the end of life or the end of history, will come with sudden, unexpected swiftness. All the postponement and preliminaries notwithstanding, as at Jericho, when the moment of reckoning comes, it will be with quick severity. "At the sound of the trumpet . . . "

The Salvation from Judgment. As intimated earlier, deliverance from YHWH's dreadful visitation was also demonstrated at Jericho. A highly unlikely candidate for deliverance, perhaps, the prostitute Rahab, along with her family, was spared out of the awful holocaust (Josh. 6:25). The reason for that, of course, was the fact that she had befriended two Israelite spies who furtively entered Jericho to secure information about the defenses of the city.[47] Not only did she protect them from certain capture; but, sensing YHWH's sovereign presence and purpose in the invading army, she also declared her submission to the Lord and her loyalty to Israel (Josh. 2:9-13). In response, the two spies instructed Rahab to tie "this scarlet cord" to the window through which she effected their escape (Josh. 2:18).[48]

Many have observed the possible symbolism of the Hebrew word *shānî* (שָׁנִי), "scarlet." Noting the use of scarlet materials in tabernacle trappings (Ex. 26:1,31; 28:5), Hermann J. Austel added the following comment:

> But it also seems to have acquired a symbolic significance in that it was used in such purification ceremonies as in the cleansing of the leper (Lev. 14:4,6) and the leprous house (Lev. 14:49,52), and for general ceremonial uncleanness (Num. 19:6). Since *shānî* was the color of blood it would be its natural symbol in such a ceremony.[49]

The explicit designation of such a distinctive and significant color suggests that some importance should be attached to its use. However, while the crimson tint of Rahab's "lifeline" is certainly reminiscent of the offerings in Yom Kippur and consistent with their symbolism, the "scarlet thread" alone does not provide a complete basis for the doctrine of blood sacrifice in atonement. That truth must be established elsewhere.

Not to be overlooked in preoccupation with the symbolism of *shānî* is the importance of the display of the designated item. Rahab and her family, even with the "scarlet cord" in their possession, might have been slain along with their neighbors had it not been for their explicit exhibition of allegiance. To be custodian of the redemptive design is not enough. Faith, to be worthy of the name, demands an overt demonstration of loyalty and devotion. It involves active commitment, not passive meditation. The ruby-tinted ribbon that fluttered from a solitary window overlooking the walls of Jericho still signals the message of faith's irrevocable abandon and pledge.

ADDENDUM

The Economy of Penal Judgment

> This is what the Lord Almighty says: "I will punish the Amalekites for what they did to Israel when they waylaid them as they came up from Egypt. Now go, attack the Amalekites and totally destroy everything that belongs to them. Do not spare them; put to death men and women, children and infants, cattle and sheep, camels and donkeys."
> 1 Samuel 15:2–3

Like the command to destroy Jericho, the charge to exterminate the Amalekites seems to invoke an extreme measure, one fraught with bloodthirsty vindictiveness. In the modern emphasis on individual freedom and human rights, there is a tendency to disregard any hint of accountability to sovereign Deity. We are inclined to think of ourselves as the exclusive master of our own fate and completely independent of any responsibility to God. So, when the biblical account reports historical incidents of divine judgment, there is an impulse to view these as an unacceptable infringement on human privilege as if God had exceeded the limits of divine authority.

To be sure, the Lord of glory needs no earthly forum to approve or justify the integrity of His acts. Through the prophet, He chided, "My thoughts are not your thoughts, / neither are your ways my ways . . . / As the heavens are higher than the earth, / so are my ways higher than your ways / and my thoughts than your thoughts" (Isa. 55:8-9).[50] Accordingly, His deeds transcend our capacity to fathom or understand. It does not follow, however, that because His activity is beyond human reason, it is unreasonable. So, although His providences require no vindication, a consideration of the setting for His command to destroy may put some matters in perspective.

For one thing, the sentence of destruction against Israel's Canaanite neighbors did not occur in a religious, moral, or historical vacuum. The inhabitants of the land and region were notoriously wicked.[51] The Amalekites were hostile toward Israel and rebellious against Israel's God.[52] Their judgment, therefore, was neither random nor capricious. Instead, it was retributive and based on legitimate accountability.

Biblical evidence for the worship of YHWH outside the context of the Abrahamic Covenant is meager but intriguing. The enchanting figure of Melchizedek, the ancient king of Salem and a messianic "type" (Gen. 14:18-20),[53] surely discloses the evidence of YHWH worship apart from that of Abraham. Laban, Abraham's kinsman in Paddan Aram, was apparently a worshiper of YHWH (Gen. 24:50), although he did not share directly in the Abrahamic Covenant. Moses' father-in-law, Jethro, was termed the "priest of Midian" (Ex. 3:1) without explanation as to his particular religious orientation. However, as one interpreter summarized, "it is altogether possible that Jethro knew and worshiped God as Yahweh before visiting Moses' camp."[54]

Balaam, the mercenary soothsayer from Pethor, was obviously knowledgeable about YHWH, although his character and conduct indicate he was not a YHWH worshiper (Num. 22:1—23:30).

Second, as noted earlier, the annihilation of Canaanite inhabitants was a justifiable visitation that had been postponed for four centuries.

Third, the death of those who perished under the cutting edge of Israelite swords was inevitable. In the two-dimensional time-plane of human discernment, the elusive reality of death appears somehow avoidable. But the termination of life is not just a strong probability. It is an inescapable, unavoidable fact. In other words, all the citizens of all the towns and villages of all the regions in and around Canaan were going to die sooner or later. That was not a negotiable factor in the situation. Given, then, the invariable certainty of their eventual demise anyway, the imposed death penalty had primarily to do with the "when" and "how," not the "whether" or "if."

Fourth, the destruction of the area's pagan population was decisively protective in nature. Peter C. Craigie noted with perception that "if the Canaanites survived, their unholy religion could turn Israel aside from serving the Lord."[55] The regrettable truth is that pagan influences did eventually lead to the eradication of both Israel and Judah. When the Hebrews entered the land, they were, in effect, surrounded by belligerent nations that were infected with a deadly, spiritual disease. Like demented monsters or a pack of rabid wolves, Israel's neighbors constantly threatened the peace and well-being of the people of YHWH. Accordingly, the devastation of foreign city-states and populations was designed to shield Israel against their contaminating and potentially lethal influence.

Finally, with the foregoing as a frame of reference, the LORD's economy for the destruction of selective pagan centers and people may be perceived as essentially redemptive in nature. He not only punished, but He also protected and preserved. Through that extended protection plan, He ultimately provided a Redeemer—for all peoples.

All of these, in some measure, indicate that there was at least some general information about the Creator-God of the

Old Testament who identified Himself as YHWH. However, on the basis of biblical information alone, we do not know to what extent, or for how long, YHWH worship may have prevailed in the ancient Near East. We can only speculate, therefore, as to the amount and degree of spiritual understanding possessed by the Canaanites of Joshua's time. However, the Old Testament does suggest that an awareness of YHWH was not necessarily restricted to Abraham and his descendants.

The extrabiblical evidence is as sparse as the biblical data, if not more so, and just as tantalizing. For example, the Karen people of Burma have nurtured a monotheistic worship of a deity designated as "Y'wa." According to Don Richardson:

> Granted, their name for God—Y'wa—suggests influence from the Jewish Yahweh, but no equivalents for Abraham and Moses, the second and third most important figures in Judaism have been reported by compilers of Karen tradition. Surely Jewish influence would have emphasized Abraham and Moses.[56]

In similar fashion, Richardson rejected the notion of Christian influence on the Karen religion because of the absence of any mention of "a Redeemer dying for man's sin."[57] He then concluded:

> Could it be that Karen beliefs about Y'wa predate both Judaism and Christianity? Did such beliefs spring from that ancient root of monotheism which characterized the age of the early patriarchs? The answer is almost certainly—yes![58]

Just as riveting is the observation: "it appears that the primitive religion of China was monotheistic with worship of a heavenly Creator and living God."[59] This unexpected disclosure is all the more astounding when the title for the ancient Chinese Creator-God is revealed as *ShangTi* ("Heavenly Emperor,"上帝). The meaning of the designation is significant enough, but its phonetic value may be of even greater importance. Nelson made this startling suggestion:

> *ShangTi* surely appears to be one and the same as the God of the Hebrews. In fact, one of the Hebrew names for their God was EL SHADDAI, phonetically very similar to SHANGTI, especially in the Cantonese dialect which pronounces the name "SHANGDAI." Cantonese, incidentally, is thought to be closest to the original spoken Chinese.[60]

Without evaluating the SHANGDAI = SHADDAI phonetic equation, suffice it to say at this point that *ShangTi* may have been the universally accepted name for the Creator-God prior to the historical emergence of the Hebrew peoples.

Conclusive evidence concerning the scope of knowledge in the ancient Near East about the one true God is simply not available.[61] However, on the basis of what *is* known, and in the light of the consistent moral nature and benevolent character of YHWH, we may safely assume that His judgment directed against any and all ancients was both righteous and justifiable.

Notes

[1]Abraham Malamat, "How Inferior Israelite Forces Conquered Fortified Canaanite Cities," *Biblical Archaeology Review*, vol. VIII, no. 2 (March/April 1982): 32 (journal hereafter cited as *BAR*).

[2]William G. Dever, "Archaeology and the Bible," *BAR*, vol. XVI, no. 3 (May/June 1990): 53. In discussing historiography in the ancient Near East, Veenhof noted, "Ancient historiographical compositions were as a rule not written out of pure scientific interest or to record the past objectively." He explained that "many texts are politically or ideologically focused," adding, "a biased writing of history does not necessarily imply that the information is wrong or spurious; it does mean that the information is slanted, interpreted, and selected in order to achieve the intended goal." See K. R. Veenhof, "History of the Ancient Near East to the Time of Alexander the Great," trans. Sierd Woudstra in *The World of the Bible*, ed. A. S. van der Woude (Grand Rapids: William B. Eerdmans Publishing Company, 1986), 204-205. Walton acknowledged the Old Testament's affinity with its historical and literary context but noted its distinctiveness: "With regard to purpose, Israel does share a didactic use of history with her neighbors but does not evidence anything like the propagandistic intention visible in the royal annals. The fact that some of the narrative may be used in a self-serving way is not denied, but neither does that make a conclusive case. It is also certain that the historiographers of Israel were selective in what they presented ... but selectivity is expected when there is a didactic agenda. This is different from distortion or embellishment." See John H. Walton, *Ancient Israelite Literature in its Cultural Context* (Grand Rapids: Zondervan Publishing House, 1990), 119.

[3]For a brief summary of the archaeological history of Tell es-Sultan, see John R. Bartlett, *Jericho*, 1st American edition (Grand Rapids: William B. Eerdmans Publishing Company, 1983), 27-36.

[4]Bryant G. Wood, "Did the Israelites Conquer Jericho?" *BAR*, vol. XVI, no. 2 (March/April 1990): 47.

[5]Ibid., 49.

[6]For an identification of dates and terminology, see the editor's chart, "Chronological Terms Used by Bienkowski and Wood," *BAR*, vol. XVI, no. 5 (September/October 1990): 45. Note the associated debate between Piotr Bienkowski and Bryant G. Wood.

[7]Wood, "Conquer," *BAR*: 49.

[8]Bartlett, *Jericho*, 6-7.

[9]For a different perspective, see John J. Bimson, *Redating the Exodus and Conquest*, in *JSOT Supplement*, no. 5 (Sheffield: JSOT Press, 1978).

[10]Wood, "Conquer," *BAR*: 53.

[11]He holds a Ph.D. in Near Eastern Studies (Major: Syro-Palestinian Archaeology; First Minor: Hebrew Language and Literature; Second Minor: Mesopotamian Archaeology) from the University of Toronto, and has participated in archaeological expeditions in Egypt, Israel, and Sinai. His written contributions include his Ph.D. thesis entitled *Palestinian Pottery of the Late Bronze Age: An Investigation of the Terminal LB IIB Phase*.

[12]Yigael Yadin, "Is the Biblical Account of the Israelite Conquest of Canaan Historically Reliable?" *BAR*, vol. VIII, no. 2 (March/April 1982): 16-23; Abraham Malamat, "How Inferior Israelite Forces Conquered Fortified Canaanite Cities," *BAR*, vol. VIII, no. 2 (March/April 1982): 24-35.

[13]Malamat, "Israelite Forces," *BAR*: 32.

[14]Ibid., 33.

[15]Erika Bleibtreu, "Five Ways to Conquer a City," *BAR*, vol. XVI, no. 3 (May/June 1990): 37-44.

[16]John Garstang, *Joshua—Judges* (Grand Rapids: Kregel Publications, 1978), 140.

[17]Garstang, *Joshua*, 141. Garstang, of course, cited the KJV's translation ("compass").

[18]In a footnote he cited Cooke's translation, "do thou surround it with the men of war round about." Robert G. Boling translated the LXX (σύ δὲ περίστησον αὐτῇ τοὺς μαχίμους κύκλῳ), "And the army shall form a circle around the city"; see Robert G. Boling, *Joshua*, in *The Anchor Bible*, ed. William Foxwell Albright and David Noel Freedman (Garden City: Doubleday and Company, 1982), 202.

[19]KB proposes both **umstellen** ("surround") and **umgehen** ("go round"); see KB, 3:698. Compare BDB, 685.

[20]יַסֵּב is a *Hiph'il* based on סָבַב and seems to be purely causative in force.

[21]Note also the use of the participle הֹלֵךְ (Josh. 6:9,13). Trent Butler's translation ("was moving along") reflects the precise verbal force. See Trent C. Butler, *Joshua*, in vol. 7 of *Word Biblical Commentary*, ed. David A. Hubbard, Glenn W. Barker, John D. W. Watts, Ralph P. Martin (Waco, TX: Word Books, Publisher, 1983), 64.

[22]Garstang, *Joshua*, 143-44.

[23]Wood, "Conquer," *BAR*: 56. Wood's article also includes a helpful artist's sketch (with explanation) of the possible format of Jericho's shattered walls (47).

[24]Garstang, *Joshua*, 146.

[25]The noun (חֵרֶם) occurs in 6:17, and the *Hiph'il* verb (וַיַּחֲרִימוּ) appears in 6:21.

[26]Snaith, *Distinctive Ideas*, 33.

[27]Leon J. Wood, "חָרַם," *TWOT*, 1:324.

[28]Marten H. Woudstra, *The Book of Joshua*, in *The New International Commentary on the Old Testament*, ed. R. K. Harrison (Grand Rapids: William B. Eerdmans Publishing Company, 1981), 112-13.

[29]Trent C. Butler, *Joshua*, vol. 7 in *Word Bible Commentary*, ed. David A. Hubbard and Glenn W. Barker (Waco, TX: Word Books, Publisher, 1987), 71.

[30]Robert G. Boling, *Joshua*, in *The Anchor Bible*, ed. William Foxwell Albright and David Noel Freedman (Garden City: Doubleday and Company, 1982), 207.

[31]Walter C. Kaiser, "A Response to Author's Intention and Biblical Interpretation," in *Hermeneutics, Inerrancy & the Bible*, ed. Earl D. Radmacher and Robert D. Preuss (Grand Rapids: Zondervan Publishing House, 1984), 441.

[32]Walter C. Kaiser, Jr., *Toward an Exegetical Theology* (Grand Rapids: Baker Book House, 1981), 132.

[33]Ibid., 152.

[34]The total campaign report stretches across chapters 2—6, nearly half of the total description of Canaan's conquest. Chapters 13—22 focus on tribal allotments.

[35]See chapter 9 of this book.

[36]For example, the destruction of Sodom and Gomorrah (Gen. 19:24-25) and the fate of Korah (Num. 16:1-32).

[37]See Isaiah 24—25 and 2 Thessalonians 1:7-10.

[38]Garstang, *Joshua*, 143.

[39]Ibid.

[40]Ibid.

[41]The text ἤδη κέκριται suggests, "he is already judged."

[42]The Greek clause features the present tense (μένει).

[43]See the section drawing in Wood's article, "Conquer," *BAR*: 55.

[44]See John 19:26; 13:23; 20:2; 21:7,20.

[45]See chapter 4 of this book.

[46]Speiser, *Genesis*, 113.

[47]That is the apparent intent of their instructions (Josh. 2:1).

[48]For a discussion (and diagram) of the possible location of Rahab's house, see Wood, "Conquer," *BAR*: 47,56.

[49]Hermann J. Austel, "שׁנה," *TWOT*, 2:942.

[50]Compare Isaiah 40:13-14.

[51]For a hint of the carnal nature of Canaanite religion, see J. C. de Moor, "Systems of Writing and Nonbiblical Languages," in *The World of*

the Bible, ed. A. S. van der Woude, trans. Sierd Woudstra (reprint, Grand Rapids: William B. Eerdmans Publishing Company, 1986), 106 and A. D. H. Mayes, *Deuteronomy* in *New Century Bible Commentary*, ed. Ronald E. Clements and Matthew Black (Grand Rapids: William B. Eerdmans Publishing Company, 1971), 184.

[52]Compare 1 Samuel 15:2 and Exodus 17:8-16.

[53]See Milton S. Terry, *Biblical Hermeneutics*, 9th printing (Grand Rapids: Zondervan Publishing House, 1981), 338.

[54]C. P. Gray, "Jethro," *The Zondervan Pictorial Encyclopedia of the Bible*, ed. Merrill C. Tenney (Grand Rapids: Zondervan Publishing House, 1977), 3:583-85. See Exodus 18:1-12.

[55]Peter C. Craigie, *The Book of Deuteronomy* (Grand Rapids: William B. Eerdmans Publishing Company, 1976), 276.

[56]Don Richardson, *Eternity in Their Hearts* (Ventura, CA: Regal Books, 1981), 81.

[57]Ibid.

[58]Ibid., 82.

[59]C. H. Kang and Ethel R. Nelson, *The Discovery of Genesis* (St. Louis: Concordia Publishing House, 1979), 19.

[60]Ethel R. Nelson and Richard E. Broadberry, *Mysteries Confucius Couldn't Solve* (Dunlap, TN: Read Books Publisher, 1986), 18.

[61]For an analysis of religious consciousness in the ancient Near East, see John H. Walton, *Ancient Israelite Literature in Its Cultural Context*, 2nd reprint (Grand Rapids: Zondervan Publishing House, 1990), 236-47.

11

Deliverance in Zion

Everyone who calls on the name
of the LORD will be saved!

Joel 2:32

"Fellow Jews and all of you who live in Jerusalem, let me explain this to you; listen carefully to what I say. These men are not drunk, as you suppose. It's only nine in the morning! No, this is what was spoken by the prophet Joel:

'In the last days, God says,
  I will pour out my Spirit on all people.
Your sons and daughters will prophesy,
    your young men will see visions,
    your old men will dream dreams.
Even on my servants, both men and women,
    I will pour out my Spirit in those days,
    and they will prophesy.
I will show wonders in the heaven above
    and signs on the earth below,
    blood and fire and billows of smoke.
The sun will be turned to darkness
    and the moon to blood
    before the coming of the great and glorious day of the
      Lord.
And everyone who calls
    on the name of the Lord will be saved" (Acts 2:14-21).

What an electrifying introduction to an unforgettable sermon! Preceded by the sound of "a violent wind," mystifying "tongues of fire" resting on the followers of Jesus, and their phenomenal declaration of the "wonders of God" in multiple languages and dialects (Acts 2:1-11), Simon Peter's Pentecostal message was extraordinary and attention-getting, to say the least. The opening "salvo" of his explosive communication was especially stunning, for with his initial statement he declared that the "Day of the Lord" was officially inaugurated. That marvelous, eschatological era predicted by the prophets[1] had finally dawned. The long-awaited "Golden Age" had arrived!

To authenticate his pronouncement, Peter cited a promise recorded in the Book of Joel. While the appeal to biblical authority was appropriate, somehow his quotation from Joel seems to be, at least on the surface, a little off target. For one thing, although the reference to the outpouring of the Spirit was certainly fitting, the item about the astronomical upheaval that would precede the Day of the Lord was strangely missing from the program. Moreover, despite the suitable element of correspondence between Joel's word and some of the Pentecostal events, Peter's announcement had to do with an era that was distinctly messianic in character.[2] It seems a little odd, therefore, that he would, on such a meaningful messianic occasion, turn to an Old Testament passage that had no messianic content. Or was that really the case?

I am convinced that a careful examination of the quote from Joel will reveal that the absence of celestial phenomena at Pentecost creates no real difficulty and does not require some strained "double fulfillment" interpretation. In addition, when the excerpt from Joel is restored to its original context and evaluated, a truly remarkable messianic orientation may be discerned.

Syntactical Analysis of Joel 2:21-32

A major difficulty in "restoring" the Joel citation to its original context for study has to do with the question of syntactical parameters within the context. William S. Prinsloo acknowledged the relative ambiguity of the situation in the second chapter of Joel: "The demarcation of this pericope poses a number of problems." Then, following the analysis of John A. Thompson,[3] he concluded, "there are sufficient grounds to regard 2:18-27 as a demarcated pericope."[4] My analysis of the passage will disagree with both Prinsloo and Thompson, as well as others.[5] But rather than critique diverse approaches, I will simply attempt to explain my own understanding of the Joel passage.

Transition Evidence. A key factor in observing transition in a written text is the recognition of syntactical devices that reveal alterations and shifts. Walter C. Kaiser cautioned, "If the scope of the work has not been laid out in definite terms" (which is certainly true in this case), "then an x-ray type of approach must be taken." He added, "In this approach the interpreter will make use of a variety of clues to locate the slightly exposed seams which mark off specific sections of the book."[6] Kaiser also listed eight possible "x-ray" devices to expose the "seams" that mark change and transition. The list included, "A change in the tense, mood, or aspect of the verb perhaps with a change in the subject or object may be another clue that a new section is beginning."[7] According to Kaiser, then, a distinct change in verb aspect, as well as subject and object, may disclose a transition.

The first four predicates in verses 18-19 (be jealous, take pity, reply [actually, answer . . . and say]) are fashioned by verbs in the imperfect tense (or prefix conjugation) with "*waw* consecutive."[8] In this case, the *vāv*[9] denotes sequential development[10] and describes a circumstance that would follow Israel's compliance with the preceding call to repentance. Those four verbs are followed by a direct discourse in which YHWH promised blessing and protection to "his people" (Joel 2:19-20). The discourse is introduced by a participle (v. 19*b*) and is elaborated by three verbs in the perfect tense with "*vāv* conjunctive,"[11] three imperfects, and an infinitive construct. YHWH is the subject of the verbal action until the "northern army" and its stench (v. 20) become the subject matter, with YHWH the subject again in the final verb formula.

Verse 21 reveals a sharp contrast. The verbs in the main clauses in verses 21-22 are in the volitional mood (two imperatives and two jussives) rather than the indicative. This, of course, marks a clear change in verbal aspect. Moreover, in marked contrast with the preceding, the subjects of the imperative-jussive verbs are "O land" and "O wild animals." The volitional mood spills over into verse 23 as the first two verbs there are also explicitly imperative in form. However, the subject of the verb evolves from "land" and "wild animals" to "people of Zion," a striking progression and one that indicates cohesion. Accordingly, I submit that the major line of demarcation in chapter 2 is between verses 20 and 21.

Syntactical Cohesion of 2:23-32. Having called attention to what we believe to be the main "seam" in chapter 2 of Joel, let us pause briefly to evaluate the time reference. A major hurdle for the new student of biblical Hebrew is the language's apparent indifference to time or tense. Despite efforts to unmask a primitive "preterite" verb form in Hebrew,[12] the fact remains that the past, present, and future tenses are not marked by distinctive morphemes. Waltke and O'Connor commented on this often frustrating situation, "Biblical Hebrew has no tenses in the strict sense; it uses a variety of other means to express time relations."[13]

The "other means," as might be expected, may be the use of adverbs or other concrete time references.[14] Unfortunately, those convenient "time arrows" are not always present; and, in such instances, less explicit contextual evidence must be weighed. Even then, conclusive time decisions may not be possible.

The entire second chapter of Joel is almost totally free of those "other means." However, the whole passage seems to point to the future, at least from Joel's frame of reference. The grotesque invaders described in 2:1-11, for example, seem to represent some latter-day incursion of robotic, invincible predators rather than an invasion already experienced.[15] In like fashion, all the imperatives of the chapter, though featuring different agents, appear to be looking to the future. Indeed, imperatives in general, almost by the very nature of the case, seem to gear to the future.

Accordingly, I submit that the complete chapter is essentially future-oriented from the standpoint of original writing or utterance. Therefore, just as developments emanating from the injunctions in 2:12-17 are translated as future (2:19-20), so the benefits elaborated after the exhortations of 2:21-23a should be construed as future (2:21-32). Specifically, then, neither the "great things" in 2:21-22 nor the "autumn rains in righteousness" in 2:23 can be viewed as either "past" or "present" with consistency.

Now we can observe how the "futuristic" bundle of 2:23-32 is packaged syntactically. The twofold instruction in verse 23a is followed by two verbs, a free-standing perfect[16] and a "consecutive imperfect."[17] In the light of the tense ambiguity already noted, nothing prevents the perfect from being construed as future. Waltke and O'Connor explained the time flexibility of this verb form, "Referring to absolute future time, a perfective form may be *persistent* or *accidental*." They added, "This use is especially frequent in prophetic address (hence it is also called the 'prophetic perfect' or 'perfective of confidence')."[18] I submit that this is the exact force of *nātan* (נָתַן, "he *shall* give").

The imperfect verb, *vayyōred* (וַיּוֹרֶד), is the *Hiph'il* (or causative) form of *yārad* (יָרַד), "to come down," and designates a consequential development out of the preceding action. I recommend this translation: "he will give for you[r benefit] . . . and he will send down for you[r benefit]."

Scattered across verses 24-32 is a sequence of distinctive verb constructions that involves a perfect with prefixed *vāv*. This particular verbal pattern has created considerable discussion and divergent opinion among students of Hebrew syntax. Ronald J. Williams, for example, explained, "By analogy, *waw* occurs with the perfect. Since it was a later development, the conjunction suffered the normal later vowel reduction, becoming *wᵊ*."[19] Suggesting that "this is equivalent to the imperfect aspect in initial position in a clause,"[20] he also commented, " 'Simple' *waw* with the perfect may occur in biblical Hebrew when two or more verbs are in a *closely related series*" (italics added).[21]

A more traditional approach was outlined by A. B. Davidson in the nineteenth century: "In the more ancient and classical language *vav* with perf. is almost invariably conversive."[22] He, too, noted a peculiar modification in that "vav with perf. occasionally expresses an action not consequential or successive to what precedes, but *co-ordinate with it* (italics added)."[23]

S. R. Driver, on the other hand, believed that he perceived two patterns, *"The Perfect with* Waw *Consecutive,"*[24] and *"The Perfect . . . with Weak* Waw."[25] He acknowledged the difficulty of his distinction:

> However difficult it may appear to find a satisfactory explanation of this waw consecutive with the perfect, one thing is perfectly clear, and ought most carefully to be borne in mind: a real *difference* of some kind or other exists between the use of the perfect with simple *waw*, and the use of the perfect with waw consecutive, and the external indication of this difference is to be found in the *alteration of the tone* which constantly attends and accompanies it.[26]

Leslie McFall has called attention to problems associated with Driver's position,[27] so additional evaluation is not necessary. Suffice it to say that Driver himself recognized a weakness in his position.

A more recent grammar has projected a "reversing vav" formula:

> In the Bible, sequences of verbs are commonly used to recount events. . . . When such sequences of verbs appear, the Bible usually uses a device called the **reversing vav**. The reversing vav is the letter ו, which is attached to the verbs which make up a sequence and reverse their tense. When a verb is in the imperfect tense, the addition of the reversing vav changes its meaning to that of the perfect tense. When a verb is in the perfect tense, the addition of the reversing vav changes its meaning to that of the imperfect tense. The reversing vav is used only with verb forms in the perfect tense and the imperfect tense.[28]

Following Driver somewhat, Waltke and O'Connor distinguish two functions, the *"waw-relative"* (sometimes called "waw-conversive" or "waw-consecutive") and *"waw-copulative."* Acknowledging that the two have identical forms, they explain the difference: "The two constructions are formally distinguished by accentuation, *though only in some forms* (italics added)."[29] Calling attention to the fact that "scholars are agreed that the *wǝqataltí* construction usually (though not always) signifies succession (temporal or logical)," they add that "after the perfective conjugation . . . *waw*-relative does not represent a chronologically successive situation but rather *explicates* the *one represented as a single whole* (italics added)."[30] Then they contrast the use of "relative waw" and "copulative waw" (with the "suffix conjugation") in this statement:

Whereas relative *wəqtl* represents one situation as subordinate to another, copulative *wəqtl* represents *two situations as coordinate with one another* [italics added]. The two constructions are distinguished by stress (in first singular and second masculine singular) and by semantics.[31]

The foregoing should explain why some students of biblical Hebrew throw up their hands in despair and why translations often differ. The performance or significance of this particular construction seems to be all but lost in a maze of accents, semantics, and complicated syntactical esoterica. Reflecting on the problem, J. Wash Watts concluded, "The confusion that prevails in the minds of students of the old theory is evidence that its logic is not merely so baffling as to overwhelm the majority of students but actually unsound."[32] Watts not only rejected earlier syntactical models of the Hebrew conjunction *vāv*; he also proposed a rather revolutionary alternative. His theory of the *vāv*, though not widely accepted, still offers a remarkably perceptive and simple pattern of usage.

In the first place, Watts insisted that there was a "fundamental distinction between *waw* conjunctive and *waw* consecutive." He explained that the *waw* consecutive (וַ, *vāv* with *patah* followed, usually, by *dagesh forte*) "appears always to indicate a sequence. It is the only form of *waw* used with consecutive imperfects."[33] On the other hand, *waw* conjunctive (וְ, *vāv* with simple *shewa*) "appears always to indicate a parallel. It is the only form of *waw* used with perfects."[34] He added that the *waw* conjunctive might either coordinate, subordinate, or correlate, depending on the nature of the verb to which it is attached.[35]

Watts insisted that when the *waw* conjunctive (וְ) was appended to a verb in the perfect, it created a very special syntactical function which he designated "correlative." He explained its performance in terms of its special, unique relationship to the preceding verb:

In a word, the two things belong to each other and are coexistent. Such a relationship is the correlative relationship. . . . The antecedent may present a general idea, while correlatives supply the details; it may give only a part, while correlatives describe other parts. In any case correlatives designate a state as a fixed part of a larger unit. The unity of the whole is the fundamental concept of this relationship. No matter whether the antecedent appears in a statement of fact, a conditional statement, a command, or an exhortation, details presented by this idiom fill out the picture and appear as fixed parts of it.[36]

Watts's theory finds support in the fact that a "correlative perfect" (*vāv* with a perfect, Waltke and O'Connor's *wǝqataltí* or *wǝqtl*) frequently introduces the expected conclusion in a conditional sentence. As Waltke and O'Connor noted, "The proposed original function of the *wǝqataltí* construction to signify the apodosis of a conditional clause shines through almost all of its uses in Biblical Hebrew."[37] The intimacy between a "correlative perfect" and its preceding verb is confirmed by a connection that persists whether the statement is declarative or conditional.

The Watts approach is attractive for three different reasons: (1) it is simple and direct; (2) it exhibits a single, unifying principle; (3) it fits a wide range of syntactical situations. For the most part, according to Watts's system, dual syntactical roles do not hide behind the same grammatical form.[38] Since there is no ambivalence regarding the form or function of a perfect plus *vāv*, the presence and significance of a "correlative perfect" is relatively uncomplicated.

On the second count, what others only observed in passing, Watts perceived to be the essential genius of the perfect plus *vāv*. Williams suggested that this pattern (perfect plus *vāv*) may occur "when two or more verbs are in a closely related series."[39] Davidson touched on the same connection when he described the pattern's potential coordination.[40] Waltke and O'Connor suggested that the pattern might represent "two situations as coordinate with one another."[41] Even Driver noted this function:

> Accordingly we find it used . . . upon occasions when a writer wishes to place two facts in *co-ordination* with one another, to exhibit the second as simultaneous with the first rather than as succeeding it.[42]

Although Watts differentiated between coordination and correlation, his meaning (of correlation) is basically the same as that of other writers who used the term "coordination." His concept, though, is not quite the same as Driver's notion of a verbal circumstance that is "simultaneous with the first" (verb). Watts did not construe the *vāv* plus perfect as a second simultaneous event, but as an extension of the preceding verbal action.

Watts represented the function of "consecutive imperfects" with a diagram that suggested a string of connected but sequential occurrences: ⌊⌋⌊⌋. He illustrated the force of the "correlative perfect," however, with the diagram of a circle that enclosed its parts: ⊕. The circle itself represents the total concept of the preceding verb (the pie), while the internal quadrants (individual pieces) picture conceptual expansion provided by "correlative perfects."

In essence, consecutive imperfects are like movie images. "Moving pictures" are composed of a series of individual photos that were filmed in deliberate and rapid sequence in order to project a visual narrative. "Correlative perfects," on the other hand, are like composite "still pictures" that feature no visual or temporal progression. The totality of the picture is captured, in effect, by the preceding (or initial) verbal action, while the "correlative perfects" supply the individual or "local" specifics of the whole.

In some respects, the performance of the Hebrew "correlative perfect" is analogous to what might be described as ancient "combat photography." The accounts of exploits and victories accomplished by rulers in the ancient Near East were frequently preserved by being engraved on walls and monuments. The stone records not only included written text, but they also often featured pictures of conquest and battle, chiseled in stone. The "lithograph" reproduction of the successful siege of any enemy city, for example, might depict the approach of the invading army (on the left of the "mural"), the actual assault on the foreign stronghold and the successful entry (in the center), followed by the return of the victorious army bringing booty and captives to present to the conquering king (on the right).[43] All of the pathos, fear, courage, pain, death, defeat, victory, despair, and exuberance of the entire event are captured in one timeless moment—frozen in stone.

The scene is depicted without regard to time, though the total event is recorded. Just so, the Old Testament prophets employed "correlative perfects" to accomplish the syntactical equivalent when they attempted to report future (not past) events, especially those that project an eschatological scenario. The sweep of events, not sequence, is recorded. As we shall presently see, Joel used that very device in the passage under consideration.

Obviously, no one syntactical model or paradigm will fit every linguistic situation. Too many variables are involved in the use of any language for a single system to apply universally. Nevertheless, Watts's "correlative perfect" concept does seem to explain the function of most verb forms that are composed of a simple *vāv* plus a "perfective." Exceptions occur, to be sure. But, once more, exceptions may lend credence to the rule.

As previously noted, the correlative perfect occurs strategically in verses 24-32. It is used seven times through verse 28a, followed by a subset of correlatives in 28b-32. While the interlocking system of correlatives is clear, the preceding primary verb is a bit uncertain. It could be "he shall give" (a simple prophetic perfect), or, just as legitimately, "he will send down" (a consecutive imperfect indicating sequential development from "he shall give"). Either way, the meaning is not altered significantly, and the following structural design is possible:

he will give			he will send down	
will be filled	will overflow		will repay	
will . . . eat	will praise	will know	(it shall be)	
	will prophesy	will show	(and it	shall be)

Significance of *'et hammōreh litsĕdāqāh*

A comparison of versions will demonstrate that translators have been uncertain as to the exact force of this two-noun formula in Joel 2:23. It is composed of the untranslatable "sign of the definite object"[44] followed by the nouns *mōreh* (מוֹרֶה) and *tsĕdāqāh* (צְדָקָה, preceded by the preposition לְ, "to"). A brief couplet like this should present no real problem. Unfortunately, such is not the case.

Translation Options. Both nouns have created some degree of difficulty for translators. The second noun, *tsĕdāqāh*, is usually translated as "righteousness."[45] However, in this particular situation, variation or flexibility is reflected in patterns such as "moderately" (KJV), "in just measure" (ASV), "for posterity" (BDB, 842) and "in righteousness" (NIV). The first of the two nouns also presents a problem. In fact, uncertainty about the meaning of the first term is probably the real reason for difficulty with the second noun. The word in question, *mōreh*, has been translated as "rain," "archer,"[46] and "teacher" or "oracle giver."

Uncertainty about the force of the respective nouns has inspired the following representative translations:

the autumn rains in righteousness	(NIV)
the former rain moderately	(KJV)
the early rain for your vindication	(Thompson)[47]
food as (a token of your) justification	(Bewer)[48]
the teacher for righteousness	(Keil)[49]

The translation question, of course, hinges on the translator's perception of the meaning of *mōreh*; and that is an interesting issue indeed.

The Force of mōreh. We concur with those who construe *mōreh* to mean "teacher" rather than "early rain." The usual term for the rain "which falls in Palestine from the last of October until the first of December" is *yōreh* (יוֹרֶה),[50] not *mōreh*. Although the word (יוֹרֶה) occurs only three times in the Old Testament (Deut. 11:14; Jer. 5:24; Hos. 6:3), in each instance it is used in connection with other terms for precipitation[51] so it obviously refers to moisture falling from the skies.

Mōreh, on the other hand, occurs ten times. In three instances it is a "place name," so its precise meaning is obscure (Gen. 12:6; Deut. 11:30; Judg. 7:1). Four times it clearly means "teacher" (Prov. 5:13; Job 36:22; Isa. 30:20 [twice]). Three times it may mean "early rain." Two of the three possible references to rain are found in Joel 2:23. The other occurrence is in Psalm 84:6(7). While "early rain" is probably correct, even there the contextual evidence is not altogether decisive.

Accordingly, the two occurrences of *mōreh* in this single verse are of considerable importance. In the second use of the term, at the end of the verse, it very clearly refers to rainfall. There *mōreh* follows *geshem* (גֶּשֶׁם, "rain showers") and is used parallel to *malqōsh* (מַלְקוֹשׁ, "latter rain"). At this point, Sawyer's explanation is germane:

> *Polysemy* is the name given to the use of the same word in two or more distinct senses in such a way as to produce, in effect, two separate words. It is caused by the parallel development of two applications of a word.[52]

I suggest that not only did *mōreh* develop two different meanings, but that Joel, in a delightful illustration of polysemy, deliberately employed both meanings in the same immediate context to highlight their contrast.

While the second *mōreh* is nestled between two meteorological expressions, the first *mōreh* is distinguished by having the definite article attached to it. Gösta Werner Ahlstrom argued that the term "probably does not mean rain in both places" and concluded "the determinative form . . . may refer to a person, the one Yahweh will give to the people."[53] Although the presence of the article may be overemphasized, it is employed on occasion to stress singularity.[54] Its use in Joel 2:23 clearly discriminates the first *mōreh* from the second.

An awareness of the distinction in meaning between the words resolves the redundancy created by the apparent repetition of the same word, which goes beyond the normal conventions of Hebrew parallelism. The usual pattern features functional synonyms in parallel (Prov. 16:18), not explicit duplication. Moreover, the recognition of a "person" reference in *mōreh* solves the problem of how to understand the force of *litsĕdāqāh*.

Tsĕdāqāh is, conventionally, a religious or ethical term. Though it was used to describe "honest" or "just" scales (Lev. 19:36), it is difficult to understand how it might be applied to rainfall.[55] Conversely, the use of *tsĕdāqāh* to designate or modify a moral creature ("teacher") is quite normal and is consistent with the larger context. In addition, *tsĕdāqāh* is a concept prominently associated with YHWH. Harold G. Stigers wrote that words derived from the root (*ts-d-q*) may be used "as a descriptive characteristic of God . . . as just and righteous, the standard being his own will and nature as the supreme being."[56]

Referring to another noun built on the same root, Snaith wrote:

> *Tsedeq* is that which God Himself established as the proper norm, and which, on that account, is firm and straight, steady and immovable. It is the norm which God set up in the beginning, by which also He will judge the world.[57]

The use of *tsĕdāqāh* in conjunction with *mōreh* then not only invokes an aura of deity, but it also hints at the moral standard by which persons are to be judged. Thompson added that the term "also has the derived meaning of God's **vindication** . . . of those who are righteous. In this sense it is often parallel to and practically synonymous with God's 'salvation.'"[58]

In the light of the foregoing evidence, translations that construe the first use of *mōreh* as rain seem to ignore a very important ingredient in the text. I am convinced that the phrase *'et hammōreh litsĕdāqāh* should be translated as "the teacher for righteousness." While the descriptive title implies that the teacher possesses the quality of righteousness, it does not denote "the righteous teacher." That would have been expressed by *hammōreh hattsĕdāqāh* (הַמּוֹרֶה הַצְּדָקָה). Instead, the label designates an instructor who teaches or imparts righteousness. Incidentally, Cecil Roth is likely correct in assuming, "This, then, was the title that the leader of the Qumran sect naturally assumed for himself, or his followers applied to him."[59]

The Identification of hammōreh. Given the presence of a "personal" reference in 2:23, the identity of the figure becomes a matter of importance. As might be expected, a number of proposals have been suggested. Roth offered this equation:

> Furthermore: the True Teacher according to both Hosea and Joel was to arise immediately before the Day of the Lord, helping to prepare the way for it. He was not therefore necessarily the Messiah, the Lord's Anointed, who was to become manifest later, after the final triumph. Conceivably, the two were considered to be or would be identical: but this identity cannot be assumed.[60]

Jacob Weingreen, on the other hand, rejected the Qumran connection. "It does not seem likely that this title was coined by the Qumran sect for the exclusive designation of their leader." Instead, he suggested that the formula was a reference to the rabbinic office.[61] Ahlstrom proposed that *hammōreh* "designates the leader and the covenant mediator of the Jerusalem temple cultus," indicating that the leader "was the king in the pre-exilic era and the high-priest in post-exilic times."[62]

Theodore Laetsch offered this summary:

> The article demands "the" Teacher, that Prophet foretold in
> Deut. 18:15-19. Hence not Joel . . . who certainly would not
> have used such language of himself; nor a series of prophets,
> including the Messiah (Keil); that would conflict with the
> definite article and the context speaking of the marvelous re-
> sult of this gift already promised to mankind in Gen. 3:15.[63]

I concur with Laetsch. "The Teacher for righteousness"
must surely be a messianic symbol. Despite Prinsloo's disclaimer that the concept "seems to accord ill with the context since the immediate framework is that of concrete,
earthly blessings,"[64] the messianic emblem fits beautifully
into Joel's literary design. Furthermore, the symbol incorporates both a human and a divine aspect ("teacher" =
human/"righteousness" = divine). Similar to Isaiah's characteristic human/divine couplets (for example, "Holy One of
Israel," Isa. 1:4), the formula anticipates the incarnation.

Theological Analysis of Joel 2:23–32

Joel demonstrated considerable literary artistry in his
use of parallels or "overlay." Notice, for example, his dual
description of "invasion" in chapters 1—2. Then he applied
a double meaning to *mōreh*; and in the description of con-
current provisions accompanying the Teacher, he employed a similar rhetorical technique. Perhaps there is
more than meets the eye.

Benefits Provided by the Teacher for Righteousness. Prinsloo was accurate in describing the immediate framework
(2:24-32) as that of "concrete, earthly blessings."[65] Sometimes, however, the Old Testament prophets were all but
forced to use concrete terms to describe spiritual and/or eschatological realities. That was especially true in their description of salvation and the era of the coming Messiah.
The principle is classically illustrated in Isaiah 35. There
the Jerusalem prophet characterized the LORD's salvation (Isa. 35:4),[66] starting with concrete, botanical allusions
that shifted quickly to descriptions of physical healing.
Consequently, verses 1-7 feature a unique blend of concrete
and abstract, literal and metaphorical.[67]

Isaiah concluded the chapter with a dazzling forecast of
the glorious climax to the redemptive process, in the mag-

nificent, sorrow-free Zion. In similar fashion, Joel projected the provisions that would be available in the Teacher's institute in terms of the physical and concrete, but with a metaphorical "overlay" of meaning.

The interlocking correlative perfects in the passage offer the following blessings: abundance (v. 24, two correlatives); restoration of lost blessings (v. 25); satisfaction (v. 26a); praise (v. 26b); knowledge about the person, position, and presence of YHWH (v. 27); and the inauguration of the Day of the Lord[68] (v. 28). The presence of the final correlative perfect (וְהָיָה, "and it shall be") in the initial syntactical unit of the passage must not be ignored, for it provides the critical link which connects the messianic symbol of 2:23 with the scenes in 2:28-32. This, in turn, marks the total unit as messianic in orientation. Simon Peter, as well as his audience, must surely have been aware of that when he quoted from Joel.

Results of the Outpouring of the Spirit. The last correlative perfect in the series (vv. 24-28) is also the first verb in verse 28. The second verb in verse 28, an imperfect, is *'ešpōk* (אֶשְׁפּוֹךְ), " I will pour out." In turn, *'ešpōk* is followed by three correlative perfects, thus producing a secondary subunit that "interfaces" with what precedes.[69] The first correlative in the subunit is "(they) will prophesy"; the second is "I will show (wonders)." These two verb forms indicate that proclamation and divine authentication were activities concomitant with the outpouring of the Spirit.

The third correlative, another "and it shall be," has a noun clause for its subject. The clause is, "everyone who calls on the name of the Lord will be saved." The third result of the outpouring of the Spirit, then, was the extension of the offer of salvation. Accordingly, the message of the outpouring of the Spirit (2:28) and the offer of salvation (2:32) are structurally interlocked with the messianic symbol of 2:23.

The Force of liphnē bō' yōm YHWH. The "compound preposition" *liphnē* (לִפְנֵי) is formed by the addition of the preposition *lĕ* (לְ) to the masculine plural construct form of the word for "face" (פְּנִים). The idiom literally means "to the faces of." While the preposition may mean "before" in the sense of "prior to," its primary nuance, as the very construction suggests, is "before," in the sense of "in the presence of."[70] The same ambiguity prevails in the English "before," but the Hebrew preposition is more positional in emphasis than temporal.

As a result, the problem generated by forcing the temporal meaning of the term on either Joel or Peter is really quite unnecessary. The language does not demand that the astronomical upheaval (described by Joel and repeated by Peter) had to occur prior to the dawn of the Day of the LORD. Therefore, the clause could legitimately be translated, "in the presence of the Day of the LORD to come." The focus then shifts from what would transpire prior to the *beginning* of the Day of the LORD to what will occur before the *end* of it.

Universal Salvation? The qualifiers in 2:32 that delimit the scope of the salvation call appear to exclude "outsiders." "Deliverance" seems to be restricted to Jerusalem, to those among the (Hebrew) "survivors." The reference to "Mount Zion," a remarkable redemptive symbol, expands the focus and anticipates Isaiah's "New Zion Order" (see Isa. 60—66).

While we cannot read the universal scope of "Isaiah's Zion" into the Book of Joel, Joel's use of "Zion" in the larger context (see 3:9-17) certainly suggests an expanded meaning for the expression. In its historical context (our primary concern in this study), the promise of "deliverance in Zion" was surely applicable to Joel's original audience. For them supremely, despite its eschatological overtones, the word of redemption was the occasion for an immediate, evangelical hope. At least for some, the significance of "calling on the name of the LORD" was more soteriological than liturgical.

Perhaps it was appropriate that, like Peter, Paul appealed to Joel to authenticate his gospel proclamation, "Everyone who calls on the name of the Lord will be saved!" (Rom. 10:13).

Associations and Implications

The message in Joel 2:23-32 was not only magnificent in its own time and context, but it was also amazingly appropriate for the Pentecostal address. The passage, in its original structure and entirety, exhibited a striking messianic emblem. Its subject matter included the Day of the Lord, judgment, deliverance, and the majestic motif of Mount Zion. Accordingly, it featured a memorable blend of messianic, eschatological, and soteriological themes. It was fitting, therefore, that Simon Peter turned to this citation in Joel as an introduction to the first proclamation of the gospel with its marvelous message of the Teacher for righteousness!

With its "end time" orientation, though, did this passage truly contain a salvation hope for the original recipients of Joel's message? Could an eschatological gospel have any meaning for an ancient audience? The truth is that the gospel has an eschatological orientation for any and every audience. The New Testament invitation is for an immediate response, to receive a forgiveness and a relationship that begin immediately. Inevitably, though, the consummation of the redemptive design transcends time, space, and history. In any generation the salvation promise concludes, "shall not perish but have eternal life" (John 3:16).

However, the final words of verse 32 ("the LORD calls," יְהוָה קֹרֵא) offer a tantalizing possibility. The verb (the predicate of the clause) is actually a participle that "distinguishes itself by emphasizing a durative circumstance and thus by not representing modal/temporal or volitional action . . . may involve repeated action."[71] Accordingly, although the "calling" by YHWH might look to a future circumstance, the dominant emphasis of the participle is not "modal," "temporal," or "volitional." Rather, its stress highlights "durative circumstance" or "repeated action." In the light of that focus on *"continuous manifestation,"*[72] and on the basis of an appeal (or "call") already extended in the larger context (2:12), verse 32 may conclude, "on Mount Zion and in Jerusalem / there will be deliverance, / as the LORD has said, / among the survivors / whom the LORD *is calling*" (italics added).

The implication, therefore, is that the LORD, even then, was inviting persons to turn from judgment to immediate as well as eschatological deliverance—a deliverance based on the fabulous benefits of the coming Teacher for righteousness. A continuing invitation based on a timeless provision! "Everyone who calls on the name of the LORD will be saved." Then—now!

Notes

[1]See Obadiah 1:15; Zephaniah 1:7; Zechariah 14:1; Malachi 4:5.

[2]See Amos 5:18; 9:11; Malachi 4:2-5.

[3]John A. Thompson, *The Book of Joel*, vol. 6 of *The Interpreter's Bible*, ed. George Arthur Buttrick (New York: Abingdon-Cokesbury Press, 1951-57), 749.

[4]Willem S. Prinsloo, *The Theology of the Book of Joel* (Berlin: Walter de Gruyten and Company, 1985), 62.

[5]See Theodore Ferdinand Laetsch, *Bible Commentary: The Minor Prophets* (St. Louis: Concordia Publishing House, 1956), 120-27; Carl Friedrich Keil, *The Twelve Minor Prophets*, vol. 16 of *Biblical Commentary on the Old Testament*, Part 1, ed. C. F. Keil and F. Delitzsch, trans. James Martin and others (Grand Rapids: William B. Eerdmans Publishing Company, 1949), 199-218. The different approaches in analysis indicate the lack of consensus.

[6]Walter C. Kaiser, Jr., *Toward an Exegetical Theology* (Grand Rapid: Baker Book House, 1981), 71.

[7]Ibid., 72.

[8]J. Wash Watts, *A Survey of Syntax in the Hebrew Old Testament* (Grand Rapids: William B. Eerdmans Publishing Company, 1964), 39-42. Waltke and O'Connor's label is *waw*-relative (*Syntax*, 543-47).

[9]Many Hebrew grammars recommend that the conjunction ו be pronounced as the English "w" and use the transliteration "*waw*" (or "*wāw*"). See C. L. Seow, *A Grammar for Biblical Hebrew* (Nashville: Abingdon Press, 1987), 2 and Thomas O. Lambdin, *Introduction to Biblical Hebrew* (New York: Charles Scribner's Sons, 1971), XXIII. Some recent grammarians, however, assign a "v" pronunciation value to ו and transliterate it as "vav." Compare Bonnie Pedrotti Kittel, Vicki Hoffer, and Rebecca Abts Wright, *Biblical Hebrew: A Text and Workbook* (New Haven: Yale University Press, 1989), 1 and Ethelyn Simon, Nanette Stahl, Linda Motzkin and Joseph Anderson, *The First Hebrew Primer for Adults* (Oakland, CA: EKS Publishing Company, 1983), 3. Following modern Hebrew pronunciation, we have opted to transliterate the Hebrew spelling וָו as "*vāv*," with a long "a." See Harry Blumberg and Mordecai H. Lewittes, *Modern Hebrew*, rev. ed. (New York: Hebrew Publishing Company, 1974), 1:369.

[10]Watts called this a *waw* consecutive of "temporal sequence" (or "logical result"), *Syntax*, 98. Waltke and O'Connor suggest a *waw*-relative of "succession" (*Syntax*, 547-50).

[11]Compare Waltke and O'Connor's nomenclature, "*waw-relative*" and "*waw-copulative*" (*Syntax*, 519). We will return to this concept later.

[12]See Anson F. Rainey, "The Ancient Hebrew Prefix Conjugation in the Light of Amarnah Canaanite," *Hebrew Studies*, 27 (1986): 4-19.

[13]Waltke and O'Connor, *Syntax*, 347. Compare Lambdin, *Hebrew*, 38-39, 100, 107-109; Williams, *Syntax*, 29-33; and Watts, *Syntax*, 6-8.

[14]Note, for example, אַחֲרֵי־כֵן ("afterward") in Joel 3:1 (Eng. 2:28) and בַּיָּמִים הָהֵמָּה ("in those days") in Joel 4:1 (Eng. 3:1).

[15]Note the contrast with the "locust" invasion of Joel 1:1-11.

[16]That is, it has no prefixes (conjunction) or suffixes.

[17]Watts, *Syntax*, 39-42.

[18]Waltke and O'Connor, *Syntax*, 489-90.

[19]Williams, *Syntax*, 33.

[20]Ibid.

[21]Ibid., 34.

[22]A. B. Davidson, *Hebrew Syntax* (Edinburgh: T & T Clark, 1894), 84.

[23]Ibid.

[24]S. R. Driver, *A Treatise on the Use of the Tenses in Hebrew*, 3rd ed. (Oxford: Clarendon Press, 1969), 114.

[25]Ibid., 158.

[26]Ibid., 115.

[27]See Leslie McFall, *The Enigma of the Hebrew Verbal System* (Sheffield: The Almond Press, 1982), 136-50.

[28]Ethelyn Simon, Nanette Stahl, Linda Motzkin and Joseph Anderson, *The First Hebrew Primer for Adults* (Oakland, CA: EKS Publishing Company, 1983), 134.

[29]Waltke and O'Connor, *Syntax*, 519-20.

[30]Ibid., 525.

[31]Ibid., 540.

[32]Watts, *Syntax*, 88. Watts, who wrote his syntax in 1951, was not familiar with current analyses and opinions.

[33]Ibid., 85.

[34]Ibid.

[35]Ibid., 90.

[36]Ibid., 94.

[37]Waltke and O'Connor, *Syntax*, 525.

[38]The major exception is the use of an imperfect with a "*waw* conjunctive." In that situation the *vāv* may either coordinate or subordinate (Watts, *Syntax*, 91,96).

[39]Williams, *Syntax*, 34.

[40]Davidson, *Syntax*, 84.

[41]Waltke and O'Connor, *Syntax*, 540.

[42]Driver, *Tenses*, 159.

[43]For such a portrayal, see David Ussishkin, *The Conquest of Lachish by Sennacherib* (Tel Aviv: Tel Aviv University, The Institute of Archaeology, 1982), 78-88.

[44]J. Weingreen, *A Practical Grammar for Classical Hebrew* (Oxford: At the Clarendon Press, 1952), 52.

[45]BDB, 842.

[46]Gösta Werner Ahlstrom, *Joel and the Temple Cult of Jerusalem*, in *VT Supplement 21* (Leiden: E. J. Brill, 1971), 99.

[47]John A. Thompson, *The Book of Joel*, vol. 6 of *The Interpreter's Bible*, ed. George Arthur Buttrick (New York: Abingdon-Cokesbury Press, 1956), 750.

[48]Julius A. Bewer, *Commentary on Joel* in *The International Critical Commentary*, ed. Samuel Rolles Driver, Alfred Plummer, and Charles

Augustus Briggs, 3rd impression (Edinburgh: T. & T. Clark, 1948), 115. Bewer followed the Septuaginal reading, τὰ βρώματα εἰς δικαιοσύνην.

[49]Karl Friedrich Keil, *The Twelve Minor Prophets*, vol. 16 of *Biblical Commentary on the Old Testament*, Part 1, ed. C. F. Keil and F. Delitzsch, trans. James Martin and others (Grand Rapids: William B. Eerdmans Publishing Company, 1949), 204. Laetsch translated the phrase as "the Teacher unto Righteousness" (*Minor Prophets*, 125). E. B. Pusey also favored this meaning; see *The Minor Prophets: A Commentary* (Grand Rapids: Baker Book House, 1956), 1:190. J. Weingreen prefers that the expression not be translated at all, though he construes it to designate a legitimate judge. See Jacob Weingreen, "The Title Moreh Sedek," *Journal of Semitic Studies* 6 (1961): 174.

[50]See BDB, 435 and KB, 2:386 (**Frühregen**, "early rain"). BDB lists both יוֹרֶה and מוֹרֶה under יָרָה.

[51]Both מָטָר, a general word for rain, and מַלְקוֹשׁ, "latter rain," are present in Deuteronomy 11:14. גֶּשֶׁם, "showers," and מַלְקוֹשׁ are present in Jeremiah 5:24 and Hosea 6:3.

[52]Sawyer, *Semantics*, 51.

[53]Ahlstrom, *Joel*, 108.

[54]See הַסְּנֶה (Ex. 3:2) and הָעַלְמָה: (Isa. 7:14).

[55]Despite Ahlstrom's attempt to connect "righteousness" and "rain" in Psalm 72:5-6 (*Joel*, 104-105).

[56]Harold G. Stigers, "צֶדֶק," *TWOT*, 2:754.

[57]Snaith, *Distinctive Ideas*, 76.

[58]Thompson, *Joel*, 751.

[59]Cecil Roth, "The Teacher of Righteousness and the Prophecy of Joel," *Vetus Testamentum* 13 (1963): 94.

[60]Ibid., 95.

[61]Jacob Weingreen, "The Title Moreh Sedek," *Journal of Semitic Studies* 6 (1961): 173.

[62]Ahlstrom, *Joel*, 109.

[63]Laetsch, *Minor Prophets*, 126.

[64]Prinsloo, *Joel*, 66.

[65]Ibid.

[66]Note יָבוֹא וְיִשְׁעֲכֶם, "he will come to save you."

[67]Note the Master's response to John the Baptist (Matt. 11:4-5).

[68]Note use of the term in Joel 1:15; 2:2; 3:14.

[69]See the chart in this chapter.

[70]See BDB, 816-19. KB noted the parallel to "akk. *lapān*" (KB, 3:888).

[71]Waltke and O'Connor, *Syntax*, 624.

[72]Driver, *Syntax*, 165.

12

Though Your Sins Are Like Scarlet: An Analysis of Isaiah 1:18–20

Come now, let us reason together.

Isaiah 1:18

"Inspiration extends to all and every part of Scripture, even to the very words."[1] This concept of the verbal inspiration of the written Record, however, does not insist that the words of the biblical text (be they Hebrew, Aramaic, or Greek) are intrinsically and independently inspired. It does not follow that all the Hebrew words in a Hebrew lexicon, even reproductions of biblical forms, are inspired. "Verbal" inspiration, then, does more than designate the words of the text. It includes the unique and particular way in which they were originally arranged in the autographs by the human writers under Holy Spirit supervision.

To be sure, the fundamental meaning of individual words is a matter of critical concern to the exegete who believes that the Bible is the verbally inspired word of God. His concern, however, must also extend to the specific grammatical forms and syntactical arrangements that those words assume in the biblical text.

Vern S. Poythress summarized the issue:

> I can put the matter in another way. Hebrew and Greek are not "holy" languages, nor is their vocabulary stock "holy." It is not essentially easier in Hebrew than in English to tell the truth or to lie, to deceive or to enlighten, to be holy or to sin. What *is* holy, yes *divine*, is the particular message sent forth in a particular historical context by putting together, in

the order specified in the Bible, words from Hebrew vocabulary—or Aramaic or Greek as the case may be. Each significant choice of one word or construction rather than another
conveys a *divine* decision to say just this, not that.[2]

The student of Scripture who approaches the Bible from
this perspective, then, must handle the divine text rever-
ently, prayerfully, and intelligently. While one must give
attention to the independent meaning of individual words,
he must also observe the significance of the strategic use
of grammatical forms and syntactical structures. To be
sure, one needs to be cautious so as not to extract too
much from the text. Still, critical syntactical shifts and
nuances contained in the divine Word require painstaking
scrutiny.

Caution and care are especially mandatory when God
speaks directly and explicitly from the biblical record. If
so, then the "says the LORD" of verse 18 and "the mouth
of the LORD hath spoken" of verse 20 underscore the importance of a correct reading and understanding of Isaiah
1:18-20. The two formulas also suggest that these verses
need to be handled as a unit.

Setting of the Invitation

Although the magnificent offers of deliverance contained
in the Bible have a beautiful timelessness that transcends
immediate circumstance, an awareness of the original setting of a given appeal enriches one's appreciation of divine
grace.[3] Moreover, the original situation may provide
worthwhile interpretative clues. This is especially true in
the moving invitation in Isaiah 1.

Historical Situation. Verses 7-9 reveal that Isaiah's beloved Judah had been ravaged by an unnamed invader.
The dramatic immediacy of the prophet's description of
the scene suggests that Jerusalem was currently under attack.[4] In commenting on verse 9, John D. W. Watts offered
this evaluation of the possible historical circumstance:

In view of the description of Israel's problems given in
vv. 4-7b, the period under discussion must come during one
of Assyria's incursions into the land before the final fall of
Samaria in 721 B.C. The language of this verse describes

Jerusalem's isolation when the emperor's marauding armies were in the neighborhood.[5]

However, Isaiah's threefold simile (applied to Jerusalem) in verse 8 accords remarkably with Sennacherib's report of his siege of the city during the Assyrian campaign against Judah in 701 B.C.[6] Whether the invasion carnage was current or not, the succor offered in 1:18-20 and the benefits guaranteed (vv. 19-20) vividly reflect that setting.

Spiritual Condition. Even more graphic is the analysis of the deplorable moral circumstances in Judah. Speaking through the son of Amoz, the LORD charged his people with rebellion (vv. 2, 4), depravity (v. 10), and hypocrisy (vv. 11-15). More stupid than cattle and as degenerate as the ancient inhabitants of Sodom and Gomorrah, Isaiah's compatriots in Israel were severely castigated for the empty meaninglessness of their ancient liturgy. The ceremonial nomenclature Isaiah used does not suggest idolatrous worship; rather, it reflects legitimate ritual prescribed in the Torah. Watts noted the propriety of the liturgical terminology:

> Worship actions include: (v. 11) זבחים "sacrifices," the general word; עלות אילים "whole burnt offerings of rams"; חלב מריעים "fat of fed beasts"; דם פרים וכבשים ועתודים "blood of bulls, of lambs and he goats." This is a comprehensive list of the types of blood sacrifice. Leviticus speaks of them in terms of function, "sin offering, guilt offering," etc. But the same sacrifices are intended.[7]

Accordingly, the LORD denounced the deplorable spiritual condition of Judah's worshipers rather than the ceremony associated with their worship. "The failure to accompany sacrificial and festal worship with a lifestyle of justice and righteousness is the problem. The latter invalidates the former."[8]

Admonition. In view of the appalling political situation and moral circumstance of Judah, the prophet vigorously encouraged his nation to abandon evil and "do good" (Isa. 1:16-17). Formal ritual could not be substituted for inner integrity; sacrifice and ceremony without submission and personal piety were unacceptable! Thus Isaiah challenged his people to repent, and his call to repentance introduces the great invitation of our text.

Nature of the Invitation

Critical elements in the LORD's appeal to Judah include both lexical and syntactical features that deserve careful evaluation. While these matters may appear to be technical or abstruse, diligent study of the specifics of the text can be highly rewarding. Since these features are an integral part of God's Word, let us persevere.

Appeal Elements. Explicit items in the text disclose that 1:18-20 constitutes an offer, not an order. The first verb in verse 18 is indeed an imperative; but the volitional force of the form is tempered by the meaning of the verb and the addition of the particle of entreaty, *nā'* (נָא). This terse, monosyllabic term defies a definite analysis. Although it may be "used to emphasize a demand, warning, or entreaty,"[9] it is also "frequently added to the imperative, as to the jussive, sometimes to soften down a command, or to make a request in a more courteous form."[10] The nuance contributed to the expression by the addition of *nā'* must be evaluated in light of additional components in the text.

The ambiguity of *nā'* calls attention to the meaning of the verb to which it is attached. The preceding imperative (לְכוּ, "come") constitutes a rather common idiom[11] that may function as a "mere introductory word."[12] This relatively perfunctory use of "come" strongly suggests that *nā'* is a part of the idiom and that the two terms, as in English, comprise a salutatory introduction to the invitation that follows.

The primary verb in the opening line of verse 18 (נִוָּכְחָה) is a *Niph'al* form of *yākah* (יָכַח), which is translated "reason together" in KJV.[13] Paul R. Gilchrist insists that the term has a "juridical notion" and that its "forensic use is clearest in the covenant lawsuit context."[14] In discussing this verse, Gilchrist adds:

> However, the most familiar passage where *yakah* occurs is in Isa. 1:18 which is within a covenant lawsuit. . . . Within this context then we should understand the expression "let us reason together" (KJV, NIV [*sic*]) as meaning "let us debate our case in court."[15]

In Isaiah 11:3–4 (יוֹכִיחַ and הוֹכִיחַ, in the *Hiph'il* stem instead of the *Niph'al*) the verb is used in parallel with "judge." In the other two Old Testament *Niph'al* uses of the verb (both outside the Book of Isaiah),[16] judicial discernment is likewise indicated.

The significant feature of this verb, though, is its grammatical form and syntactical function in the sentence. As will be noted presently, verbal mood is not always precisely indicated by verb form;[17] but the structure and meaning of this particular verb are explicit and clear. Called a "cohortative," the form is fashioned from the first-person pattern of the imperfect (also known as the "prefix" or "imperfective" conjugation[18]) by the addition of a long *a* vowel and an *h* consonant (ה). The resultant morpheme is distinctive and, in this instance, unmistakable.[19]

The meaning or force of any cohortative is relatively straightforward. Waltke and O'Connor observed:

> The cohortative expresses the will or strong desire of the speaker. In cases where the speaker has the ability to carry out an inclination it takes on the coloring of resolve.... In other cases, where the speaker cannot effect a desire without the consent of the one addressed, it connotes request ("May I ... ").[20]

Davidson commented that when a speaker is dependent on others, his use of the cohortative "expresses a wish or request."[21] As Waltke and O'Connor pointed out, the cohortative (first common singular) may reflect the speaker's intense determination to implement his will or strong desire. The first common plural form of the verb in verse 18, however, excludes the possibility that it might be construed as a "cohortative of determination"[22] but demands that it be understood as an exhortation.[23] Accordingly, the opening statement in verse 18 constitutes an appeal for the "consent of the one(s) addressed" and invites a desired response.

The remainder of verses 18-20 must be evaluated in view of the prospect that the issues presented are to be determined by the reaction of the audience addressed. These verses constitute an invitation, not an edict. They are contingent on factors external to the speaker (YHWH).

Conditional Structures. One of the major exegetical challenges in Old Testament interpretation is presented by the puzzle of Hebrew conditional sentences. As GKC noted, the complexity of Hebrew conditional formulas has resulted in appraisals that frequently depend "on the subjective judgment of the speaker."[24] The ambiguity of conditional structures is perpetrated, at least in part, by the plurality of introductory and transitional particles,[25] the abbreviation of some formats, and the lack of temporal and modal precision in the biblical Hebrew verb system. The problem has been further compounded by the relative neglect of scholars in dealing with the difficulties involved.

One of my former students, Michael R. Spradlin, has written a dissertation that evaluates the possible levels of certainty in Hebrew conditional patterns. His research provides new data for consideration. The accompanying chart summarizes most of the significant research and evaluation of conditional structures by Hebrew grammarians to the present time. His analysis of the potential significance of particles and verb forms provides a welcome insight into the total conditional puzzle.[26]

Furthermore, he has called attention to the fact that conditional sentences involve (or imply) verbs in both the protasis and apodosis positions and that, consequently, they require dual evaluation.[27] In other words, a conditional structure includes both a circumstance (protasis) and a conclusion (apodosis). Therefore, the relative degree of certainty or probability of each (in the mind of the speaker or writer) needs to be considered.

The verbs (in both the protasis and apodosis) in the two conditional sentences in verse 18 occur in the "imperfect" or "prefix" conjugation.[28] Independent of the issue of time, the imperfect "tense" is somewhat more complex than the perfect[29] because it may function in the indicative, volitional, or subjunctive mood.[30] While insisting that to describe the action of the imperfect as "incomplete or unfinished" is not entirely accurate, Lambdin conceded that the imperfect is "used to describe action conceived by the speaker as general, non-specific, habitual, potential, or to some degree probable."[31]

The tentative nature of the imperfect conjugation would suggest that this verbal form might well designate a dubious circumstance or conclusion. Moreover, when present in both components of the conditional structure, the imper-

CONDITIONAL STRUCTURE AS
INTERPRETED BY VARIOUS GRAMMARIANS

Grammarian	One	Two	Three	Four
Williams	Real	Unreal		
Gesenius	Capable of Fulfillment	Incapable of Fulfillment		
Yates	Perfect of Condition	Perfect of Concurrency	Subjunctive Mood	
Watts	Taken for Granted	Contrary to Fact	More Probable	Less Probable
Ferguson	Assumed Real	Assumed Probable	Indefinite	Impossible
Joüon	Juxtaposition	Volitional Mood	Waw Relation	Particle
Driver	Real	Indefinite	Improbable	Impossible
	Conditions 5 and 6 in Driver are rare forms of 4			
Waltke/ O'Conner	Real	Irreal		
Lambdin	Real	Irreal		

fect might indicate a heightened level of uncertainty. Just so, Henry Ferguson wrote:

> When the hypothesis is *indefinite* and the conclusion merely considered *possible*, or when the supposition is extremely *improbable*, but yet *possible* (Class III), the *Imperfect* is usually found in both clauses.[32]

Watts suggested that if both imperfects (in protasis and apodosis) are construed as indicative in mood, then the overall format may be understood as "More Probable"; but if they are viewed as subjunctive, then the conditional structure constitutes a "Less Probable" circumstance.[33]

Of course, the problem associated with Watts's proposal is that the Hebrew subjunctive has no explicit verb form. The subjunctive mood can be discerned in the imperfect only on the basis of context. The distinction in mood is the difference between the actual "is" or "will be" (in English) of the indicative and the potential "may" or "might be" of the subjunctive.

Construed as indicative, the protasis imperfects in verse 18 could be translated "(if your sins) are . . . /(if they) become . . . " and "(if they) are red . . . /(if they) become red. . . . " In light of the preceding description of Judah's moral and spiritual decay, the imperfects could certainly be understood as describing a present circumstance. However, as Ferguson noted, the situation in this kind of supposition is at best "indefinite" if not improbable.

The indecisive nature of the imperfect seems to suggest the tentative disposition of the protasis or hypothesis. If understood as subjunctive in mood, the two verbs could read "(if your sins) may/might/should be (or become) . . . " and "(if they) may/might/should be (or become) red. . . . "[34] In any event, the use of the imperfect (in both protases) seems to reflect strongly the uncertainty of the projected circumstance.

The insecure status represented by the imperfect should also be noted in the two apodoses of verse 18. The context of verbal chastisement, condemnation, and admonition combines with the rudiments of biblical theology to cause Bible students to reject totally the equation created by construing the two final imperfects as indicative. That formula would translate "then they (your sins) will become white as snow . . . then they will be as wool." If these two conclusions represent certain (or even probable) consequences of the conditions described in their respective protases, then "scarlet sin" and "crimson depravity" must surely pave the fast track to cleansing and purification. Such a notion is not only repugnant; it is completely inconsistent with the biblical record and the character of God. Mankind is never encouraged to pursue sin as an avenue to forgiveness (see Rom. 6:1-2).

We must, therefore, conclude that these conditional sentences do not guarantee a mechanical, automatic purging geared to human depravity. Rather, they offer the prospect of forgiveness despite human depravity—an offer based on divine grace. Accordingly, we suggest that the imperfects in both protasis and apodosis be construed as subjunctive, with the following translation:

"If your sins should be as scarlet, they may be made white as snow. If they should be red like crimson, they may become as wool."

The conditional sentences in verses 19-20, however, are quite different in format and emphasis from those in verse 18. Although the verbs in the two protases are in the imperfect conjugation (as in verse 18), the verbs in the apodoses (conclusions) appear in the perfect conjugation and are prefixed by a *vāv* (waw) "conjunctive"[35] ("waw conversive") which functions as a transitional participle.[36] The more stable, definite character of the perfect[37] and the distinctive flavor of the particle influenced Ferguson to label this formula as "assumed probable." He explained:

> If the condition imply probability, we shall usually find the imperfect in the protasis, followed by the perfect with waw conversive in the apodosis, if the verb stand first in the clause.[38]

Watts labeled this kind of structure as "more probable,"[39] suggesting that the protasis imperfect be construed as indicative in mood rather than subjunctive. If one then applies the concept of the "more" or "assumed probable" format to the conditional structures in verses 19-20—in other words, the pattern of an indicative imperfect in the protasis followed by a perfect with a "waw conversive" in the apodosis—then a fascinating and significant change in the force of the two statements results. That shift is reflected in this proposed translation:

"If you are willing, then you will hearken; the good of the land you will eat. But if you refuse, then you rebel; by the sword you will be consumed."

Despite the somewhat startling modification in emphasis, the legitimacy of applying the concept is reinforced by the fact that the procedure duly recognizes the presence of the transitional particle (*vāv*) in both instances. This formula constitutes a classic apodosis pattern in the Old Testament. Waltke and O'Connor noted, "The proposed original function of the *weqataltí* construction to signify the apodosis of a conditional clause shines through almost all of its uses in Biblical Hebrew."[40] While a sequence of perfects with *vāv* in a conditional context may obscure the transition from protasis to apodosis,[41] the singular use of the pattern in these verses clearly indicates the shift from condition to conclusion. Accordingly, in the absence of extenuating contextual factors, the initial perfect with *vāv* is to be construed as introducing the apodosis.

Moreover, the proposed translation of verses 19–20 reflects the independent nature of the clauses that summarize both verses. That the two circumstances are syntactically distinct from their respective conditional formulas is indicated by the fact that both begin with a nominal (טוֹב הָאָרֶץ, "good of the land" and חֶרֶב, "sword") followed by a predicate. Moreover, neither clause has a transitional particle. In each of these verses, the apodosis is followed by a summary affirmation, but neither statement is an integral part of the initial conditional structure.

Spradlin has noted the ambiguity of labeling the conditional formula of verse 19 in the conventional manner:

> The protasis has an imperfect verb indicating a possible circumstance. The audience of Isaiah might not be willing. The apodosis, however, is a perfect-verb-with-*waw* indicating certainty of outcome. Apart from the protasis, it would definitely occur. So classifying this as a "possible outcome" conditional sentence describes neither the protasis nor the apodosis. A possibility exists that some of the people will be willing; and, if this happens, then they will definitely be obedient. In this situation, a doubtful protasis has been combined with a definite apodosis.[42]

Spradlin proposed a model system that provides more precise identification criteria:

	Model A	*Model B*	*Model C*
[P]	Definite	Probable	Possible
[A]	1 Definite	1 Definite	1 Definite
	2 Probable	2 Probable	2 Probable
	3 Possible	3 Possible	3 Possible
	4 Impossible	4 Impossible	4 Impossible
	5 Neutral	5 Neutral	5 Neutral

	Model D	*Model E*	*Model F*
[P]	Impossible	Neutral	Biblical Oath[43]
[A]	1 Definite	1 Definite	
	2 Probable	2 Probable	
	3 Possible	3 Possible	
	4 Impossible	4 Impossible	
	5 Neutral	5 Neutral	

Adopting his system and nomenclature, we would categorize the conditional sentences in verses 19-20 as C:1—in other words, the model featuring an uncertain protasis ("Possible") with a definite apodosis.

Critical Modifications in the Invitation

Prospect. In the light of the alteration of conditional patterns, attention should be directed to the significance of what appears to be a deliberate modification in the total entreaty (vv. 18-20). In terms of both condition and result, the invitation in verse 18 projects that which is only possible. On the other hand, the appeals in verses 19-20, with tentative conditions but definite results, suggest that which is more probable. The summary statements of the latter two verses with their indicative imperfects, however, constitute positive declarations. The progression from possible to probable to positive would seem to be quite calculated.

Subject. Another significant alteration is the shift in the nature of verb subjects. "Your sins" served as the agent of verbal action in verse 18, but in verses 19-20, "you" becomes the subject. Notice the transition: from the conceptual to the concrete, from the abstract to the personal. This focus restriction is surely not incidental.

Scenario. The change in verb agency is accompanied by a sharp shift from comparison to confrontation. The charming similes are replaced by stringent and demanding alternatives.

Verb Force. The core meaning of the verbs in the protases in verses 19-20 is of crucial significance. The first, 'ābāh (אָבָה, conjugated as תֹּאבוּ), is usually translated "be willing."[44] Leonard J. Coppes adds that the term involves "the willingness to do something under obligation or upon request."[45] The circumstance indicated by this "stative verb" denotes an internal attitude or disposition that may be influenced by external stimuli but is not totally regulated by them. The "obligation" of Coppes's definition obviously does not mean mandatory regulation in view of the additional statement, "The idea of exercising the will is expressed when one is asked to acquiesce to another's request."[46]

The independent nature of *'ābāh* is further indicated by the fact that, while it occurs in the Old Testament 112 times, it appears only twice without a negative particle.[47] In 110 out of 112 instances, then, despite any or all external influences, a willing disposition is not the response. The verbal state of *'ābāh* involves both external and internal factors, but the external does not override the internal. In addition, notice that "willingness" is equated with "hearken" (וּשְׁמַעְתֶּם).[48]

The second verb, *ma'en* מָאֵן (v. 20), is of equal importance. The word means "refuse"[49] and is frequently followed by an infinitive construct.[50] Again, by the very nature of its meaning, the concept generated by this verb indicates an internal reaction-response. The notion, to be sure, requires some kind of external initiative; but the term connotes the inherent capacity to reject that initiative. Accordingly, in this text, *ma'en* is equated with "rebel" (וּמְרִיתֶם).

The results of Isaiah's invitation on the LORD's behalf, at least in verses 19-20, depended on the internal response of "you." The circumstances, options, and possibilities had been carefully, painstakingly delineated. Now, the alternatives with their respective results were affirmed with the clear challenge to respond. The choice between acceptance and rejection of the LORD's offer of forgiveness was Judah's privilege and responsibility to exercise. Thus, the principle of the awesome human obligation to respond in trust or rebellion is articulated, in and through the conditional structures of Isaiah's appeal. The summary statements of the latter two sentences couch the invitation in its original historical context.

Theological Conclusions

In attempting to find an acceptable theological framework for this appeal (and other divine invitations), we search for a synthesis that is consistent with all the biblical evidence. We probe for a position that is compatible with all the specifics, without having to restate, modify, or add to any biblical text. We seek a principle that accommodates all possible exceptions but that is not built on exceptions.

We believe that the LORD, through Isaiah, extended an offer of salvation and preservation to Judah. The pledge of preservation, as we understand it, had a limited historical frame of reference; but the soteriological principle embedded in the grammatical and syntactical details of our text was valid, then and now. Just as surely as John 3:16 had an immediate and an abiding application, so the magnificent invitation in Isaiah's "gospel" was both timely and timeless. If so, I offer the following evaluations.

Human Accountability. First, considering the details of Isaiah's appeal, I conclude that persons can resist the divine initiative. While they may not seek God apart from a heavenly overture, people do have the capacity to reject the advances of grace.

Second, I observe that individuals are responsible for their choices.

Third, I conclude that a person's response determines assured consequences.

If the foregoing statements are not valid, the meaning of the words and the grammatical and syntactical selections in Isaiah 1:18-20 appear to be totally meaningless and either accidental or incidental. Such a conclusion hardly seems consistent with the premise that "all scripture is inspired by God."

Divine Sovereignty. These evaluations might cause some to question my conception of the sovereignty of God. I respond, however, by insisting that God is indeed sovereign, both in history and in salvation.

God is sovereign in history, but sovereignty is not tyranny. It does not dictate that foreknowledge and predetermination are one and the same. In like fashion, omnipotence, omniscience, and omnipresence do not mean omnipraxis (omni-instigation or omni-restraint). God's will *will* be done, but He does not necessarily will all that *is* done. God's will ranges from permission to purpose to pleasure. Still, He is not a despot who cannot tolerate disobedience. Rather, He is a sovereign who can effectively overrule—yes, and even use—both the rebellion of persons and the insurrection of the forces of hell. He will accomplish His ultimate design for this world, mankind, and history, not without resistance but despite any and all resistance. God is sovereign in history.

God is also sovereign in salvation. His grace is sovereign with respect to salvation's strategy. Observe His dealings with Jacob, Pharaoh, and Saul of Tarsus. These do not reflect standard individual examples of election or reprobation and constitute universal salvation models. Rather, they disclose the evidence of an overarching economy in the inception, preservation, and extension of a covenant people. They reflect the grand design of the LORD's total salvation strategy.

His grace is sovereign with regard to the basis of salvation—the redeeming efficacy of the cross. He is sovereign in salvation's initiative. Without His provision and individual appeal, by His Word and Spirit, mankind would be helpless and hopeless. He is also sovereign in the matter of the condition of salvation. He has determined that people will be saved on the basis of trust. In His Word, He has decreed that individuals will be saved by faith, the level of response that all people of all ages, of all races, and of all intellects can meet. It is so—by His sovereign choice.

Conclusion

As a result of this examination and exegesis of Isaiah 1:18-20, I conclude that people are not preprogrammed robots, helpless victims caught in the web of a hidden predestination. In the Garden of Eden, the plea "The devil made me do it!" did not absolve man and woman of their complicity in history's first act of insurrection. In like fashion, "I'm a victim of circumstance, environment, or heredity!" will not excuse. "I didn't draw a lucky number!" or "I'm not one of the elect!" or "God made me this way!" won't do either. His sovereign grace has not only made a provision for all; it also requires that all can and must make a response.

So God's invitation to Judah was just that—an invitation. It was not an irresistible mandate. The LORD declared, in effect, "The ball is in your court." By His sovereign grace, we may decide; we can decide; we *must* decide. And the decision is irreversible. We must live— and die—with our choice.

Notes

[1]H. Lindsell, "Inspiration," in *The Zondervan Pictorial Encyclopedia of the Bible*, ed. Merrill C. Tenney, 2nd printing (Grand Rapids: Zondervan Publishing House, 1977), 3:288. Compare Donald R. Potts, "Inspiration of Scripture," *Holman Bible Dictionary*, ed. Trent C. Butler (Nashbille: Holman Bible Publishers, 1991).

[2]Vern S. Poythress, "Language and Accommodation" in *Hermeneutics, Inerrancy, and the Bible*, ed. Earl D. Radmacher and Robert D. Preus (Grand Rapids: Zondervan Publishing House, 1984), 363.

[3]See Isaiah 45:22 and Revelation 22:17.

[4]"Daughter of Zion" undoubtedly refers to Judah's capital.

[5]John D. W. Watts, *Isaiah 1–33*, vol. 24 in *Word Biblical Commentary*, ed. David A. Hubbard and Glenn W. Barker (Waco, TX: Word Books, Publisher, 1985), 20.

[6]Sennacherib described his siege of Jerusalem in terms of his humiliation of Judah's king (Hezekiah): "Himself I made a prisoner in Jerusalem, his royal residence, like a bird in a cage." See *Ancient Near Eastern Texts*, ed. James B. Pritchard, 2nd ed. (Princeton: Princeton University Press, 1955), 288.

[7]John Watts, *Isaiah 1–33*, 21.

[8]Ibid., 20.

[9]GKC, 308.

[10]Ibid., 324.

[11]See Isaiah 2:3 and Exodus 3:10.

[12]BDB, 234.

[13]The force of יָכַח in the *Niph'al* stem (as used here) may be construed to have a reflexive connotation. See KB, 2:392 (**sich auseinandersetzen**) and BDB, 407.

[14]Paul R. Gilchrist, "יָכַח," *TWOT*, 1:376.

[15]Gilchrist, "יָכַח," 1:377.

[16]Job 23:7 and Genesis 20:16.

[17]For example, biblical Hebrew has no conjugational pattern that is equivalent to the subjunctive mood in Greek.

[18]See Waltke and O'Connor, *Syntax*, 496-518.

[19]Lamed-He verbs, however, preserve no distinctive cohortative ending. See Lambdin, *Hebrew*, 145.

[20]Waltke and O'Connor, *Syntax*, 573.

[21]Davidson, *Syntax*, 88.

[22]Watts, *Syntax*, 51-52. Contextual factors explain the apparent contradiction presented by the cohortatives in Genesis 22:5.

[23]Ibid.

[24]GKC, 493. Commenting on Genesis 32:9, Driver noted "that it is only the sense which shews that the apodosis begins with והיה, and not with והכהו. The same ambiguity of form occurs constantly in this type of hypothetical sentence in Hebrew." See Driver, *Tenses*, 174.

[25]I am indebted to Michael R. Spradlin for the precision of the terms "introductory" and "transitional" particles. See his "An Investigation of Conditional Sentences in the Hebrew Text of Isaiah" (Th.D. diss., Mid-America Baptist Theological Seminary, 1991), 45-57.

[26]Ibid., 56-77.

[27]Ibid., 150.

[28]Also known as the "Non-Perfective." See Waltke and O'Connor, *Syntax*, 496-518.

[29]Waltke and O'Connor, *Syntax*, 496.

[30]Ibid., 506-511.

[31]Lambdin, *Hebrew*, 100.

[32]Henry Ferguson, "An Examination of the Use of the Tenses in Conditional Sentences in Hebrew," *Journal of the Society of Biblical Literature and Exegesis* 2 (June-September 1882): 60.

[33]Watts, *Syntax*, 111-16.

[34]This tentative mood is beautifully captured in the KJV by the haunting, "though your sins be as. . . . "

[35]Watts, *Syntax*, 85-90.

[36]Spradlin, *Conditional*, 55-57. Spradlin proposed that such a feature "is intended to mark a transition between a circumstance and a consequence" (57).

[37]Compare Waltke and O'Connor's use of "completeness" (*Syntax*, 480) with Gesenius's "completion" (GKC, 309) in describing the genius of the perfect.

[38]Ferguson, "Examination," 59. The verb does stand first in both result clauses in verses 19-20.

[39]Watts, *Syntax*, 112.

[40]Waltke and O'Connor, *Syntax*, 525.

[41]See Genesis 28:20-21.

[42]Spradlin, *Conditional*, 143.

[43]Ibid., 144.

[44]BDB, 2; see also NIV and KJV.

[45]Leonard J. Coppes, "אָבָה," *TWOT*, 1:4.

[46]Ibid.

[47]Ibid. Compare Bo Johnson, "אָבָה," *TDOT*, 1:24-25.

[48]On the other hand, according to Johnson, *lo' 'abhah* is tantamount to "unwillingness." See Johnson, "אָבָה," *TDOT*, 1:26.

[49]BDB, 549.

[50]Also implied here, in other words, "refuse to be willing."

13

Man of Sorrows

My servant will act wisely.

Isaiah 52:13

" 'Tell me, please, who is the prophet talking about, himself or someone else?' Then Philip began with that very passage of Scripture and told him the good news about Jesus" (Acts 8:34-35).

According to Dr. Luke's journal, "an important official in charge of all the treasury of Candace, queen of the Ethiopians" (Acts 8:27) was returning home from Jerusalem where he had gone to worship. He was riding in his chariot and reading from Isaiah 53 when he encountered Philip, one of the first deacons in the infant church.

Sensing the Jewishness of the stranger and evidently moved by what he was reading in the Jewish Scriptures, he asked Philip about the identity of the mysterious figure whose presence loomed from the written page. The question was apropos, and the traveling deacon was far more qualified to answer the Ethiopian's query than he could possibly have imagined.

From the standpoint of our current investigation, a crucial feature of that memorable encounter is the fact that Philip responded by correlating the Isaiah text with the New Testament gospel. Undoubtedly this famous Isaian passage is soteriological in nature, and it will be the focus of this particular unit of study.

The Servant Songs in Isaiah

First, the parameters of the immediate context need to be recognized. Because of the unfortunate division between chapters 52 and 53, the unity of the material may be overlooked. The segment actually begins with Isaiah 52:13 and extends through Isaiah 53:12. In addition, the unit constitutes one of the so-called "servant songs" in the Book of Isaiah. Therefore, the soteriological message of the unit needs to be evaluated in light of its full scope and its thematic and contextual setting.

Location. Isaiah 52:13—53:12 is the final of four compositions that have been identified as servant songs or poems.[1] The other three are located in Isaiah 42:1-4; 49:1-6; 50:4-9.[2] Some have suggested that the servant songs are actually later additions and do not fit their respective contexts. In response James Muilenburg offered this rebuttal:

> An examination of the foregoing literature demonstrates quite conclusively that the excision of the four servant poems, far from resolving difficulties, has only added to them. Duhm and others have been compelled to delete contiguous verses.[3]

Muilenburg's point is well taken, and an awareness of the indigenous nature of the songs will be a key factor in our theological appraisal of the fourth poem.

Theme Analysis. Claus Westermann, feeling that the songs are basically disparate from each other, made this evaluation: "The songs thus differ completely in kind, their link being a subject in common, God's servant."[4] I would counter that the servant motif alone, especially in light of its theological significance, provides a distinctive unifying emphasis of sufficient magnitude to indicate the thematic cohesion of the songs. Furthermore, the four poems also share another singular feature. Each of them is a study in paradox, marked by a unique contrast formula. They all begin with a projection of the servant's inadequacy, but they conclude with the servant's image of success and victory. In Isaiah 42:1-4, note the thematic progression: Meekness > Universal Justice. Observe the parallel in Isaiah 49:1-6: Failure > Universal Salvation. In the latter two poems, note a similar emphasis: Humiliation > Divine Assistance (Isa. 50:4-9) and Rejection > Divine Vindication (Isa. 52:13—53:12). Not only does the servant figure dominate each of the songs. His fate is essentially the same in each case, the outcome in stark contrast to his initial profile.

Macrostructure Analysis

Although opinions vary as to the unity and authorship of the Book of Isaiah, appreciation for the literary artistry of the final product is widespread, if not unanimous. In this section, I will make no attempt to address the question of the book's composition. I will try to "sketch in" what appears to be the basic theological design within the second major component of the book, chapters 40—66.

Chapters 40—66. Analyses and outlines of these chapters are as numerous as there are analysts and "outliners." While they usually have much in common, sometimes inspiration for the analysis seems to be in "the eye of the beholder." In the absence of an outline by the author, a degree of subjectivity is probably unavoidable. However, one cannot help but wonder if the biblical writer really used the same literary and organizational techniques now perceived by the modern Western interpreter. In the light of these considerations, I must acknowledge a measure of tentativeness in any analysis of this much material.

Watts made this preliminary evaluation of Isaiah 40—66:

> Outstanding features of the teaching in "The Book of Comfort" are as follows: (1) *The occasion* for those acts of Yahweh's by which he offers comfort to Israelites; (2) *the purpose* of them; (3) *the means* by which he promises to accomplish them; and (4) *the result* of them predicted by him.[5]

With the foregoing as an analytical formula, Watts charted the content of chapters 41—66 in this format:

Chapters 41–48

Occasion	Babylonian Captivity
Purpose	Restoration to Land of Israel
Means	Cyrus
Result	Continuance of Israel as a nation

Chapters 49–59

Occasion	Sin
Purpose	Restoration to peace with Yahweh
Means	The Suffering Servant
Result	Salvation of a believing remnant of National Israel

Mighty to Save

Chapters 60–66

Occasion	Shame and Disgrace
Purpose	Restoration as a shining light in world
Means	The Glorious One
Result	Glorification of Zion where all believers share alike.[6]

If Watts's evaluation is only approximately accurate, then the major stress in chapters 49—59 is decidedly soteriological. This perception is important to the understanding of specific items.

Chapters 49—59. Watts, in addition, isolated in this unit what he perceived to be a series of problems and solutions. Granted that the "problems" and "solutions" are not specifically designated as such, still, there seems to be genuine merit in his overall analysis of the data. The following is an outline of the sevenfold problem-solution series. Although I am indebted to Watts for the insight, I have dared to alter his labels and modify his categories slightly.

Problem-Solution Series

Problem	*Solution*
(1) Failure 49:1-4	Second Servant 49:5-13
(2) Sense of Abandonment 49:14	Ensign to the Nations 49:15-26
(3) Sense of Alienation 50:1-3	The Inspired Teacher 50:4—51:8
(4) Weakness 51:9—52:12	The Arm of YHWH 52:13—53:12
(5) Desolation 54:1-17	The Sure Mercies of David 55:1—56:8
(6) Ignorance 56:9—57:14	The Inhabitant of Eternity 57:15-21
(7) Hypocrisy 58:1—59:15a	Zion's Redeemer 59:15b-21[7]

The overt complaints, the implicit evidence of disgruntled frustration, and the pleas and exhortations all combine to pinpoint the problems in the corporate psyche of Judah. In some instances, the difficulty stemmed from the spiritual and emotional feelings of the people (for example, the sense of being abandoned or alienated). In other situations, the problem was concrete (failure, hypocrisy) and objective. Whatever the manifestation, the source of the problem was intimately related to the sin factor in Judah. Incidentally, the sin-symptom connection reflected in this series has an eerie timelessness. The problems that plagued Judah are as contemporary as the evening news on television.

Another striking feature about the series is the fact that a messianic motif or emblem is enclosed in each "solution" package. Accordingly, we have opted to reflect that factor in the "solution" terminology[8] since the "Messiah imprimatur" imparts a distinct soteriological sanction to the material.

Song of the Suffering Servant

The fourth poem in the servant song series, Isaiah 52:13—53:12, has been described as the "Song of the Suffering Servant." The anguish and distress experienced by the central figure in the prophetic "elegy" certainly justify the appellation. However, although the melody was composed in the key of "Pain Sharp" (P#), harmonious overtones of victory soar above the song's dissonance of sorrow.

Servant Identification. Because of the servant's prominence in all four of the songs and his unmistakable presence elsewhere in the general context, his somewhat mysterious identity requires clarification. Fortunately, or perhaps otherwise, suggestions are not wanting.

Muilenburg, for example, while recognizing that "not a few scholars see in the servant the features of the divine king as he appears in the royal psalms and elsewhere,"[9] concluded: "If the servant songs are the work of Second Isaiah . . . then the servant of the Lord is certainly Israel."[10] Noting that "the servant of Yahweh and the servant Israel are also basically different in their character," he added (referring to Isa. 49:5-6), "Here, the servant seems to be set over against Israel so that it is difficult to identify the two."[11]

Harry M. Orlinsky, along with others, equated the servant with the writer himself (Second Isaiah). "In all the four so-called ʿebed sections—though the term ʿebed is not found in two of the four—it is the prophet himself who is the central personage."[12] Arvid S. Kapelrud called attention to the fact that other identifications have been advocated, including (First) Isaiah, Third Isaiah, Moses, Uzziah, the prophet Jeremiah, and "the ideal Israel."[13]

Kapelrud also shared his own opinion: "All the features which are delineated in the description of the Servant of Yahweh in the Songs may be applied to *the exiles, as this group was seen by those who were not exiles themselves.*"[14] Snaith agreed, essentially, with Kapelrud's assessment. "Our proposition is therefore: The Servant of the LORD is primarily the 597 exiles, but gradually it tends to widen in conception to include all the Babylonian exiles."[15]

The range and inconsistency of scholarly opinion suggest that the textual evidence is not altogether clear or decisive. A survey of the material in Isaiah 41—53 confirms that impression. In the first place, the "servant" is initially and unmistakably equated with Israel. Notice these explicit references:

"But you, O Israel, my servant, / Jacob whom I have chosen . . . " (Isa. 41:8).

"But now listen, O Jacob, my servant, / Israel, whom I have chosen . . . " (Isa. 44:1).

"Remember these things, O Jacob, / for you are my servant, O Israel, / I have made you, you are my servant . . . " (Isa. 44:21).

"For the sake of Jacob my servant, / of Israel my chosen . . . " (Isa. 45:4).

YHWH's affirmation that Israel (Jacob) is His servant is so definite and specific that the issue should be immediately settled, or so it would seem. Other references to the servant, however, indicate that a one-facet analysis may not be acceptable.

In the initial servant song (Isa. 42:1-4), the servant is not specifically designated. That should generate no confusion, though, since his identification as Israel is spelled out, both before and after the song.[16] Although the servant-Israel formula is compatible with the first verse of this poem, the meekness, gentleness, and quiet confidence of the servant's manner is hardly characteristic of other descriptions of the servant in the context.[17]

Moreover, his projected mission, establishing "justice on earth," and the prediction that "in his law the islands will put their hope" hardly correspond to other data in the larger passage. If this is, indeed, a reference to Israel's destiny, then "his law" would appear to designate the To-rah, a rather strange projection. Accordingly, although the servant profile in this first song does not contradict the servant-Israel equation, neither is it particularly consistent with it.

At this point, crucial information from outside the immediate context becomes a decisive interpretive factor. The New Testament writer-interpreter, Matthew, applied the first servant song to the earthly ministry of the Carpenter from Galilee (Matt. 12:17-21). His appraisal, based on Holy Spirit direction as well as textual analysis, helps resolve the servant-Israel tension. In addition, it leads to the evaluation that, in the first servant song, the servant is depicted as personified within Israel.[18] That designation, I believe, preserves the Israel-orientation but also anticipates a critical distinction.

An even more intricate puzzle is wrapped up in Isaiah 42:19: "Who is blind but my servant, / and deaf like the messenger I send? / Who is blind like the one committed to me, / blind like the servant of the LORD?" As in the case of Isaiah 42:1-4, Israel is not mentioned specifically in this verse, though both Israel and Jacob are referred to in verse 24. Even without that designation, though, the description of the miserable servant, blind and deaf, corresponds to the general ineptitude of Israel's performance as the LORD's servant. Jacob did seem to be blind to the LORD's purposes and deaf to His pleas.[19]

The perplexing item in the verse, though, is not the reference to blindness and deafness. Instead, the piece that does not seem to "fit" in the verse or conform to the general character of Israel's performance is the single word translated "one committed" in NIV and "he that is perfect" in KJV. Both versions reflect the Hebrew term *kiměšullām* (כִּמְשֻׁלָּם), an expression formed by the addition of the "comparative preposition" *kě* (כְּ) to the *Pu'al* participle form *měšullām* (מְשֻׁלָּם).

Built on the verbal root *š-l-m* (שׁלם) and associated with the noun *šālōm* (שָׁלוֹם), the precise meaning of this particular form is contested, primarily because two verbs are detected in the same consonantal root. BDB, for example, projects *šālēm* (שָׁלֵם, "be complete, sound") and the denominative *šālam* (שָׁלַם, "be in covenant of peace").[20] The uncertainty is compounded by the Septuagint translation "they that rule over them."[21] Muilenburg, rejecting the LXX option, summarized the major possibilities:

> The presence of the servant is not removed so simply. The word משלם is translated many different ways: "he that is at peace" (ASV), "made perfect" or "recomposed" (ASV mg.), "the purchased one" (Rosenmüller), "the devoted one" (Cheyne) ... "the befriended one" (Skinner), "one made whole" (Levy), "the perfected one" (Torrey and Buber).[22]

Somewhat surprisingly, Muilenburg reached this conclusion, "Perhaps the best solution is that proposed by Kissane, 'the covenanted one,' derived from the verb meaning 'to be in covenant of peace.'"[23]

I am persuaded that the semantic thrust of the term, consistent with its primary meaning,[24] centers in the "made perfect" or "made whole" sector. The reading "be in covenant of peace" is probably a secondary or extended meaning anyway. Even if the root is allowed that meaning, *mĕšullām* is its only *Pu'al* form that is attested in the entire Old Testament.[25] Accordingly, Kissane's proposal, despite Muilenburg's endorsement, is not convincing.

Moreover, whatever its meaning, the verb is definitely participial in form and passive in nature (*Pu'al*). This suggests two important features: (1) the action of the verb indicated a "durative circumstance,"[26] and (2) the "perfecting" process was initiated from without. I prefer, then, the following translation: "Who is blind like the one being perfected?"

Recognizing the distinctive force of verbal form and meaning, the foregoing translation offers this fourfold analysis of the servant (Israel): (1) the servant was imperfect then, (2) the servant was to become perfect, (3) the change was a process in progress at that time, and (4) the change was (and is) being wrought by YHWH. I therefore conclude that this enigmatic verse guarantees that the servant *was and is being perfected as Israel*.

The second of the servant songs (Isa. 49:1-6) makes a distinctive contribution to the expanding picture of the servant of the LORD. The opening stanza confirms the earlier description of the servant's divine selection by

YHWH (vv. 1-3). Also, the lamentable confession of failure (Isa. 49:4) accurately confirms the deafness and blindness of the inept servant reflected in Isaiah 42:19.

Then verse 5 repeats the reference to divine ordination (from [the] womb)[27] and the call to be YHWH's servant (Isa. 49:3). The content of the verse appears to be superfluous, especially in the light of "though Israel be not gathered," a translation (KJV) that seems totally contradictory. NIV and others have acknowledged the plausibility of the marginal reading *lō* (לוֹ, "to him," so the *qĕrē*[28]) over *lōʾ* (לֹא, "not," in the *kĕtīb*), substituting the preposition with a pronominal suffix for the negative particle. Edward J. Young endorsed the procedure, "It is perhaps best to render, *and Israel will be gathered to him.* Thus there is a striking parallelism and an interesting chiastic arrangement."[29] This alteration not only relieves the apparent contradiction within verse 5, but it also clarifies its evident redundancy.

Verse 5 introduces the emergence of a *second servant* who will succeed where the first servant failed miserably. The disclosure of the second servant includes a forecast of his effecting the spiritual restoration of Israel (the "blind and deaf servant") that will result in his being "honored in the eyes of the LORD" (that is, the "second" servant). Verse 6 adds that he will be "a light for the Gentiles" and extend YHWH's salvation "to the ends of the earth." This perception, in my judgment, answers the question of servant identity as expressed by Orlinsky, "It has been noted by many scholars that it is simply impossible for 'Israel' to be original both in our verse 3 and also in verse 5: how can Israel be given a mission to Israel?"[30]

In the light of the foregoing, I propose that in chapters 41—49, the servant is (progressively): equated with Israel, personified within Israel, being perfected as Israel, but also distinguished from Israel. One other important feature is present in the last of the servant songs.

The final servant poem (Isa. 52:13—53:12), like the second and third songs (Isa. 49:1-6; 50:4-9), is embedded in the proposed problem-solution series of chapters 49—59, a sequence that is essentially a sin-salvation paradigm. This location marks the material as basically soteriological in character, but it also indicates two other important features. (1) It anchors the poem's content to the sin problem in Judah, and (2) it relates the poem's content to a messianic motif.

The difficulty reflected in the fourth problem of the series was Judah's sense of weakness. The nation's spiritual frailty is disclosed by her multiple pleas for divine strength and assistance:

"Awake, awake! Clothe yourself with strength, / O arm of the LORD; / awake, as in days gone by, / as in generations of old" (Isa. 51:9).

"Awake, awake! / Rise up, O Jerusalem, / you who have drunk from the hand of the LORD / the cup of his wrath" (Isa. 51:17).

"Awake, awake, O Zion, / clothe yourself with strength" (Isa. 52:1).

Notice in particular the appeal for a demonstration of strength by the "arm of the LORD." That entreaty correlates with the expression "arm of the LORD" (Isa. 53:1) of the fourth servant song. Just as the "Inspired Teacher,"[31] offered as the solution to the problem of a sense of alienation (Isa. 50:1-3), was also the servant in the third song (see Isa. 50:10), so the solution to the problem of weakness (the arm of the LORD) was the servant in the final poem.

That interrelationship firmly links the contents of the song to the historical circumstance in Isaiah's beloved Judah. Consequently, however one may apply or "principlize"[32] the message of this incomparable "anthem," its direct, intimate connection to Judah cannot be ignored. When the prophetic "lyrics" affirm, "Surely he took up our infirmities / and carried our sorrows" (Isa. 53:4), the principle of "vicarious atonement" may have universal application; but its primary frame of reference is "Judah-centered." In other words, the original antecedent for the collective pronominal suffixes attached to words such as "transgressions" and iniquities" was Judah. The initial "we" who could be healed by "his wounds" (Isa. 53:5) were the people who first received the redemptive message. That leads us to conclude that not only is the servant distinguished from Israel (Judah), but he is also the one who suffers *for* Israel.

The textual evidence then supports this profile:

The Servant of the LORD in Isaiah 41—53

Equated with Israel (41:8; 44:1-2; 44:21; 45:4; 49:3)
Personified within Israel (42:1-4)
Being perfected as Israel (42:19)
Distinguished from Israel (49:5)
Suffering for Israel (53:6)[33]

The "Vicarious" Question. Perhaps one other item should be considered before we make a specific identification proposal. Strange as it may seem, the concept of the innocent suffering for the guilty (in the fourth servant song) has been seriously challenged. Orlinsky totally and categorically rejected the notion:

> The aspect of vicariousness has been found in our chapter by theologian and scholar alike for nigh on two thousand years. But does this aspect really obtain in our text? Is the personage in chapter 53, whoever it may be, a *vicarius*: did he really act as a substitute for the guilty who deserved punishment because of their iniquity, but who escaped it because this personage, while himself innocent of sin, bore their punishment for them?
>
> It is remarkable how virtually every scholar dealing with the subject has merely taken it for granted that the principle of vicariousness is present in Isaiah 53 . . . No one proves it, everyone assumes it.[34]

Orlinsky then cited Eissfeldt, who wrote of the song's "discovery of the significance of vicarious death" and Torrey, who described it as "the most wonderful bit of religious poetry in all literature." Orlinsky implied that Eissfeldt was guilty of a "gratuitous assumption of vicariousness in this chapter" and responded to Torrey's appraisal with the caustic, "I wonder whether anyone has read the 'religious poetry in all literature!'" He also quoted but rejected Kissane's evaluation: " 'Here the servant is a sacrificial victim chosen by God to make expiation for the sins of men by his suffering and death . . . Jahweh's purpose . . . is fulfilled by the servant's vicarious suffering and death.'"[35]

It is interesting to note that Orlinsky refutes two thousand years of study and research by "theologian and scholar," flatly rejecting their evaluations. Furthermore, it apparently never occurred to him that the evidence in Isaiah 53 for vicarious suffering is so overwhelming that no one has felt obligated to "prove" it. Vicariousness has not been "assumed" in the text as Orlinsky charges; rather, it has simply been acknowledged—by practically everyone except Orlinsky!

Orlinsky's iconoclastic approach may be summarized in this statement:

> It is our contention that the concept of vicarious suffering and atonement is not to be found either here or anywhere else in the Bible; it is a concept that arose in Jewish and especially Christian circles of post-biblical times.[36]

Indeed, if Orlinsky cannot find vicariousness in Isaiah 53, one would hardly expect him to discover its presence anywhere else in the Bible.

Orlinsky's argument for rejecting vicarious suffering is basically two-fold. First, he appealed to the priority of the covenant with the Law's guilt-punishment pattern as an interpretive paradigm. He insisted that this fundamental model precluded a concept of vicariousness and added:

> Nowhere in the Hebrew Bible did anyone preach a doctrine—which would have superseded the covenant!—which allowed the sacrifice of the innocent in place of and as an acceptable substitution for the guilty.[37]

That statement is absolutely amazing since the concept of the sacrifice of the innocent as an acceptable substitute for the guilty is prominently featured in the Yom Kippur rites.[38] The Day of Atonement ceremony was, of course, a major religious observance associated with the covenant. Its symbolic provisions broke the fatalistic chain of guilt and penalty that would otherwise remain in effect. Accordingly, a salient feature of the covenant was a profound liturgy that pictured the resolution of the human sin problem in terms of the "sacrifice of the innocent."

Orlinsky evidently ignored the association, however, for, as evidence for the "absence of vicariousness in Second Isaiah," he cited Lattey's comment, " 'From the scapegoat I turn naturally to Isa. liii, which hardly calls for much expostion [sic], being such a clear case of vicarious solidarity.' "[39] Amazing, indeed!

Second, although Orlinsky transcribed (in English and Hebrew) the critical data in Isaiah 53:4-6, 11-12, his refutation of their obvious vicarious content consisted of the proposal that, had substitution been intended, the preposition *bě* (בְּ) would have been attached to the nouns (our) "transgressions" and (our) "iniquities" instead of the preposition *min* (מִן).[40] He completely disregarded "Surely he has borne our sickness and carried our pains" (Orlinsky's translation) of verse 4 and "he shall bear their iniquities" and "he bore the sins of many" in verses 11-12.

While Orlinsky may speculate about the change of prepositions, one wonders how he would imagine the author's language if he had intended to describe sacrificial substitution. It is difficult to anticipate how the writer of Isaiah 53 could have been any more explicit and precise. Ironically, Orlinsky is guilty of his own criticism. He assumes something but proves nothing.

Perhaps the major question, though, is, "Who is the prophet talking about?" John D. W. Watts offered a "dual identity" in his interpretative (amplified?) translation of Isaiah 53:10-12:

> Yahweh willed to bruise him.
>   He caused his sickness.
> If he (Darius) considers his soul a sin offering,
>   he (Darius) will see seed.
>   He will prolong days.
> And the will of Yahweh
>   succeeds in his (Darius') hand.
> Because of the travail of his (Zerubbabel's) soul,
>   he (Darius) will see. He will be satisfied.
> In knowing (about) him (Zerubbabel), he (Darius)
>   will justify (many).
> My servant (Darius) becomes a righteous one
>   for many,
>   and will forgive their wrongs.
> Therefore I allot to him (Zerubbabel) a share with
>   the many.
>   And he will share an allotment with the healthy,
> because he poured out his soul even to death
>   and was numbered with rebels.
> He himself bore the sins of many
>   and interceded for rebels.[41]

In a rather classic example of understatement, Watts acknowledged, "The arrangement adopted by this commentary places this passage in a specific historical setting."[42]

Watts's appraisal notwithstanding, and despite Orlinsky's charge of unscholarly dogmatic assertion, I am convinced that Young's identification (as cited by Orlinsky) is essentially correct:

> Who is the Servant? The answer, we believe, is that He is the
> redeemer Messiah whom God had long ago promised to His
> people as their Deliverer from sin. In other words, the Ser-
> vant is Jesus Christ. . . . The righteous Servant suffering for
> the sins of those who are unrighteous is a conception which
> could never have been conceived by the unaided mind of
> man. . . . If, therefore, we are to look for the sources of the
> idea of the Suffering Servant, we shall find them not in the
> religions of antiquity, but in a special revelation from God.[43]

"My Servant Will Act Wisely." The opening line to the
fourth servant song is remarkable. It makes a claim for
the servant (see "arm of the LORD," Isa. 53:1) that is both
magnificent and mystifying. The featured verb, a *Hiph'il*
built on the root *s-k-l* (שׂכל), is marked by a wide semantic
range. BDB lists six translation options: (1) "look at,"
(2) "consider," (3) "have insight," (4) "give insight," "teach,"
(5) "act prudently," and (6) "prosper," "have success."[44]
Louis Goldberg reports, "Of the seventy-four times the
verb form is used, all but two appear in the Hiphil stem."[45]
The two exceptions are 1 Samuel 18:30 (*Qal*) and Genesis
48:14 (*Pi'el*). BDB lists the *Pi'el* form under a hypothetical
s-k-l root,[46] but since the Genesis location is the only occurrence, such a distinction seems highly unlikely. Perhaps the basis for their distinction stems from the unusual
(apparently) meaning of the *Pi'el* usage, as opposed to the
more conventional meaning of the *Qal*.

In Genesis 48:14, the *Pi'el* participle of *s-k-l* was used to
describe the action of Israel's hands as he pronounced the
patriarchal blessing on the two sons of Joseph. The phrase
sōkkēl 'et yādāyv (שִׂכֵּל אֶת־יָדָיו) is translated by NIV as
"crossing his arms," which is preferable to KJV's "guiding
his hands wittingly." Joseph's positioning of Ephraim and
Manasseh (Gen. 48:13) was, in effect, canceled when Israel
placed his right hand on the head of the younger son and
his left on the elder. Obviously, then, the force of *sōkkēl 'et
yādāyv* explains the crossing of his hands in order to assign the elder's portion to Ephraim.

Any attempt to associate the divergent meanings of "exhibiting prudence" or "succeeding" with "lay crosswise" or
"plait" would be highly conjectural with the evidence now
available.[47] Still, the idea of weaving or blending dissimilar components together as a nuance of *yaskīl* ("act wisely")

fits beautifully in this servant song. The poem, like the other servant songs, is a study in paradox. The "Suffering Servant" (who is the arm of the Lord, an example of paradox) exhibits his timeless skill in the harmonizing of discordant contrasts. Muilenburg called attention to that distinctive pattern by observing that "the whole poem is dominated by the contrast between humiliation and suffering on the one hand, and exaltation and triumph on the other."[48]

If one accepts Muilenburg's analysis that the song is composed of five three-verse strophes,[49] then a striking chiastic structure (based on contrasts) may be projected. Note the skillful blending of apparent "irreconcilables":

Exaltation	52:13-15	Humiliation
Weakness	53:1-3	Strength
Peace	53:4-6	Punishment
Submission	53:7-9	Honor
Life	53:10-12	Death[50]

The Destiny of "My Servant." The immeasurable riches of this passage absolutely defy an acceptable analysis. At best, one can only conduct a surface exploration. Yet, even in a superficial examination, some extraordinary truths assert themselves. For example, in the first strophe (Isa. 52:13-15), the unmistakable emphasis is on the surprise created by the servant. Despite his appalling appearance (v. 14), even kings will shut their mouths because of him as they come to see and understand what they have not been told or heard. Thus he will "startle" ("sprinkle," according to NIV) many nations (v. 15).[51] "Marred" and "disfigured," the servant will astound earthly rulers and human wisdom, an amazing and unexpected feat indeed!

The second strophe (Isa. 53:1-3) emphasizes the strength of the servant who is the very arm of the LORD. Again, what a contrast! Like a "suckling" offshoot clinging to a parent stock or a fragile sprout out of dry, stony soil, the delicate "might" of the servant will hardly inspire awe or confidence. To the contrary, he will be without appeal or beauty. Despised and rejected, he will be characterized as a "man of sorrows." No wonder, then, that the prophet lamented, "Who can believe our message and to whom can the arm of the LORD be revealed?"[52] What a contradiction! As a later rabbi observed, "The weakness of God is stronger than man's strength" (1 Cor. 1:25).

While the specter of suffering lurks in every shadow of the poem, the third strophe (Isa. 53:4-6) focuses on the frightful element of pain. The verbs that characterize his suffering in verses 4-5 are awesome: "stricken" (נָגוּעַ), "smitten" (מֻכֵּה), "afflicted" (מְעֻנֶּה), "pierced" (מְחֹלָל), and "crushed" (מְדֻכָּא). The agony which the servant will endure, however, is not the consequence of his own misconduct. Rather, he will bear the infirmities and sorrows of others. The truly astounding result is that his punishment will provide peace and healing for others.

The fourth strophe (Isa. 53:7-9) calls attention to the willful submission of the servant to the brutal cruelties to be imposed upon him. According to the prophetic portrait, despite the flagrant violation of his human rights and monstrous misapplication of the judicial processes, the servant would go silently to his doom, like a "lamb to the slaughter." Then, in the ultimate travesty, despite his innocence, he would be cut off from the land of the living to be "assigned a grave with the wicked, and with the rich in his death." A veritable paragon of paradox!

The fifth and final strophe (Isa. 53:10-12) confidently predicts the salvation to be provided by the servant. Despite his pain and grief, in fact *because* of his vicarious pain and grief, the redemptive "will of the LORD will prosper in his hand" (v. 10). As a result of "the suffering of his soul" and the pouring out of his "life unto death," the righteous servant will come to justify many (vv. 11-12) by his knowledge. Ultimately the servant will be vindicated and, triumphant over death, will emerge victorious.

The Soteriological Application

By way of summary, let us evaluate some of the soteriological implications of this remarkable servant song. Volumes could be written on the subject, but at least two key items demand attention.

The Messianic Motif. Isaiah 52:13—53:12 is the last of the servant songs in the book, but it is also an integral component of the fourth solution in the problem-solution series of chapters 49—59. Accordingly, though it is a part of the total sequence, it is intimately and vitally connected to the "savior-solution" pattern of the series. As pointed out earlier, a messianic emblem is associated with each of the savior-solution models, so that the servant in this final poem is part of this kind of equation:

Problem vs. Solution = Messianic Symbol = Suffering Servant

Distinctive Associations. The final servant song prominently features the concept of vicarious suffering. That element was previously noted in our study of Yom Kippur in Leviticus 16, so the idea of substitutionary atonement is not altogether new in the unfolding salvation message. The song also indicates that faith is the basis for salvation: "by his knowledge my righteous servant will justify many" (v. 11). This, too, is a concept that was previously established.[53] So, while neither of these concepts is independently new, the Song of the Suffering Servant aligns them in a new and different way. According to this epic poem, salvation is to be experienced on the basis of *faith in a suffering redeemer* so that both faith and its legitimate object are correctly identified and associated.

One may reasonably ask, "But what distinguishes salvation in the Old Testament from that of the New Testament if the people of both covenants are saved on the basis of faith in a suffering and justifying redeemer?" The answer is simple: "Only time." The believers of the Old Testament were saved because they looked forward in faith to the coming Suffering Servant. We of the New Testament are saved because we look back in faith to the finished work of Calvary's Redeemer. All believers of all ages are saved because they look up in faith to the "Man of Sorrows."

> "Man of Sorrows!" what a name
> For the Son of God who came
> Ruined sinners to reclaim!
> Hallelujah, what a Savior!
>
> Bearing shame and scoffing rude,
> In my place condemned he stood;
> Seal'd my pardon with his blood;
> Hallelujah, what a Savior![54]

Notes

[1]See James Muilenburg for a discussion of the range of scholarly opinion about the number and location of the servant songs, "Introduction," in *The Book of Isaiah: Chapters 40—66*, in *The Interpreter's Bible*, vol. 5, ed. George Arthur Buttrick (New York: Abingdon-Cokesbury Press, 1951-57), 406.

[2]For opinions about individual song limits, see Muilenburg, "Introduction," 406. Note especially John Watts's reluctance to characterize Isaiah 50:4-9 as a "servant song" and his identification of the "speaker" in the text as "Darius's advocate and defender in Jerusalem," namely, Zerubbabel. See John D. W. Watts, *Isaiah 34—66*, vol. 25 in *Word Biblical Commentary*, ed. David A. Hubbard and Glenn W. Barker (Waco, TX: Word Books, Publisher, 1987), 197, 201.

[3]Muilenburg, "Introduction," 406.

[4]Claus Westermann, *Isaiah 40—66: A Commentary* (London: SCM Press, 1969), 20.

[5]Watts, *Teaching*, 286.

[6]Ibid.

[7]Compare with Watts's chart, *Teaching*, 293.

[8]See the chart "Problem-Solution Series" in this chapter.

[9]Muilenburg, "Introduction," 412.

[10]Ibid., 408.

[11]Ibid.

[12]Harry M. Orlinsky, "The So-Called 'Servant of the Lord' and 'Suffering Servant' in Second Isaiah," in *Studies on the Second Part of the Book of Isaiah* (Leiden: E. J. Brill, 1977), 118.

[13]Arvid S. Kapelrud, "The Identity of the Suffering Servant," in *Near Eastern Studies in Honor of William Foxwell Albright*, ed. Hans Goedicke (Baltimore: Johns Hopkins Press, 1971), 309–10.

[14]Ibid., 311.

[15]Norman H. Snaith, "Isaiah 40–66: A Study of the Teaching of the Second Isaiah and Its Consequences," in *Studies on the Second Part of the Book of Isaiah* (Leiden: E. J. Brill, 1977), 174.

[16]The Septuagint has Jacob (Ιακωβ) in Isaiah 42:1.

[17]See Isaiah 42:19; 49:4.

[18]Kapelrud noted that "the sharp distinction between individual and collective interpretation did not exist in ancient time." See Kapelrud, "Identity," 312. John Watts's attempt to identify the servant of Isaiah 49:1 with Cyrus (John Watts, *Isaiah 34—66*,117,119) is unconvincing. Granted, Cyrus is designated as YHWH's "shepherd" (Isa. 44:28) and His "anointed" (Isa. 45:1); but he is nowhere explicitly tagged as "servant." Moreover, despite the positive features attributed to Cyrus, he scarcely fits the magnificent profile projected in Isaiah 42:1-7. The self-descriptive boast, "I am Cyrus, king of the world, great king, legitimate king, king of Babylon, king of Sumer and Akkad, king of the four rims" contradicts the description of Cyrus as "quiet, pervasive, sensitive" (*Isaiah 34—66*, 119). See *Ancient Near Eastern Texts*, 2nd ed., ed. James B.

Pritchard (Princeton: Princeton University Press, 1955), 316. Compare Isaiah 42:6-7 with 9:2; 11:10; 61:1.

[19]See Isaiah 43:22-28.

[20]BDB, 1022-23. KB proposes **vergolten werden** (KB, 4:1421).

[21]LXX has οἱ κυριεύοντες αὐτῶν.

[22]James Muilenburg, "Exegesis," in *The Book of Isaiah: Chapters 40—66*, in *The Interpreter's Bible*, vol. 5, ed. George Arthur Buttrick (New York: Abingdon-Cokesbury Press, 1956), 476. Compare John Watts, *Isaiah 34—66*, 125-26.

[23]Muilenburg, "Exegesis," 476.

[24]See BDB, 1022 and KB, 4:1419 (**fertig, vollendet werden**). Note the *Pi'el* use of the verb in 1 Kings 9:25. The idea of "requite, recompense, reward" is likely an extended meaning.

[25]See BDB, 1023.

[26]Waltke and O'Connor, *Syntax*, 624.

[27]מִבֶּטֶן in verses 1, 5.

[28]See GKC, 65-67.

[29]Edward J. Young, *The Book of Isaiah* (Grand Rapids: William B. Eerdmans Publishing Company, 1978), 3:274.

[30]Orlinsky, "Second Isaiah," 85.

[31]A title "inspired" by the expression "an instructed tongue" (לְשׁוֹן לִמּוּדִים), Isaiah 50:4.

[32]Kaiser, *Exegetical Theology*, 152.

[33]Compare John Watts's identification of the servant as Israel, Cyrus, and "the believing and obedient worshipers who delight in Yahweh's new city that was built by the Persians for loyal Jews and their God" (returning exiles?). See John Watts, *Isaiah 34—66*, 117.

[34]Orlinsky, "Second Isaiah," 51.

[35]Ibid., 51-53.

[36]Ibid., 54.

[37]Ibid., 55.

[38]See chapter 8 of this book.

[39]Orlinsky, "Second Isaiah," 52.

[40]Ibid., 57.

[41]John D. W. Watts, *Isaiah 34—66*, vol. 25 in *Word Biblical Commentary*, ed. David A. Hubbard and Glenn W. Barker (Waco, TX: Word Books, Publisher, 1987), 225.

[42]Ibid., 233. Commitment to the immediate Persian historical context for correspondence has forced Watts, in our opinion, to draw strained and unwarranted parallels. He has allowed history to interpret the text rather than permit the text to affirm its own message. The result is "historical eisegesis."

[43]Orlinsky, "Second Isaiah," 66.

[44]BDB, 968. KB offers four options: (1) **verstehen**, "understand," (2) **Einsicht haben**, "have discernment," (3) **klug machen**, "show prudence," and (4) **Gelingen haben**, "have success" (KB, 4:1238).

[45]Louis Goldberg, "שָׂכַל," *TWOT*, 2:877.

[46]BDB, see under "II. שָׂכַל," 968.

Mighty to Save

[47]In a simple nomadic culture, however, the weaver's skill (note Arabic, *"plait* locks of hair" cited in BDB, 968) might be extended to include prudence and prosperity.

[48]Muilenburg, "Exegesis," 615.

[49]Muilenburg, "Introduction," 417.

[50]I am indebted to seminar notes under J. Wash Watts and J. Hardee Kennedy for this analysis.

[51]John Watts's comment explains the translational ambiguity, "MT יַזֶּה may be from נזה 'sprinkle' (BDB, 633, I) or may be a *hap. leg.* from an identical root related to Arab *nazā* 'startle,' 'cause to leap' (BDB, 633, II). LXX θαυμάσονται 'they will wonder' may suggest the latter derivation. . . . Read MT with the meaning 'startle.'" See John Watts, *Isaiah 34—66*, 225.

[52]Watts proposed that this is an example of a contrary-to-fact rhetorical question (*Syntax*, 48-49).

[53]See Genesis 4:26; 15:6.

[54]Philip P. Bliss, HALLELUJAH! WHAT A SAVIOR, 1875.

14

The Everlasting Covenant

Come to the waters.

Isaiah 55:1

The Old Testament has a subtle way of speaking to the universal by addressing the specific. The principle is illustrated in the opening invitation of Isaiah 55. The appeal to "all you who are thirsty" is formulated in concrete, "literal" terminology, but its implication obviously transcends mere physical thirst.

Yet, how appropriate is the analogy! Few appetites or drives compare to the compulsive desire for water that consumes one who is completely without liquid nourishment. Fortunately, not many are ever subjected to the ordeal of extended thirst. All who have endured that kind of privation can readily understand the attachment of adjectival modifiers like "blazing" or "raging" to the term "thirst." This kind of description is not altogether hyperbole or simply metaphorical. Rather, such terms accurately describe the burning urge for moisture. So this monumental invitation addresses the characteristic yearning and longing of the human spirit in terms of an appeal to the "thirsty." Immediate and concrete but, at the same time, ageless and universal!

Covenant Occasion

The invitation of Isaiah 55:1 introduces the offer of a covenant that is designated as "everlasting." The essential ingredients of the pledge are contained in Isaiah 55:1-7. As fascinating as the contents of this section alone may be, the context is of vital importance to a correct understanding of the "everlasting covenant."

The covenant package of Isaiah 55 is part of the larger "problem-solution" series in chapters 49—59, a sequence already noted.[1] As the prior analysis suggests, the pledge that featured the "sure mercies" of David (Isa. 55:3, KJV) is the response (solution) to the sense of desolation (problem) expressed by Judah (Isa. 54:1). Accordingly, the nature of Judah's difficulty that prompted the covenant offer justifies consideration.

The Desolation of Barrenness. The sense of desolation that plagued Judah, though not specifically defined, is graphically depicted in chapter 54 by three figures or images. The first is the figure of the childless Hebrew wife (a barren woman[2] who never bore a child, Isa. 54:1). On the surface, that unique dilemma might seem to have a highly restricted field of application. Still, the example of childless Hebrew wives in the Old Testament is worth noting. Sarai (Sarah), for example, was so distraught about her barrenness that she constrained her husband, Abram (Abraham), to bear children by her maidservant, Hagar (Gen. 16:1-4).[3] Later, Rachel, fretting under the embarrassment of childlessness and jealous of her fruitful sister, Leah, made an unreasonable demand of Jacob: "Give me children, or I'll die!" (Gen. 30:1). Even the saintly Hannah agonized under the burden of barrenness (1 Sam. 1:1-18).

In an age of growing disdain for the sacred responsibility of marriage and family, how is one to understand this strong preoccupation with childbearing? Perhaps the Old Testament itself contains a clue. Mark the word from the psalmist, "Sons are a heritage from the Lord, / children a reward from him" (Ps. 127:3). The simple, terse statement transfers the producing of offspring from the realm of "freedom of choice," home economics, tax deductions, and financial responsibility to a decidedly religious and spiritual domain. Moreover, ancient Israelite women, like the three mentioned above, evidently understood that and recognized their motherhood role as a distinct badge of honor with a special YHWH ("Source of Life") connection.

To women like that, the veritable miracle of fostering life was considerably more than a fringe benefit (or burden) of the marriage arrangement. For them, it was part of their unique contribution to life itself. Bearing children was not a duty to be endured; rather, it was an honor to be cherished. Therefore, when an ancient Hebrew wife found herself to be childless, evidently she felt that she was missing a vital part of the very purpose of life. That perspective would explain the tortured anguish of a woman like Hannah.

In our modern, sophisticated culture, not many will find much in common with an ancient, childless Hebrew wife. If we perceive her problem to be related to her understanding of the meaning and purpose of life, we suddenly have more in common than we might like to admit. Even the young ponder the haunting questions, "Who am I and why am I here? What does it all mean?" Young and old alike, we are hounded by the nagging suspicion that life is passing us by. So we worry, "Have I missed the boat?" Then, as if to avoid the answer, we grasp frantically for straws of pleasure, bravely shout, "Bring on the clowns!" and struggle to live life to its fullest. Yet, in the inevitable crunch of pain, grief, and death, we find ourselves desolate—like "the barren woman who never bore a child."

The Desolation of Widowhood. Judah's sense of desolation is further defined by the reference to "the reproach of your widowhood" (Isa. 54:4). Again, a common point of contact seems highly elusive. At best, the modern individual can scarcely imagine the fear, anxiety, and emptiness that an Israelite wife must have felt following the loss of her husband. Her sense of isolation was probably intensified by the relatively primitive culture of her day (no garden clubs, tour groups, or single-parent organizations). Even today, the loss of a spouse can be devastating. While I cannot fully empathize with a woman's grief over the loss of her husband, I can, through painful experience, sense the hollow, empty feeling that numbs the soul and spirit when the companion of the years lies silent in death. Life and the future loom like some dark, bottomless pit when one is left alone. That brings us to the key word: "alone."

"Alone," of course, identifies the concept of loneliness, conceivably the most chronic "social disease" of our time. Loneliness involves considerably more than simple seclusion, as debilitating as isolation may be. It is possible to be lonely in a crowd; indeed, throngs of people may only intensify the inner sense of quarantine and separation. Being alone does not necessarily produce loneliness, but loneliness definitely spawns a sense of being alone. So, regardless of time, setting, or gender, anyone who feels lonely will have a lonesome point of contact with the "reproach of . . . widowhood."

The Desolation of Affliction. NIV has translated the feminine 'ăniyyāh (עֲנִיָּה, Isa. 54:11) as "O afflicted city." The gender of the term corresponds to that of city ('îr, עִיר) and Zion or Jerusalem, though none of those words are used in the immediate context. Still, the references to "foundations," "battlements," "gates," and "walls" (Isa. 54:11-12) would appear to presuppose one (or all) of the above. However, all the feminine gender terms used until verse 11 seem to apply to the "desolate woman" of verse 1.[4] It may be possible, then, that one metaphorical symbol merges into another in verse 11.

In any event, the stress of "affliction" is described as the equivalent of "being storm tossed" (סֹעֲרָה).[5] While the verb (סָעַר) may characterize the savage activity of a tempest in the Book of Jonah (Jonah 1:11), it also describes, as in this instance, the impact of its fury. "Affliction," then, is to be construed in terms of the turbulence produced by a rampaging storm. That imagery, plus the extension "not comforted" and the parallel in Jonah, combine to suggest a disturbance at sea. That scenario is more compatible with the personal metaphor (desolate woman) than a geographical or institutional identification (city or Zion).

The "ocean gale" setting also corresponds to the simile used later in the larger context: "But the wicked are like the tossing sea, / which cannot rest, / whose waves cast up mire and mud. / 'There is no peace,' says my God, 'for the wicked'" (Isa. 57:20-21).[6]

Perhaps only those who have felt a ship shudder under the crushing impact of rolling, mountainous, wind-driven waves, or watched the heaving, restless billows of the open sea in constant motion can fully appreciate the analogy. The concrete expression describes more than tossing waves; it also captures the intrinsic and internal turbulence of the ungodly. "The wicked are like the tossing sea, / which cannot rest" (Isa. 57:20). Even so, the "storm-tossed" (the wicked) experience no rest, no tranquillity, no serenity, no peace.

Is it possible, then, that the ancient recipient of the message in Isaiah 54 (like the modern reader) slowly realized that its subject matter had to do with more than lonely women and storm-weary sailors? For those who recognized the meaninglessness, loneliness, and restlessness of their own lives, the offer of the "everlasting covenant" must have provided a marvelous word of hope.

Covenant Distinction

The formula "everlasting covenant," a translation of *běrīt ʿōlām* (בְּרִית עוֹלָם), is a rather unique expression, but it occurs often enough in the Old Testament to require some clarification. Accordingly, a brief survey of its use is in order. In Genesis 9:16, *běrīt ʿōlām* was used to designate God's pledge to Noah and "all living creatures of every kind on the earth" to refrain from sending another flood. In Exodus 31:16 and Leviticus 24:8 it was applied to Sabbath observance and ceremony, with *ʿōlām* apparently meaning "perpetual" or "lasting" rather than "eternal."

David, reflecting on the promise made to him by YHWH,[7] described it as a *běrīt ʿōlām* (2 Sam. 23:5), and his perception is confirmed in Psalm 89:28,34. In Jeremiah 32:40 the formula refers to an arrangement with a restored Israel,[8] and in Jeremiah 50:5 it is part of a statement attributed to returning exiles. Restored Jerusalem and reunified Israel and Judah are the respective beneficiaries in Ezekiel 16:60; 37:26. In Psalm 105:9-10 and 1 Chronicles 16:16-17 *běrīt ʿōlām* refers to the promise made to the patriarchs concerning possession of the land of Canaan.

The use of the expression in Isaiah 24:5 is especially important, for there it is described as being broken (*hēperu*, הֵפֵרוּ) by the people of earth. Franz Delitzsch suggested that in this instance *běrīt 'ōlām* may refer to the covenant with Noah,[9] while Young proposed:

> The frustrating of the covenant is something universal. For this reason we may adopt the position that the eternal covenant here spoken of designates the fact that God has given His Law and ordinances to Adam, and in Adam to all mankind.[10]

As stated previously,[11] I have difficulty accepting the concept of an Adamic Covenant in the early chapters of Genesis since nothing in the text mentions or even alludes to a covenant. Still, Young's awareness that in Isaiah 24 the covenant violation is "something universal" correlates with the tenor of the context. Despite R. B. Y. Scott's insistence that "it is highly unlikely that the inhabitants of the whole earth are held responsible for transgressing **the laws, . . . the statutes . . . the everlasting covenant** of Israel,"[12] the terminology and scenario of the chapter are decidedly cosmic in scope.[13]

The universal accountability reflected in the Isaian text then corresponds rather remarkably to Paul's sweeping indictment that "men are without excuse" (Rom. 1:20). The comment by F. Leroy Forlines (on Rom. 2:14-15) is apropos:

> By nature refers to that which is designed by God into the moral constitution of a human being. It is that which he knows in his own rational and moral constitution apart from having received the written revelation of God. . . .
> The law of the heart does not speak with the clarity of written law. But it does speak with a force that cannot be totally silenced. Men need the clarification that the written law gives, but whenever the written law is presented, to those who have never heard it, it will never be addressed to a moral blank.[14]

I submit, therefore, that the *běrīt 'ōlām* in Isaiah 24 refers to mankind's "moral constitution," making this particular use of the term unique and special.

The various uses of *běrīt 'ōlām* make it clear that identical form (much less similar form) does not necessarily guarantee identical meaning. Critical factors in each context must be examined and attention directed to differences as well as parallels, whatever their nature. I conclude, therefore, that *bĕrīt 'ōlām* as employed in Isaiah 55 is distinct from the other uses of the term that we have considered, including the meaning in Isaiah 24.

Ḥasdē dāvid. The association of David with *bĕrīt 'ōlām* in Isaiah 55 would seem to contradict the foregoing evaluation. However, the label alone (*Ḥasdē dāvid*, חַסְדֵי דָוִד) does not signify per se that this is a reference to the Davidic Covenant. As a matter of fact, the personal name is used in connection with the preceding word, creating a special syntactical arrangement called a construct chain. Lambdin explained the meaning of the phenomenon:

> There is in BH no preposition having the same range of meaning expressed by English "of." The of-relationship, the genitive case of the classical languages, has its correspondent in the construct chain. . . . The simple juxtaposition of two nouns serves to mark a modifying relationship. The first noun in such a chain is said to be in the construct state. In more modern terminology, the first noun occurs in a bound form as opposed to the normal or free form (absolute) used elsewhere.[15]

As a result of this syntactical bond, the two terms must be understood as a single expression.

The word linked with "David" is the plural form of the masculine noun, *hesed*. In this instance, NIV translated *hesed* as "faithful love." Translations vary, even within the same version.[16] Snaith, however, while acknowledging that *hesed* might include "loving-kindness" and "mercy," offered the opinion that its basic thrust was much stronger than that. He wrote:

> The original use of the Hebrew *chesed* is to denote that attitude of loyalty and faithfulness which both parties to a covenant should observe towards each other. . . . The word means "faithfulness" rather than "kindness," for we find the word to involve, in almost every case, a substratum of fixed, determined, almost stubborn steadfastness. If therefore we were compelled to choose one word in a case where the exact significance was not made clear by the context, we should choose "faithfulness" in preference to "kindness." The best word is "covenant-love."[17]

I concur, essentially, with Snaith's appraisal but prefer to link the obvious covenant orientation of the term with its "faithfulness" aspect. I therefore suggest the translation, "covenant loyalty."

George A. F. Knight called attention to the fact that the term is plural in Isaiah 55:3:

> Finally we should note an interesting grammatical question. The word for *steadfast love* here is written in the plural in the Hebrew. This is an unusual form. Most expositors regard it as an intensive plural. It may very well be such. Yet it may also be what grammarians call a distributive plural. If so, then by means of it DI declares the oneness of God's covenant love, first, between himself and David and, second, between himself and each and every member of Israel as the people of God.[18]

Knight's understanding of the force of the construct chain (*hasdē dāvid*) matches the interpretative translation of NIV, "my faithful love promised to David."

However, the case is not "open and shut." Waltke and O'Connor cautioned about the flexibility of this type of arrangement:

> English periphrastic genitives, in fact, show some of the same complexity of meaning characteristic of Hebrew construct chains. The phrase "love of God" . . . is ambiguous in both languages; it may mean either "God's love (for someone)" or "(someone's) love for God."[19]

Consequently, while the couplet might describe the "covenant loyalty" promised to or enjoyed by David, it could also reflect the covenant loyalty demonstrated by David. The incident with Mephibosheth, for example, not only illustrates the covenant connection of *hesed*. It also exhibits David's faithfulness regarding his pledge to the deceased Jonathan.[20] Either way, the use of *hasdē dāvid* communicates the certainty of the covenant provisions and guarantees its dependability.

Covenant Scope

The invitation to covenant participation is couched in universal and expansive language. Introduced by the interjection *hōy* (הוֹי), the appeal echoes the ringing call of a street peddler, hawking his wares. Young directed attention to a parallel: "In Oriental countries where water is scarce, water is sold by a vendor, who calls out attracting attention to his ware."[21] Here, however, the great covenant

Vendor is none other than YHWH Himself. The call is first directed (Isa. 55:1*a*) to all who experience thirst, a recurrent and common need. It is then expanded to include the hungry and the dissatisfied (Isa. 55:2). The astounding feature of the appeal, though, is the fact that "water," "wine," "milk," and "bread" are offered "without money and without cost."

Whatever the symbolism of the advertised goods may be, two things about the invitation are clear. (1) The offer is directed to any and all who have need, and (2) the covenant benefits are free! These features clearly distinguish the *bĕrīt 'ōlām* of Isaiah 55 from most of the other everlasting covenants in the Old Testament.

Covenant Appeal

The announcement of the marvelous provisions of this Everlasting Covenant is framed in a series of verb forms expressing the divine volition. These verbs include imperatives, jussives, and a solitary but significant cohortative. The imperative "come" (לְכוּ) is used four times (three times in the first verse alone). "Buy" (שִׁבְרוּ) occurs twice. Other imperatives are "listen" (שִׁמְעוּ), "eat" (אִכְלוּ), "give ear" (הַטּוּ אָזְנְכֶם), plus "seek" (דִּרְשׁוּ) and "call" (קְרָאֻהוּ) in verse 6.

The strong thrust of these multiple imperatives is moderated a bit, however, by the four jussives that are interspersed (in vv. 2,3,7). Although the final verb in verse 2 has no distinctive jussive ("short form"),[22] KJV's translation ("let . . . delight") of *vĕtit'annag* (וְתִתְעַנַּג) is preferable to that of NIV, which reflects the indicative mood ("will delight"). The simple *ševa* (*shewa*) attached to the imperfect form communicates either subordination ("in order that [your soul] may delight") or coordination that would, in this case, indicate a mood that is parallel (or coordinate) with the preceding verb, an imperative.[23] The case for a jussive interpretation of the final verb in verse 2 is strengthened by the fact that the verb *ūtĕḥi* (וּתְחִי) in verse 3 (also with "your soul" as its subject) is an explicitly shortened jussive form with a simple *shewa*. Without question *ūtĕḥi* is a jussive,[24] and I suggest that the translation of the jussives should read, "let your soul delight . . . " and "let your soul live."

Waltke and O'Connor described the potential force of the jussive: "When a superior uses the jussive with reference to an inferior the volitional force may be command, . . . exhortation, . . . counsel, . . . or invitation or permission."[25] In the light of the options suggested, the exact force of these jussives remains vague. The possible nuance of *větit'annag* and *ūtĕḥi* is conditioned by the influence of the cohortative *vě'ekrĕtāh* (וְאֶכְרְתָה) in verse 3. The verb is unquestionably cohortative in form and probably "connotes request."[26] Young's translation indicates, "let me make with you an eternal covenant."[27] Accordingly, I propose that the combination of jussives and the cohortative soften the imperatives and transform an edict into an entreaty.

Covenant Provisions

The blessings promised in the Everlasting Covenant[28] are noteworthy. Although covenant features center in Isaiah 55:1-7, key items in chapters 54 and 56 must also be acknowledged.

Peace. Isaiah was a master of introducing a thought or concept in abbreviated "seed form" and then elaborating its significance later. An example of this rhetorical device is illustrated in his use of the word "glory" (כָּבוֹד). In Isaiah 4:5 he introduced the expression in cryptic fashion ("over all the glory will be a canopy") without any clear suggestion as to its range of meaning. Later he returned to the glory concept, embellished it with messianic connotation in 40:5, and then used it as the theme of the closing chapters of his book (chapters 60—66), the magnificent "glory stanzas."

The slightly enigmatic phrase (בְּרִית שְׁלוֹמִי), "my covenant of peace" (Isa. 54:10), is perhaps another demonstration of the literary technique just described. Nothing in the (immediate) preceding context provides any kind of antecedent for this use of covenant.[29] Because of the perceived unity of the passage (Isa. 54:1 – 56:8), I submit that this is an anticipation of the Everlasting Covenant which is formally introduced in the following chapter. Otherwise, two separate covenants are present in the same context without any explanation or evidence of discrimination.

If that is true, then "peace" is to be construed as a distinctive hallmark of the Everlasting Covenant. That benefit serves as an appropriate counterpoint to the legacy of the wicked to be cited later (Isa. 57:20–21) and addresses the "storm-tossed" of Isaiah 54:11. The peace element also hearkens back to the prophet's earlier declaration, "You will keep in perfect peace / him whose mind is steadfast, / because he trusts in you" (Isa. 26:3).[30] However one may perceive the meaning of peace (*šālōm*, שָׁלוֹם), be it absence of strife (Isa. 32:18), "rest" (Ps. 38:3, KJV), "welfare" (Gen. 43:27, KJV), or as a general description of the redemptive state,[31] *šālōm* is a major (and precious) provision of the Everlasting Covenant. Somehow the words of the Teacher from Nazareth seem to fit this context: "Peace I leave with you; my peace I give you" (John 14:27).

True Satisfaction. The appeal chides those who squander their "labor on what does not satisfy" (Isa. 55:2). In direct contrast, the Everlasting Covenant promises guaranteed satisfaction. Genuine gratification is promised by the formula "delight in the richest fare." Actually, "let your soul delight itself in fatness" (וְתִתְעַנַּג בַּדֶּשֶׁן נַפְשְׁכֶם) is closer to the concrete language of the text.[32] Although the idiom is hardly attractive to Western palates, the expression offered the prospect of a savory and delectable feast to the ancient oriental. Knight commented:

> To *delight yourselves in fatness* meant enjoying what, to the easterner, was the best of the meat, the fatty parts of the fatted calf or sheep, or else any food that has been cooked in olive oil. For these were both considered the greatest delicacies of which a humble farm worker or artisan could hope to partake.[33]

Young offered this evaluation:

> *Fatness* stands for the best of luxuriant food, in contrast to the leanness and nothingness of what the people were striving after, just as *good* in contrast to *not bread* signifies what is genuinely good.[34]

The force of the expression represents the prospect of satisfaction to the fullest. Again, a word delivered by the Galilean leaps quickly to mind: "I am the bread of life. He who comes to me will never go hungry, and he who believes in me will never be thirsty" (John 6:35).

Life. The encouragement to let "your soul . . . live" (Isa. 55:3) clearly extends the promise of life in and through the covenant. Arthur Sumner Herbert, calling attention to the parallel in John 10:10 ("I have come that they may have life, and have it to the full"), proposed an expanded translation. "The Hebrew might be translated 'you shall have abundant life.'"[35] Although no specific term is in the text to support Herbert's recommendation, neither is there anything present to preclude his interpretation. In any event, the invitation to life is a remarkable response to the choking death mist that evidently swirled around the bereft widow of Isaiah 54:4. As in other soteriological scenarios of the Old Testament,[36] life is a salvation benefit of the Everlasting Covenant.

Abundant Pardon. NIV has reflected the clause *yarbeh lislōaḥ* (יַרְבֶּה־לִסְלוֹחַ, Isa. 55:7b) in the translation "freely pardon." Young's translation preserves the presence and force of the infinitive construct (*lislōaḥ*), "he will multiply to pardon."[37] Either way, the stress is on the magnitude of forgiving, redeeming grace in the covenant. As the need was great, the scope of pardon was greater. Even in ancient Judah, "Where sin increased, grace increased all the more" (Rom. 5:20).

Universal and Full Acceptance. A truly revolutionary aspect of the Everlasting Covenant is presented in Isaiah 56:3-8. The magnanimous and expansive invitation strongly suggested a universal offering (Isa. 55:1-3), but the specific historical setting and restrictions of the context hinted that "universal" meant "universal within Judah." However, these verses decisively and explicitly extended covenant participation to "foreigners" (בֶּן־הַנֵּכָר) and "eunuchs" (הַסָּרִיס), thus indicating that it was both international and fully universal in the truest sense.

The alien and the maimed had been denied ritual participation under the old code (Deut. 23:1-3), but now they were specifically included in the Everlasting Covenant (designated "my covenant" in Isa. 56:4,6). The language was unmistakable: no racial distinctions or physical disqualifications. Observe the degree of acceptance and the magnitude of pardon, "To them I will give within my temple and its walls / a memorial and a name / better than sons and daughters; / I will give them an everlasting name/ that will not be cut off" (Isa. 56:5). Remarkable indeed!

To be sure, the Everlasting Covenant is firmly locked into its original setting, meaning that it was directed primarily to beleaguered Judah. However, as if it anticipated the focus of the gospel in the New Testament ("first for the Jew, then for the Gentile," Rom. 1:16), the Everlasting Covenant expanded the parameters of grace to embrace those "who were far away," even "foreigners and aliens" (Eph. 2:17,19). Perhaps it is not incidental, then, that the first "outside" convert to the Christian faith was an Ethiopian eunuch (Acts 8:36-39).[38]

Covenant Agent

Another striking feature of the Everlasting Covenant is the elusive presence of a character who plays a vital part in the implementation of the covenant. Projected as the means by which benefits are to be confirmed, he is simply designated as "David."

Identification. Even if one assigns this verse (Isa. 55:3) to the pen of Isaiah, the eighth-century (B.C.) prophet of Jerusalem, David the son of Jesse had already been dead for over two hundred years.[39] It seems highly unlikely that the writer had Saul's successor to the throne of Israel in mind. In what way, then, is one to understand the reference to David? Muilenburg offered this counsel:

> Is this a reference to the Messiah, the messianic David (Jer. 30:9; Ezek. 34:23–24)? Many scholars (Duhm, Haller, Skinner, Torrey) think so. But the construction of the strophe shows very clearly that the emphasis falls not primarily on David but upon the people of Israel.[40]

As Muilenburg noted, however, other prophetic materials clearly catalogued "David" as a messianic symbol. The locations that he cited (but did not quote) present convincing evidence that both Jeremiah and Ezekiel used the "David" label in a messianic sense. Jeremiah, for example, forecast that a restored and reunited Israel and Judah (Jer. 30:3) would come to "serve the LORD their God / and

David their king,/ whom I will raise up for them" (Jer. 30:9). Through Ezekiel (in a similar context of restoration, Ezek. 34:13-14), the Lord promised:

"I will place over them one shepherd, my servant David, and he will tend them; he will tend them and be their shepherd. I the LORD will be their God, and my servant David will be prince among them. I the LORD have spoken" (Ezek. 34:23-24).

The eschatological framework of both passage helps to identify a messianic flavor in the Davidic motif. Other examples could illustrate the same concept (Hos. 3:5; Amos 9:11), but these are sufficient to demonstrate the prophetic application of the term.

Although a general prophetic pattern would not necessarily dictate Isaiah's use of the term, earlier references in the Book of Isaiah strongly suggest that he employed the label in much the same way as his colleagues. That is surely demonstrated in one of Isaiah's most memorable citations:

"For to us a child is born, / to us a son is given, / and the government will be on his shoulders. / And he will be called / Wonderful Counselor, Mighty God, / Everlasting Father, Prince of Peace. / Of the increase of his government and peace / there will be no end. / He will reign on David's throne / and over his kingdom, / establishing and upholding it / with justice and righteousness / from that time on and forever" (Isa. 9:6-7).

In another impressive messianic passage, Isaiah declared, "A shoot will come up from the stump of Jesse; / from his roots a Branch will bear fruit" (Isa. 11:1). The allusion to the offspring of Jesse, coupled with the "Branch" emblem (also a messianic label),[41] provides a specific "David = Messiah" equation. Accordingly, these instances establish a clear messianic antecedent in Isaiah for the use of the name David in chapter 55.

Another factor in the identification process is the witness of the larger context: the problem-solution series in Isaiah 49—59. As previously noted,[42] a messianic emblem is prominently associated with each of the solution elements including: (1) the Second Servant (Isa. 49:5), (2) the Ensign to the Nations (Isa. 49:22),[43] (3) The Inspired Teacher (Isa. 50:4), (4) the Arm of YHWH (Isa. 53:1),

(5) the Sure Mercies of David (Isa. 55:3, KJV), (6) the Inhabitant of Eternity (Isa. 57:15), and (7) Zion's Redeemer (Isa. 59:20). The "David" reference is fifth in the series, and the messianic motif is so pronounced in the overall sequence that to reject the David = Messiah equation is unwarranted. Roland Kenneth Harrison construed the use of David in chapter 55 as a vital link in the messianic king-servant motif:

> Thus the Messiah, who had appeared in earlier passages as a king of the Davidic lineage, was subsequently described in terms of the divine Servant. Yet the fact that David was referred to in Isaiah 55:3 makes it clear that the earlier concept had not been abandoned in favor of the later one.[44]

I therefore conclude that the total evidence confirms that the David reference in Isaiah 55:3 was an unmistakable description of Messiah. Accordingly, this is a designation of the "Second" or "Ideal David."[45]

Performance. A performance analysis of the David in Isaiah 55 supports the Messiah connection. In the line "I have made him (*nĕtattīv*, נְתַתִּיו[46]) a witness to the peoples," the pronoun "him" obviously refers back to David. Consequently, the Ideal David is projected as a witness, leader, and commander of the peoples (Isa. 55:4). This strategic role coincides with other Isaian descriptions of the messianic destiny (Isa. 49:6).

Verse 5, however, presents something of a problem. Despite Muilenburg's insistence that the strophe (of which this verse is a part) "shows very clearly that the emphasis falls" on Israel,[47] the precise force of the text is not altogether certain. NIV has this translation (with slight editing for the sake of clarity): "Surely *you* will summon nations *you* know not, / and nations that do not know *you* will hasten to *you*, / because of the LORD *your* God, / the Holy One of Israel, / for he has endowed *you* with splendor" (Isa. 55:5).

The first five pronouns that are underlined in the translation (two are a part of the verbal conjugation and three are pronominal suffixes) are second masculine singular in form. Apparently the antecedent for these pronouns it the "him" of verse 4 that, in turn, is derived from "David" in verse 3. These would then refer back to David.

The problem centers, though, in the final pronoun, you. Knight construed the form as second feminine singular.

"DI suddenly and unexpectedly employs the feminine form of the word *you*. In this context, *you* can naturally be no other than Zion, the people whom God has chosen to be his Servant and his Bride at once."[48] While I would reject his identification of Zion with the Servant in this context, I concede that the *you* of the text might indeed be second feminine singular. Actually a pronominal suffix attached to the verb (*pē'ǎrāk*, פְּאֲרָךְ), the vocalized form could be feminine singular, but according to GKC the pattern is rare.[49] If that position is adopted, the nearest antecedent in the text would have to be the second feminine singular suffix in Isaiah 54:17 that alludes to the "desolate woman-Jerusalem-Zion."

The form could also be second masculine singular because the word occurs at the end of the verse and is, thereby, "in pause," a factor that influences the normal vocalization of the word.[50] The form, as vocalized, is unclear; it could be either feminine or masculine. However, if the masculine gender of the pronoun is accepted, then the use of the conjunction (*vāv*) with "Holy One of Israel" takes on additional possibilities. Normally used in the sense of coordination (the equivalent of the English "and"), the Hebrew conjunction may also function with an *"explicative"* or *"emphatic"* sense.[51] If that is its function here, then it probably refers back to the "him" of verse 4 and the "David" of verse 3. That premise is reinforced by the singular use of *lěma'an* (עְ"מ"ל) preceding YHWH,[52] suggesting this translation: "nations that do not know you will hasten to you, even the Holy One of Israel, because of the Lord your God, for he will endow you with splendor."

Admittedly, the evidence is not conclusive, but it is certainly admissible. Furthermore, it provides a plausible translation and interpretation that are consistent with the grammatical and syntactical data in the text.

Covenant Conditions

While the magnificent appeal of the covenant was universal in scope and addressed to all in need, it also included significant requirements.

Timely Response. The imperatives "seek" and "call" in verse 6 are modified by the two temporal clauses "while he may be found" (בְּהִמָּצְאוֹ) and "while he is near" (בִּהְיוֹתוֹ קָרוֹב). The restrictions did not impose ritualistic, religious, or moral limitations on the covenant invitation. "Seek," like "call," implied the dimension of trust and surrender rather than suggesting some merit to be earned.[53] The clauses did, however, spell out a temporal and circumstantial condition. The covenant, if accepted at all, would be on God's terms. As generous and extravagant as the overtures of His grace might be, it was clear that people must respond to His divine initiative, at the season of His choice.

True Repentance. It is interesting to observe that the verse which specified "abundant pardon" also spelled out the requirement of repentance (Isa. 55:7). The limitation focused on intent, not conduct. It did not require that the "wicked" actually change "his way" or that the "evil man" master "his thoughts." It did specify, though, that "turning to the LORD" (וְיָשֹׁב אֶל־יְהוָה) involved the intentional abandonment of acts ("his way," דַּרְכּוֹ) and attitudes of disobedience ("his thoughts," מַחְשְׁבֹתָיו). To participate in the Everlasting Covenant, one had to make a fundamental choice of loyalty and allegiance.

Covenant Guarantee

"Money-back guarantee" is a popular sales slogan. Still, despite the appealing phraseology, common sense assures us that on product is better than the integrity of its manufacturer. That consideration would certainly suggest that the Everlasting Covenant was based on more than grandiose promises, especially in light of the information contained in Isaiah 55:8-13.

Superior Design. According to Isaiah 55:8-9, the genius that inspired the covenant provisions was superior to conventional human inspiration as "the heavens are higher than the earth" (v. 9). Since the designer of the Everlasting Covenant was the master Architect of the Ages, surely the design would be infinitely superior to any and all other options. The superlative quality of this particular "merchandise" calls to mind Isaiah's earlier haunting questions, "Whom did the Lord consult to enlighten him, / and who taught him the right way? / Who was it that taught him knowledge / or showed him the path of understanding?" (Isa. 40:14). On the basis of the "quality control" of the end "product," then, one would have to conclude that the covenant was superior on the basis of its origin.

Certain Pledge. Now and again, the slogan just mentioned is reinforced by the word of a salesman, a celebrity, or even a CEO-type with the highly convincing, "I personally guarantee it." Pardon the technical expression, but, "Wow!"

In Isaiah 55:10-11, YHWH Himself laid His personal powerful, productive, and eternal Word on the line in support of His covenant pledge. In this instance, a promise "as good as his word" was not some ludicrous, hollow boast. Mountains may crumble, seasons may change, grass may wither, and flowers may fall, but the "word of our God stands forever" (Isa. 40:8).

Eternal Warranty. Warranties are frequently geared to time, mileage, and / or use, with strictly "unlimited warranty" a rare commodity indeed. Since a guarantee is no better or durable than the manufacturer that stands behind it, very few (if any) goods are pledged to last forever. Contrast that with the description of the Everlasting Covenant in Isaiah 55:12-13, with italics added:

"You will go out in joy / and be led forth in peace; / the mountains and hills / will burst into song before you, / and all the trees of the field / will clap their hands. / Instead of the thornbush will grow the pine tree, / and instead of briers the myrtle will grow. / This will be for the LORD's renown, / for an *everlasting sign*, / *which will not be destroyed*."

Wonder of wonders, the marvelous benefits of the Everlasting Covenant, conveyed in terms of the transformation of nature, would be immutable and eternal! Till the end of time and beyond, the blessing of covenant participation will endure.

Covenant Application

běrīt 'ōlām quite clearly encompassed an expanded and profound soteriological truth. The understanding and response of Isaiah's original audience to its challenge is unknown, but the covenant's disclosure remains a highwater mark in the Old Testament's widening and deepening stream of salvation.

Immediate Application. By virtue of the syntactical and rhetorical cohesion of the total context, I must insist that the covenant beamed its redemptive message directly to Judah. This covenant was not the codification of some abstract theological speculation. The need it addressed was immediate and urgent; even so, the deliverance it promised was immediate and urgent. The prophet's appeal and exhortation were as heartfelt and impassioned as any evangelist's use of Romans 10:13 in a revival-meeting altar call.

Just as immediate and current was the covenant's pledge of acceptance to the "disenfranchised," the alien and the eunuch. Inclusion of the nations in YHWH worship was not a totally new concept in the Old Testament,[54] but the full participation offered in the Everlasting Covenant was close to revolutionary.

Extended Application. The total soteriological scope of the covenant was and is extraordinary. Its focus was messianic, so that the David of Isaiah 55 and the Gospel's "Son of David" bear a striking resemblance to each other (Matt. 12:23). I then conclude that the Everlasting Covenant, even with its immediate appeal to Judah, was nonetheless fundamentally Christological.

In the light of the general sweep of its invitation and its specific appeal to foreigners, the covenant is revealed as universal and missionary. Granted, the performance of Israel (Judah) did not reflect an awareness of the covenant's missionary implications. Still, their corporate conduct was no clue to covenant truth, any more than the disposition of the English church to the dream of William Carey confirmed the Great Commission.

Finally, although covenant provisions were securely anchored to the sin problem in Judah, their abiding durability indicate the endurance of the promise. Therefore, the redemptive pledge was both temporal and timeless. How appropriate, then, is the designation *běrīt 'ōlām*—the Everlasting Covenant!

Notes

[1]See chapter 13 of this book.

[2]"Barren woman" reflects עֲקָרָה, "unfruitful." Consult KB, see under "עָקַר," 3:828.

[3]Independent of the question or propriety, Sarai's proposal indicated the measure of her distress.

[4]Though "desolate woman," in turn, may represent Jerusalem.

[5]Note the use of the participle, BDB, 704. KJV has "tossed with tempest."

[6]See also Isaiah 48:22.

[7]See 2 Samuel 7:12-16. The promise guaranteed that the Davidic throne would be established forever.

[8]See Jeremiah 32:36-39.

[9]Franz Delitzsch, *Biblical Commentary on the Prophecies of Isaiah* in *Biblical Commentary on the Old Testament*, vol. 2, ed. C. F. Keil and F. Delitzsch, trans. James Martin (Grand Rapid: William B. Eerdmans Publishing Company, 1954), 427.

[10]Edward J. Young, *Isaiah*, 2:158.

[11]See the Excursus in this book (chap. 3).

[12]R. B. Y. Scott, "Exegesis," in *The Book of Isaiah: Chapters 1—39*, in *The Interpreter's Bible*, vol. 5, ed. George Arthur Buttrick (New York: Abingdon-Cokesbury Press, 1956), 298.

[13]See Isaiah 24:15,16,19-23.

[14]F. Leroy Forlines, *Romans*, 1st ed. (Nashville: Randall House Publications, 1987), 56-57.

[15]Lambdin, *Hebrew*, 67.

[16]Note the offerings of "sure mercies" (Isa. 55:3), "goodness" (Ex. 34:6), and "mercy" (Ex. 34:7) in KJV; compare "faithful love" (Isa. 55:3) and "kindness" (2 Sam. 9:1) in NIV.

[17]Snaith, *Distinctive Ideas*, 99-100.

[18]George A. F. Knight, *Servant Theology* (Grand Rapids: William B. Eerdmans Publishing Company, 1984), 193-94. For another example of plural usage, see Psalm 89:1-2.

[19]Waltke and O'Connor, *Syntax*, 141.

[20]Compare 2 Samuel 9:1-13; 1 Samuel 20:11-17.

[21]Young, *Isaiah*, 3:374.

[22]See Waltke and O'Connor, *Syntax*, 566-67.

[23]Watts, *Syntax*, 91-92.

[24]Mysteriously ignored by both NIV and KJV.

[25]Waltke and O'Connor, *Syntax*, 568.

[26]Ibid., 573.

[27]Young, *Isaiah*, 3:374.

[28]To distinguish the *bĕrīt 'ōlām* of Isaiah 55 from other arrangements, we shall capitalize the expression hereafter.

[29]The covenant of Isaiah 49:8 is rather distant (in location and application).

[30]"Perfect peace" represents a simple *šālōm, šālōm*, "peace, peace."

[31]Compare Isaiah 32:17; 52:7; 53:5; 57:19; 66:12.

[32]Muilenburg, "Exegesis," 644.

[33]Knight, *Servant*, 191.

[34]Young, *Isaiah*, 3:376. Apparently the ancients were not particularly concerned with cholesterol.

[35]Arthur Sumner Herbert, *The Book of the Prophet Isaiah: Chapters 40—66* (London: Cambridge University Press, 1975), 123.

[36]See chapter 3 of this book.

[37]Young, *Isaiah*, 3:379. Compare John Watts, *Isaiah 34—66*, 241, 243.

[38]John Watts noted the significance of Philip's "early convert to Christianity." John Watts, *Isaiah 34—66*, 249.

[39]1 Samuel 16:1-13. Of course, if one presumes that the material was written by a post-Exilic prophet, the time gap would be considerably longer.

[40]Muilenburg, "Exegesis," 646.

[41]Notice the same combination in Jeremiah 23:5.

[42]See chapter 13 of this book.

[43]Compare Isaiah 11:10.

[44]Roland Kenneth Harrison, *Introduction to the Old Testament* (Grand Rapids: William B. Eerdmans Publishing Company, 1969), 777.

[45]John Watts's nomination of Darius as the "new leader to assume the mantle and responsibilities of David" is unconvincing. See John Watts, *Isaiah 34—66*, 246.

[46]This is undoubtedly a prophetic perfect and could be translated, "I shall make him." See Waltke and O'Connor, *Syntax*, 490.

[47]See chapter 13 of this book.

[48]Knight, *Servant*, 195.

[49]GKC, 155.

[50]Ibid., 97. See also Delitzsch, *Isaiah*, 2:357.

[51]Waltke and O'Connor, *Syntax*, 649.

[52]Compare its repetition in 1 Kings 11:13,32; Isaiah 37:35.

[53]See Genesis 4:25-26; Joel 2:32.

[54]See Solomon's dedicatory prayer (1 Kings 8:41-43) and the experience of Jonah.

15

The Standard Bearer

The Spirit of the LORD shall lift up a standard.

Isaiah 59:19, KJV

"In the beginning God created the heavens and the earth. Now the earth was formless and empty, darkness was over the surface of the deep, and the Spirit of God was hovering over the waters" (Gen. 1:1-2).

In the late twelfth century A.D., an oriental chieftain named Temujin unified and organized the scattered Mongol tribes of central Asia into a formidable military force. Assuming the title of Genghis Khan, he launched an ambitious campaign with his horde of Mongol warriors that resulted in the conquest of much of the heartland of Asia. His grandson, Kublai Khan, extended the limits of the Mongol Empire until it ultimately reached from the Pacific on the east to the Danube on the west.

Like the youthful Macedonian Alexander of an earlier era, Kublai Khan looked for new fields to conquer. His imperial gaze focused on the island kingdom of Nippon, Japan. Kublai Khan forced subjugated Koreans to build a flotilla of 450 ships and, in 1274, dispatched a force of 15,000 to 25,000 troops to mount an invasion of Japan. The Japanese islands of Tsushima and Ikishima in the straits between Korea and Japan were occupied, and a bridgehead was established on the northern coast of Kyushu. Following inconclusive battle, however, a storm sank some of the invasion ships; and the Mongol invaders were forced to withdraw back to the mainland.

Undaunted, the Khan constructed another, more formidable invasion armada. In the summer of 1281 he launched an army of approximately 100,000 men aboard a fleet of 4,000 ships, probably the most massive amphibious strike force until the Allied landings in Normandy during World War II. In a two-pronged attack from both Korea and China, the Mongol invaders stormed ashore on north Kyushu again. The ensuing savage battle lasted more than fifty days—until another rampaging tempest pounced violently on the invasion flotilla, destroying most of its ships and leaving the marooned invaders to be slaughtered by the Japanese defenders.

Japanese words comprised of Chinese characters (*Kanji*), in many instances, may have two different pronunciation possibilities. For example, the name of the indigenous religion of Japan is composed of two characters, one for god or deity and one meaning "way" or "road." When the "*on*" or Chinese pronunciation of the symbols is followed, the term is pronounced "*shintō*" (Shinto, 神道). However, when the strictly Japanese pronunciation is used, the possessive particle "*no*" is inserted between the two symbols and it becomes "*kami no michi*" (かみのみち). In either instance, the literal meaning is (the)[1] "Way of (the) Gods."

So the Japanese, using the "*on*" pronunciation, might have labeled the tempest that sank the ships of the Mongol invaders "*shinfū*" ("divine wind," 神風). Instead, they preferred the distinctive Japanese sounds and called it (the) "Wind of the Gods," *kamikaze* (かみかぜ).[2]

Some have suggested that in Genesis 1:2 *rūaḥ 'ĕlōhīm* (רוּחַ אֱלֹהִים) should be translated as "divine wind" or "strong wind,"[3] as if one were dealing with some kind of primordial "kamikaze." While רוּחַ may indeed mean "wind" or "breath" as well as "spirit," such meaning hardly fits Genesis 1:2. In most instances, when רוּחַ is used with אֱלֹהִים or יהוה, it means "Spirit" with a capital "S." Moreover, the absence of meteorological terminology (words such as "blow," etc.) and the use of the verb רָחַף, apparently meaning to "hover" as in protection or supervision,[4] strongly suggest that "Spirit," not "wind," is intended. In addition, the multiple use of the jussive verb forms in the context further confirms the "Spirit's" presence as personality rather than raw, mechanical energy.

Accordingly, the Holy Spirit is introduced in the opening stanza of the Old Testament. As the Old Testament revelation unfolds, He is further depicted as involved in the selection of Israel's judges (Judg. 11:29), the equipping of individuals for special tasks (1 Chron. 12:18), the energizing of prophets (Mic. 3:8), the nomination of kings (1 Sam. 16:13), and the implementation of the coming of Messiah (Isa. 11:2). In fact, a great deal is said about the person and work of the Holy Spirit in the Old Testament. What is *not* said, however, is sometimes puzzling and tantalizing.

Isaiah 59 contains a striking notice about the soteriological activity of the Holy Spirit. While the text is not as explicit as one might wish, still, it provides a glimpse of the Spirit's role in the redemptive design. Exegesis of a key verse (Isa. 59:19) is influenced by the value assigned to *rūaḥ YHWH* (רוּחַ יְהוָה) and the interpretation of *nosesah* (נֹסְסָה). I will attempt, therefore, to address these matters with care and discrimination.

The Problem

Isaiah 58:1—59:21 constitutes the seventh and final entry in the problem-solution series of chapters 49—59.[5] This concluding unit in the sequence features hypocrisy as the problem, with Zion's Redeemer as the messianic-symbol solution. Our analysis of these two chapters will need to keep that context in focus.

Occasion. The description of the deplorable moral condition of Isaiah's Judah (chapters 58—59) might be described as "a walk on the dark side." Actually, the spiritual profile in this passage is an extension of the prophet's prior analysis of his nation (recorded in chapters 1—5). Chapter 58 inspires the "hypocrisy" label with charges such as this: "For day after day they seek me out; / they seem eager to know my ways, / as if they were a nation that does what is right / and has not forsaken the commands of its God" (Isa. 58:2).

Despite the external evidences of piety, the people of Judah were, at best, only "going through the motions" of religion. Accordingly, YHWH, through Isaiah, vigorously denounced their hollow and meaningless pretense: "Your fasting ends in quarreling and strife, / and in striking each other with wicked fists. / You cannot fast as you do today / and expect your voice to be heard on high" (Isa. 58:4).

Consequence. Sin, of course, generates devastating and damnable results. The connection endures, even in the case of hypocrisy, as Isaiah 59:1-16 graphically and painfully attests. Judah's silly religious "charade" produced alienation from YHWH—not a sense of alienation but the actual condition of separation. Accordingly, the prophet warned, "But your iniquities have separated / you from your God; / your sins have hidden his face from you, / so that he will not hear" (Isa. 59:2). Thus, regardless of formal covenant affiliation with the LORD, the people of Judah were without God.

The people, in effect, acknowledged their deplorable circumstance: "We look for light, but all is darkness; / for brightness, but we walk in deep shadows. / Like the blind we grope along the wall, / feeling our way like men without eyes. / At midday we stumble as if it were twilight; / among the strong, we are like the dead" (Isa. 59:9-10).

They admitted that they were stumbling about in moral and spiritual darkness, like the blind. Indeed, they conceded that they were like the dead. What a chilling and ominous confession!

The statement in verse 11 is enigmatic: "We all growl like bears; / we moan mournfully like doves. / We look for justice, but find none; / for deliverance, but it is far away." The exact meaning of the reference to bears and doves is not altogether clear. Muilenburg offered this interpretation: "In their distress and perplexity they growl **like bears** filled with ominous dread and fear . . . They **moan like doves** . . . in plaintive sense of foreboding."[6] Westermann suggested that the verse may communicate a "mood of bitter disenchantment and despondency."[7] His assessment finds support in a comparable simile that appears in a Babylonian prayer to Ishtar, "I mourn like a dove night and day. I am beaten down, and so I weep bitterly."[8]

These lines, plus the general tenor of the prayer, indicate the dismay and disappointment of the supplicant. However, that meaning cannot be arbitrarily imposed on the Isaian text, especially since the growling of bears is not necessarily associated with bitterness. Beasts and birds do emit their characteristic sounds or songs, though, whenever they are aroused or disturbed. So while any estimate must remain tentative, the figure of speech may be designed to express frustration. The thwarted anticipation of justice and deliverance (reflected in the second half of the verse) may communicate that nuance.

Another result of the sin of hypocrisy is posed by this frightening appraisal: "So justice is driven back, / and righteousness stands at a distance; / truth has stumbled in the streets, / honesty cannot enter. / Truth is nowhere to be found, / and whoever shuns evil becomes a prey" (Isa. 59:14-15).

Judah had apparently regressed to the deplorable religious, cultural, and social condition that had plagued the Hebrew tribes before the installation of the monarchy. That remote chaotic, turbulent period was summarized in this report: "In those days Israel had no king; everyone did as he saw fit" (Judg. 21:25). Now the kingdom had come full cycle. Once again moral anarchy prevailed, and truth and righteousness languished.

The appalling spiritual sickness was apparently terminal. "The LORD looked and . . . there was no one to intervene" (Isa. 59:15b-16). Left to their own devices and resources, the people of Judah were helpless, incapable of rescuing themselves. The sin problem was so deeply ingrained that without divine intervention, they were both helpless and hopeless. YHWH's magnificent response can only be appreciated in light of the magnitude of that deplorable situation.

The Solution

The record speaks for itself across the pages of Scripture and throughout the ages: the LORD has repeatedly and faithfully involved Himself in mankind's chronic and lin-

gering sin difficulty. The principle is beautifully illustrated in the climactic solution to this final sin problem
cataloged in Isaiah 49—59.

The Strength of the Savior. The expression "he was ap-
palled" (*vayyiŝtōmēm*, וַיִּשְׁתּוֹמֵם) in Isaiah 59:16 does not
suggest that YHWH was either surprised or puzzled.[9]
Rather, it means that He was disturbed that there was no
intercessor (*mapgīa'*, מַפְגִּיעַ), "no one to intervene." So He
determined to use "his own arm" to provide the intercession and deliverance needed.

"Arm," of course, was a symbol of might, power, and
strength. The metaphor proposed that the LORD was prepared to "flex His muscle." However, "his own arm" in Isaiah 59:16 cannot be evaluated apart from the more
elaborate and formal disclosure of the "arm of the LORD"
in Isaiah 53. The profile of the Arm's supernatural
strength in that context, though, was not apt to inspire
confidence.

There, the arm is likened to "a root out of dry ground"
(v. 2), "a man of sorrows" (v. 3). He is described as
"stricken by God" (v. 4), "pierced for our transgressions"
(v. 5), one who will bear "the iniquity of us all" (v. 6), and
a lamb of slaughter (v. 7). He is to be "cut off from the land
of the living" (v. 8), entombed with the wicked and the rich
(v. 9), to become a "guilt offering" (v. 10), and be "num-
bered with the transgressors" (v. 12). Yet, despite such ig-
nominious prospects, the Arm of the LORD was ordained
to provide the intercession and the salvation that Judah
so sorely needed.

A subtle messianic aura accompanies the projection of
the Arm's career in verses 17-20 of chapter 59. The description of His glorious redemptive activity that culmi-
nates in vindication and victory (vv. 17-18) connects to
another messianic symbol, the "ensign" (v. 19), and concludes with the "redeemer" motif (v. 20). This messianic
connection and the latent significance of "redeemer" (*gō'ēl*,
גָּאַל)[10] combine to suggest that not only would the Arm of
the Lord provide the necessary intervention and salvation
demanded by Judah's helplessness. He would also, as
Zion's sympathetic Redeemer, recover life's lost opportu-
nities for Judah.[11]

Centuries after the day of Isaiah, the Redeemer came to Zion. He surveyed Jerusalem and agonized over the inhabitants of the city (Luke 13:34; 19:41-44). As in Isaiah's time, there was no one to intercede, to intervene, to plead the case of the helpless, to aid the stricken. So the Redeemer laid bare the mighty strength of God. Through His shame, humiliation, and exaltation He provided the intercession, salvation, and restoration that all generations of all ages have needed.

The Standard of the Spirit. Earlier I alluded to the presence of the messianic symbol "ensign" (*nēs*, נֵס) in verse 19. The NIV version does not reflect that presence: "From the west, men will fear the name of the Lord, / and from the rising of the sun, they will revere his glory. / For he will come like a pent-up flood / that the breath of the Lord drives along."

The language and meaning of the first part of the verse are relatively clear and uncomplicated. However, the second half is somewhat cryptic; and both translation and interpretation are subject to disagreement. As previously noted, the translation-interpretation problem centers on the meaning and force of *rūaḥ YHWH* (רוּחַ יְהוָה) and *nosesah* (נֹסְסָה). Also indicated above, *rūaḥ YHWH* may mean either "Spirit of YHWH" or "wind" or "breath" of YHWH,[12] with the Hebrew word *rūaḥ* having the same element of uncertainty as the Greek counterpart, *pneuma* (πνεῦμα). Because of the ambiguity of the word *rūaḥ* and the flexibility of the expression *rūaḥ YHWH*, the context must determine the emphasis.

In this particular case, the uncertainly of *rūaḥ YHWH* is compounded by the obscurity of the verb from *nosesah*. NIV, KB, and BDB have construed the form as a *Polel* (perfect, 3fs) derived from the root *n-u-s* (נוּם, "flee," "escape").[13] That is certainly a legitimate possibility, though the precise meaning is not altogether clear since this is the only instance of a *Polel* built on *n-u-s*.[14] It may also be a *Qal* active participle (feminine singular) built on *n-s-s* (נסס), a root evidently associated with the noun *nēs* (נס), "ensign" or "standard" ("to display a standard"?).[15] However, just as *nosesah* would be the only *Polel* form if derived from *n-u-s*, it would be the only *Qal* form if derived from *n-s-s*. Apart from this instance, forms derived from *n-s-s* occur only twice in the Old Testament, both in the *Hitpoʻel* stem.[16] The vagueness of the situation is revealed in the fact that BDB lists *lĕhitnōsēs* (לְהִתְנוֹסֵס, Ps. 60:6) under both *n-u-s* and *n-s-s*.[17]

The decidedly unclear meaning of *nosesah*, then, suggests that the verb must be analyzed and defined on the basis of its subject rather than vice versa. Consequently, the more conventional meaning of "the Spirit of YHWH" for *rūaḥ YHWH* seems to accord better with "lifts up a standard" than the uncertain "drives along."

That meaning also makes sense in the context, which includes another reference to *rūaḥ* in verse 21. The possessive suffix attached to *rūaḥ* in that location equates "my Spirit" of verse 21 with the *rūaḥ YHWH* of verse 19. There is nothing decisive in this restricted passage to suggest that *rūaḥ* might mean "breath" in one location and "Spirit" in the other. Since "my breath" (or "wind") scarcely seems appropriate in verse 21, to translate *rūaḥ* as "Spirit" in both verses appears more suitable. I concur, therefore, with Young's summary:

> The thought of the verse then is that whenever the enemy comes upon God's people, like a flood of all-engulfing water racing down a narrow wadi, the Lord in the very midst of the flood raises a standard, thus showing that He is in control of the situation.[18]

Four critical factors need to be remembered. First, the agent who "lifts up" or "elevates" the "battle standard" against the enemy is the Spirit of the Lord, not some impersonal mechanism or force. Second, the connection of the verbal action in verse 19 with the noun *nēs* ("ensign," "banner") implies a strong association with a distinct messianic emblem.[19] Third, the interdicting work of the divine Spirit will be in the face of adversity, "when the enemy comes in like a flood."[20] Just as the Spirit of YHWH "put on" (*lābĕšā*, לָבְשָׁה) Gideon in the face of Midianite danger (Judg. 6:34) and "rushed upon" (*tiṣlaḥ*, תִּצְלַח) Samson during a time of Philistine oppression (Judg. 14:6), so *rūaḥ YHWH* will resist whenever hell's battalions threaten. Fourth, the activity of the Spirit in raising the standard to the nations will result in honor and glory to the ineffable

Name. "From the west" to the "rising of the sun," people will revere and praise His Name. The Spirit will glorify His majesty till "savage tribes attend his word" and "His name like sweet perfume shall rise / With every morning sacrifice."[21]

Note: The divine activity of redemption, already operational in Isaiah's day, involved the joint, cooperative work of the Redeemer (pre-incarnate) *and* the (Holy) Spirit of the Lord. We observe, then, that He is no latter-day interloper in the salvation scenario.

The Application

Verse 21 is the crucial summary to all that has been stated in chapters 58—59 and requires careful analysis: "'As for me, this is my covenant with them,'" says the Lord. "'My Spirit, who is on you, and my words that I have put in your mouth will not depart from your mouth, or from the mouths of your children, or from the mouths of their descendants from this time on and forever,'" says the Lord.

Covenant Equation. In light of the momentous covenant data encountered in chapter 55, the mention of "my covenant" in Isaiah 59:21 invites our attention. A reference to covenant is missing from the immediate context to provide an antecedent. The nearest option is the "my covenant" of Isaiah 56:4, 6, which is a "personalized" designation for the Everlasting Covenant of Isaiah 55:3.

While, perhaps, there is no specific connection between "my covenant" in Isaiah 59:21 and the covenant of chapters 54—56, the similarity in designation implies some correlation. In addition, the requirement of repentance in Isaiah 55:7 and the description of "those . . . who repent of their sins" in Isaiah 59:20 provide remarkable correspondence. Moreover, the topical unity of chapters 49—59[22] strongly suggests that the same covenant is being described, with (Second) David messianic symbol associated with the Everlasting Covenant and Zion's Redeemer the emblem connected to "my covenant" in Isaiah 59:20-21. I therefore propose the following equation:

54:10	55:3	56:4	56:6	59:21
my covenant of peace	= everlasting covenant	= my covenant	= my covenant	= my covenant

One final covenant factor needs to be noted. In Isaiah's marvelous projection of the glorified Zion that incorporates "aliens" and "foreigners" into the unified service of the Lord (Isa. 61:5-6), the radical "new order" is based on *bĕrīt 'ōlām*, the Everlasting Covenant (Isa. 61:8). The "my covenant" of Isaiah 59:21, then, seems to constitute the link between the Everlasting Covenant of chapter 55 and the Everlasting Covenant of chapter 61.

Covenant Recipients. As the quotation marks in NIV indicate, most of verse 21 is a direct discourse statement by YHWH. The "them" of the opening line, therefore, refers to "those in Jacob who repent of their sins" and respond to Zion's Redeemer (v. 20). Since these are the ones addressed by the Lord, the "you" of the remainder of the verse is a "collective singular" that also designates the repentant ones in Jacob (Judah). This explicit designation clearly defines those who will share the blessings and benefits of "my covenant." Once more, as in the case of the covenant in Isaiah 55:3, the cohesion of the total context indicates that the covenant of Isaiah 59:21 beamed its redemptive message directly to Judah. Accordingly, these covenant benefits, while exhibiting "principlization" possibilities,[23] were nonetheless firmly anchored to the historical setting.

Covenant Provisions. The consequences of covenant participation are not altogether clear in verse 21, but the somewhat enigmatic disclosures of the verse provide hints worthy of note. For example, the stirring line "my Spirit, who is on you" provides the most important affirmation in the Old Testament, if not the only one, about the work of the Holy Spirit in salvation. Obscure and cryptic though the statement may be, it furnishes a pledge of the seal of the Spirit in the redemptive application of the covenant. It thereby establishes a clear soteriological involvement by the third member of the Trinity.

The word does not pledge that the Spirit "will be" upon you, implying some future frame of reference. Instead, the item is contained in a relative clause without any form of the verb "to be" (הָיָה). This strongly infers a present circumstance, indicating that the Spirit was "on them" currently.

A second benefit is suggested by the enduring permanence of "my words . . . in your mouth." The abiding character of the divine word had been previously established in the Book of Isaiah (40:8), and its eternal luster illuminates this and every application of YHWH's utterance and self-disclosure. That implication is supported by the pledge that the covenant's revelation and the relationship that it promised would extend "from this time on and forever." YHWH's covenant thus guaranteed an eternal security, but it was a security that extended "from this time." Accordingly, I conclude that intercession, salvation, and the redemptive work of the Spirit through the Everlasting Covenant were operative in the midst of ancient Judah's urgent need.

Summary

What, then, is the difference between the work of the Holy Spirit in the Old Testament and the New? Even in the New Testament there is evidence of the Holy Spirit's activity prior to the outpouring at Pentecost (note the baptism and temptation of Jesus, Matt. 3:16-17; 4:1). The Master's proclamation is relatively clear:

"On the last and greatest day of the Feast, Jesus stood and said in a loud voice, 'If anyone is thirsty, let him come to me and drink. Whoever believes in me, as the Scripture has said, streams of living water will flow from within him'" (John 7:37-38).

We may be puzzled at John's intriguing editorial note, "By this he meant the Spirit, whom those who believed in him were later to receive. Up to that time the Spirit had not been given, since Jesus had not yet been glorified" (John 7:39). In the light of this report, we may wonder where the Spirit was and what He was doing before the time of Jesus's glorification.

Moreover, there is the paradoxical word about the Agent of comfort: "And I will ask the Father, and he will give you another Counselor to be with you forever—the Spirit of truth. The world cannot accept him, because it neither sees him nor knows him. But you know him, for he lives with you and will be in you. I will not leave you as orphans; I will come to you" (John 14:16-18). Notice how closely the Spirit is identified with the person of the Messiah. The Master said, He (the Spirit) "will be in you," but also declared, "I will come to you."

Obviously, a full disclosure of the Spirit's activity before Pentecost is simply not available. Even the data we do have may not supply all the details of His elusive but essential ministry. I believe, however, that the New Testament provides enough information to indicate that the expansion of His role in the church's era involves a work that relates specifically to the Messiah. For one thing, He is deputized to convict the world *concerning* the Messiah:

"But I tell you the truth: It is for your good that I am going away. Unless I go away, the Counselor will not come to you; but if I go, I will send him to you. When he comes, he will convict the world of guilt in regard to sin and righteousness and judgment: in regard to sin, because men do not believe in me; in regard to righteousness, because I am going to the Father, where you can see me no longer" (John 16:7-10).

As the tortured confession of David revealed (Ps. 32:3-4; 51:3-14), the Holy Spirit vigorously convicted persons about sin even in the time of the Old Testament. The distinctive new feature in His current work, however, has to do with conviction "because men do not believe in me." The sinner is now indicted, prosecuted, and judged on the basis of his response to the messianic provision of forgiveness.

In addition, the Holy Spirit currently guides persons to the truth *of* the Messiah: "He will bring glory to me *by taking from what is mine and making it known to you*" (John 16:14, italics added). In so doing, He exalts and magnifies the person and work of the Messiah. Finally, He is prepared to empower those who witness *about* the Messiah. "You will receive power when the Holy Spirit comes on you; and you will be my witnesses in Jerusalem, and in all Judea and Samaria, and to the ends of the earth" (Acts 1:8).

In the so-called "age of the New Testament," the Holy Spirit is still lifting up a banner in the face of satanic assault. Isaiah was obviously aware of the character and role of the coming Messiah, but did not know His precise, historical identity. Accordingly, he wrote about Messiah in terms of labels such as "the Holy One of Israel" and "Immanuel" and motifs such as "David" and the "Suffering Servant." If the "standard of the Spirit" in Isaiah's time featured an "emblem," perhaps it was the "star of David." If so, it was the star of "Second David"—the one who would later be called the "son of David" by the common people.

However, from that epochal day of Pentecost forward, He has continued to lift up a standard. Now it is a bloodspattered banner—emblazoned with a cross!

Notes

[1]"The" is placed in parenthesis because Japanese has no definite article.

[2]*Kenkyusha's New Japanese-English Dictionary*, new ed. (Tokyo: Kenkyusha Ltd., 1954), s.v. "kamikaze."

[3]See Robert Luyster, "Wind and Water: Cosmogonic Symbolism in the Old Testament," *Zeitschrift für die Alttestamentliche Wissenschaft* 93:1 (1981): 1.

[4]See KB, 4:1138 and BDB, 934.

[5]See chapter 13 of this book.

[6]Muilenburg, "Exegesis," 691. For the uses of הָמָה, "growl," see KB, 1:240 and BDB, 242. For הָגָה, "moan," see KB, 1:228 and KB, 211. Compare the use of הָגָה in Psalm 1:2.

[7]Westermann, *Isaiah 40—66*, 348.

[8]*Ancient Near Eastern Texts*, 2nd ed., ed. James B. Pritchard (Princeton: Princeton University Press, 1955), 384.

[9]For a lexical definition of שָׁמֵם (in the *Hithpolel* stem), see KB, 4:1448 and BDB, 1031.

[10]See chapter 9 of this book.

[11]John Watts offered this identification: "Who or what is Yahweh's arm? If this passage is like chaps. 44—45 and 49, it refers to the rising Persian emperor in this case to Artaxerxes I. He, like Darius and Cyrus before him, is a chosen agent to do Yahweh's will" (*Isaiah 34:66*, 286). This perspective, however, construes the content of the latter part of Isaiah as more political than prophetic. (Note his translation of תּוֹשַׁע as "wrought victory" [Isa. 59:16] and כּוֹבַע יְשׁוּעָה as "helmet of victory" [Isa. 59:17]; *Isaiah 34—66*, 284, 287.) While Isaiah was indeed concerned with international affairs (chapters 13—23), the primary thrust of his message focused on spiritual, moral, religious, and soteriological

issues rather than the fortunes of military adventure. (Compare Watts's identification of the theophanic figure in Isaiah 63:1-6 with Megabyzuz; *Isaiah 34—66*, 317-19 and Westermann, *Isaiah 40—66*, 350-51.) Consistently loyal to the principle of historical correspondence, Watts ultimately commented (almost reluctantly it would seem) on the climactic scene in the Book of Isaiah: "The Vision closes as it began with a scene in the heavenly court of God. It is vitally related to the happenings in Jerusalem's temple and the people who worship there. But, in these scenes at least, the point relates more to that worship and attitudes of the worshipers than to any historical issues. The Vision has come full circle" (*Isaiah 34—66*, 362). In my judgment, that was the major point all along.

[12]For an example of this relatively rare usage, see Hosea 13:15 and Isaiah 40:7 (even here, it could mean "Spirit").

[13]See KB, 3:643 and BDB, 630. For other translations that follow this identification, compare Westermann, *Isaiah 40—66*, 344; John Watts, *Isaiah 34—66*, 285; and Muilenburg, "Exegesis," 695.

[14]The LXX provides little help with ἥξει γὰρ ὡς ποταμὸς βίαιος ἡ ὀργὴ παρὰ κυρίου, ἥξει μετὰ θυμοῦ ("for wrath from the Lord will arrive like a violent river; it will arrive with anger").

[15]Both BDB and KB list a possible "denominative" root, נסס. See BDB, 651 and KB, 3:664.

[16]An infinitive construct in Psalm 60:6 (where the connection with "ensign" is clear) and a participle in Zechariah 9:16. Compare KB, 3:664 and BDB, 651. See Marvin R. Wilson, "נסס," *TWOT*, 2:583.

[17]BDB, 631.

[18]Young, *Isaiah*, 3:440.

[19]See Isaiah 11:10,12; 49:22.

[20]See NIV's footnote.

[21]Isaac Watts, DUKE STREET, 1719.

[22]See chapter 13 of this book.

[23]Kaiser, *Exegetical Theology*, 152.

Conclusion

Two questions were raised at the beginning of this investigation: (1) what is the God of the Old Testament really like? and (2) what kind of salvation is actually described in the Old Testament? The biblical evidence supports the contention that He is a God of compassion, grace, patience, and faithfulness (Ex. 34:6-7). Those warm, positive attributes are legitimately His on the basis of claim, revealed character, and sustained performance. The fact that He is a holy God who holds persons accountable for their sins does not obscure the radiant truth that He is a God of infinite mercy who has interceded on behalf of humanity, at great and unimaginable cost to Himself.

What does the evidence indicate, though, about the character of salvation in the Old Testament? How does it compare (or contrast) with the New Testament redemptive paradigm? Before attempting to summarize and evaluate the data that have been examined, perhaps we should briefly survey the material which was not included in this study.

The Psalms

The Book of Psalms, of course, was Israel's hymnal. As a consequence, it is replete with descriptions, allusions, and reflections of the salvation experience(s) of Old Testament saints. For example, classic citations such as "If you, O Lord, kept a record of sins, / O Lord, who could stand? / But with you there is forgiveness; / therefore you are feared" (Ps. 130:3-4) and "As far as the east is from the west, / so far has he removed our transgressions from us" (Ps. 103:12) are decidedly soteriological in orientation. Sin, accountability, pardon, trust, and cleansing are addressed in these brief verses.

Inner spiritual assurance and victory reverberate from this exultation: "Praise the Lord, O my soul; / all my inmost being, praise his holy name. / Praise the Lord, O my soul, / and forget not all his benefits— / who forgives all your sins / and heals all your diseases, / who redeems your life from the pit / and crowns you with love and compassion, / who satisfies your desires with good things / so that your youth is renewed like the eagle's" (Ps. 103:1-5). This one location alone almost provides enough insight into the redemptive relationship to construct a full Old Testament soteriology.

The brokenhearted prayer of the contrite David discloses something of the distress and turmoil that are generated by unconfessed sin (Ps. 51:1-19). Disobedience, even in the life of the believer, shatters the tranquility and victory of the relationship and brings calamitous results. Thus the experience of David confirmed the meaning of the New Testament line, long before it was penned, "If we confess our sins, he is faithful and just and will forgive our sins and purify us from all unrighteousness" (1 John 1:9).

The hope in an afterlife is also depicted in the Psalms. "Surely goodness and love will follow me / all the days of my life, / and I will dwell in the house of the LORD / forever" (Ps. 23:6). Even an anticipation of resurrection is hinted: "But God will redeem my life from the grave; / he will surely take me to himself" (Ps. 49:15).

As is evident, the Psalms contain (along with other theological themes) multiple references to various features of Old Testament salvation. The sheer volume of material on the subject is so great, however, that it was omitted. A study of soteriology in the Psalms would constitute, in itself, a worthwhile and extensive project. Moreover, since the Psalms material is basically experience-oriented, I made a choice (appropriate or otherwise) to concentrate instead on those passages that either teach or objectively illustrate soteriological truth.

The New Covenant

A key salvation passage in the Old Testament is contained in Jeremiah 31:31-34, a text that features *bĕrīt ḥădāšāh* (בְּרִית חֲדָשָׁה), the "New Covenant." The New Covenant, though, must be approached through the context of a "covenant controversy" provoked by certain aspects of Jeremiah's message to the people. Essentially, three covenant "categories" were involved. They included the Patriarchal Covenant,[1] the National Covenants (the Covenants of Holiness [Ex. 19—24], Entry [Ex. 34:10], and Possession [Deut. 28—30]),[2] and the Davidic Covenant (2 Sam. 7:12-16). The three categories promised, in turn, three critical provisions for the permanence of: (1) Israel, (2) Israel's occupation of Canaan, and (3) Davidic rule.

Jeremiah, however, seriously challenged those features. He predicted the demolition of the sacred temple in Jerusalem and the destruction of Judah (Jer. 7:14-16; 14:11-12; 37:9-10), a message that provoked hostile resentment against the prophet (Jer. 20:1-8). Furthermore, in apparent contradiction to YHWH's covenant pledge, he forecast the discontinuance of the Davidic line (Jer. 22:24-30). It almost seemed as if Jeremiah were trying to engender opposition as he disputed the Lord's covenant promises.

Jeremiah was himself sensitive to the surface disparity between the covenant pledges and his preaching. Nevertheless, the prophet perceived a resolution of the apparent discrepancy, a solution that his audience sadly failed to note. He sensed that although Judah would be destroyed and removed from the land and that the Davidic line through Solomon would be severed, still YHWH would keep His covenant promises. The pledges would be fulfilled through a "new" Israel (30:1-24), a "new" covenant (31:31-34), and a "new" (Ideal) David (30:9).

According to the data in chapter 30, the New Israel will feature the following: (1) restoration to the land (30:1-3);

(2) reunification of Judah and Israel (30:3); (3) rescue from trouble (30:7); (4) recognition of (Ideal) David (30:9); (5) recovery from spiritual disease (30:10-17); and (6) reestablishment as a nation (30:18-24).

In somewhat similar fashion, the New Covenant offers a distinctive profile. It will be: (1) Spiritual (31:31-33); (2) Unanimous (31:34); (3) Permanent (31:36-37); and (4) Corporate (31:31,33,36).[3]

Jeremiah's message of the New Covenant, to be sure, has a strong soteriological flavor; and its exclusion from the present investigation requires some explanation. This particular covenant was explicitly distinguished from "the covenant / I made with their forefathers / when I took them by the hand / to lead them out of Egypt" (Jer. 31:32). In addition, it was designated as becoming "operational" in the context of reunification and restoration.

Accordingly, the New Covenant that is described in Jeremiah 31:31-34 was primarily eschatological (at least from Jeremiah's point of reference) and designed specifically for the house of Israel and the house of Judah. Granted, Gentiles have been graciously permitted to participate in this covenant; but that does not alter its original and basic purpose.[4] Because of this orientation, the covenant must be construed, in its original setting, as strategic rather than soteriological. It did not include an immediate offer, an appeal, or even a contemporary application.

Jeremiah's New Covenant may be the temporal "packaging" of Isaiah's Everlasting Covenant. In any event, because of the stated objective of this study "to determine what the Old Testament had to say about salvation to the recipients of the Old Testament message(s),"[5] the New Covenant was excluded because of its eschatological perspective.

Redemptive Concepts

Reluctantly, I also ignored some beautiful salvation analogies. For example, the New Testament word for "gospel" ("good news") was imported from the Old Testament. Paul, in quoting from Isaiah 52:7, acknowledged as much. "As it is written, 'How beautiful are the feet of those who bring good news!'" (Rom. 10:15). The term "good news" (gospel) has been traditionally associated with the life, message, and redemptive work of the Messiah to the extent that the four accounts of His earthly ministry are tagged as "Gospels." The English translation "good news" is true to the semantic thrust of the Greek word *euangellion* (εὐαγγέλιον). The intriguing consideration is why the particular Hebrew word (מְבַשֵּׂר) behind *euangellion* was chosen from the Old Testament, as over against other terminology.

The Hebrew root in question, *b-s-r* (בשׂר), survives in other Semitic languages[6] and may be neutral or even negative,[7] although an optimistic flavor is the dominant nuance. The term was used in the Old Testament in connection with the announcement of the birth of a child (Jer. 20:15), victory in battle (2 Sam. 18:19), and the proclamation of royal succession (1 Kings 1:42–43). These applications of *bissar* (the *Pi'el* conjugation of *b-s-r*) correspond remarkably to salient features of the "good news" in the New Testament. Again, although the expression incorporates a striking redemptive concept, it was not included in this study because it did not relate directly to the immediate message of salvation in the Old Testament.

Other terms and concepts were also slighted. Expressions such as *bāṭaḥ* (בָּטַח, "trust"), *'ĕmūnāh* (אֱמוּנָה, "faithfulness"), *pādah* (פָּדָה, "ransom"), and *yir'at YHWH* (יִרְאַת יהוה, "the fear of YHWH") were omitted, primarily because they did not occur in the key locations that were selected for examination. For that matter, this study by no means included all of the Old Testament passages that refer to personal salvation. I hope that these limited examples will inspire readers to pursue the investigation beyond these narrow parameters.

Soteriological Wheel

This investigation has disclosed some limited data that will help to provide a general framework for a formal Old Testament soteriology. As the following summary reveals, even a cursory soteriological analysis provides significant theological information regarding theology (proper), hamartiology (the study of sin), atonement, election, justification, sanctification, and even eschatology (final destiny). In the summary of the results of the study, additional reference material, when appropriate, will be noted in passing.

Theology. The study has considered specific attributes of God. In this instance the term *theology* is used in a restricted sense, rather than in its broader (generic) application. The investigation of the creation account and evidence about the covenant deity at Sinai have provided concrete and "measurable" information about the nature of God. The evidence leads to the conclusion that the tension between the "righteousness-vengeance" factor and the "mighty to save-redemption" factor in the divine character is beautifully resolved. The incredible redemptive truth is that God Himself "bears" a person's guilt by providing a vicarious substitute in the person of His Servant. In addition, the involvement of the Holy Spirit in the salvation design has also been noted.

Hamartiology. The study has furnished information about the character (Ex. 34:7), scope (Isa. 53:6), and consequence of sin (Gen. 3:24). Other Old Testament material may expand the delineation of the sin problem,[8] but the foregoing at least sketch the general outline of humanity's moral difficulty.

Atonement. The specific meaning of *atonement* has been evaluated on the basis of a careful examination of the textual evidence in Leviticus 16. That data, plus the disclosures in the Song of the Suffering Servant (Isa. 52:13—53:12), lead to the conclusions that atonement involves the satisfaction of divine holiness on the basis of a substitutionary sacrifice.

Election. The sinner must come to the Lord at the time of divine choice (Isa. 55:6), but the God of creation holds mankind accountable for sin (Gen. 3:16-24). Moreover, as the salvation invitations of the Old Testament indicate (Isa. 1:18-20; 55:1-3,6), mankind is capable of receiving or rejecting the overtures of grace; but the individual is responsible for personal choices.

Justification. Pardon is conditioned on repentance (Isa. 55:7; 59:20) and faith (Gen. 15:6; Ex. 19:5-6), although both components are not necessarily highlighted in the same location or individual passage. This blend of soteriological requirements, of course, coincides with the teaching of the New Testament, perhaps to a surprising degree.

Sanctification. The profound alteration in the believer that accompanied personal salvation is reflected in the imputation of righteousness to Abraham (Gen. 15:6) and the phenomenal transformation of Jacob (Gen. 32:24-31). The purifying aspect of the relationship is illustrated further in the symbolism of the scapegoat in the Yom Kippur ceremony. The Old Testament redemptive "transaction" obviously involved more than religious "paperwork."

Final Destiny. The biblical record addresses the issue of mankind's final destiny. It confirms human accountability for sin and also projects the ultimate disposition of the ungodly (Josh. 6:1-25). Although the Old Testament does not provide a detailed profile of the afterlife, it anticipates a resurrection (Job 19:25-27)[9] and an ultimate glorification (Isa. 35:10) for those who trust in YHWH.

These seven features constitute the critical theological elements of the Old Testament's revelation of salvation-truth. While they may not be as precise or elaborate as the New Testament's disclosures, they do provide enough to reveal that the message of salvation sounded loud and clear to the ancient Old Testament audience. These elements may be likened to spokes radiating inward from the outer rim of a wheel that represents the totality of salvation-truth in the Old Testament. The analogy suggests something like figure 1.

The outer circumference of the wheel is supported by the spokes, just as the soteriological summary of the Old Testament is the result of the individual theological truths that sustain it. Drawn with a solid line, these components correspond with remarkable precision to their New Testament counterparts. However, in the Old Testament, the hub of the wheel is not yet in place. It is forecast with beautiful clarity, but it is still missing. Accordingly, the hub is drawn with a broken line to indicate its historical and functional absence.

The major feature to be noted, though, is the correspondence. The theological patterns in the salvation message are more than parallel or similar. They are, in essence,

Figure 1

identical. What about the difference? Without the hub, the wheel will not work! That's right. However, when the Roman legionnaires drove spikes into the Carpenter's cross, they also unknowingly hammered the hub into the wheel and completed the Old Testament picture of redemption.

Summary

In discussing "Continuing and Contemporary Issues in Old Testament Theology" John H. Hayes and Frederick C. Prussner noted that "Old Testament theology has sought to find some organizing principle, central concepts, or officially sanctioned positions in the Bible to use as a structuring center or middle from which to work."[10] They added:

> The desire to locate a single concept which runs throughout the material and could be used like Eichrodt's emphasis on the covenant in order to present a cross-section of the entire Old Testament is still held as a goal by some interpreters.[11]

They cited the views of several theologians, including Walther Eichrodt (covenant),[12] Gerhard von Rad (sacred history, *Heilsgeschichte*)[13] Walter C. Kaiser, Jr. (promise),[14] and Claus Westermann (deliverance/blessing).[15] In evaluating efforts to find a unifying theme in Old Testament theology, they called attention to the weakness, as well as the strength, of some of the theories. For example, on Eichrodt's "covenant approach," they observed, "While one may grant the novelty of his use of the covenant idea, the fact remains that he was able to apply it as an organizing principle only to a part of the religious thought contained in the Old Testament."[16] Noting the salvation-history approach's "inability to integrate Old Testament wisdom literature," they also cautioned:

> Proponents of revelation through history were forced to recognize that excluding wisdom, or seeing it as Israel's response to Yahweh's acts in history (so von Rad in his *Theology*), meant that a major area of the Old Testament could not be easily fitted into such a scheme. Surely no adequate theology could do justice to the Old Testament unless this material could be made an integral part of the picture.[17]

Still, Hayes and Prussner concluded:

> Thus it appears that even those who seem to deny a principle of unity assume some structure for approaching the material. This is to be expected and will probably continue to function, in one form or another, in any presentation of Old Testament theology.[18]

Does the Old Testament indeed embrace a central, unifying theme? Addressing that issue, Kaiser posed three pertinent questions. (1) Does a key exist for an orderly and progressive arrangement of the subjects, themes, and teachings of the OT? (2) Were the writers of the Old Testament consciously aware of such a key as they continued to add to the historical stream of revelation? (3) Can such a center be identified from the texts themselves?[19]

If such a theme does exist, what is its core or nucleus? Is it restricted to salvation history? Does it coalesce around covenant (or covenants)? Does the promise-blessing motif, as Kaiser advocates, constitute the major consolidating principle?[20]

Perhaps all of these incorporate a strong element of truth. Yet, I am convinced that each is inadequate. I proposed earlier that "the primary purpose of the Old Testament narrative was, and is, to record the unfolding redemptive acts of God in history."[21] The statement, though, was made in the context of an analysis of the Genesis narrative. Moreover, it followed the assertion that "salvation economy prevails throughout the entire Old Testament." Accordingly, when the Old Testament writers reported history, they concentrated on moral, spiritual, religious, and soteriological matters. In that respect, its theme might be construed as "salvation history."

However, the Old Testament contains more than the record of incidents in an ancient past. Indeed, at least some of its historical accounts, through the vehicle of prophetic anticipation, project events yet to occur. Accordingly, since salvation history ignores future developments as well as poetic sections of the Old Testament, it fails to qualify as the theological center of the Old Testament.

In like fashion, the promises and covenants in the Old Testament contribute to its total economy but hardly constitute a singular unifying principle.[22] Observe, though, that all of these relate to the salvation theme. Indeed, the narratives, letters, edicts, covenants, poetry, laments, hymns, proverbs, oracles, preaching, and predictions—all reflect various aspects of YHWH's grand soteriological design. I repeat, therefore, that "salvation economy prevails throughout the entire Old Testament." Moreover, that economy modifies all of the Old Testament components, the Law (תורה), the Prophets (נביאים), and the Writings (כתובים). Furthermore, I am convinced that the Old Testament writers consciously contributed to this theme and that such a center can indeed be identified from the texts themselves, though its presence may not always be immediately obvious. Accordingly, I dare to declare that YHWH's salvation strategy constitutes the central theme of the Old Testament.

In fact, I am persuaded that the LORD's soteriological design is the consolidating principle of both Testaments. It not only provides unity in diversity but also constitutes the central motif of the biblical revelation. Just as the redemptive strategy modulates the Old Testament record, it also permeates the New Testament Gospels, narrative (Acts), epistles, and apocalypse. Moreover, the grand event of the New Testament—the incarnation and all of its developments[23]—was not mere divine self-disclosure or grandiose metaphysical exercise. It was the critical feature of the redemptive plan (Rev. 13:8).

Perhaps, apart from the specific historical reference (a disclosure reserved for the fullness of time), John's editorial note would not be totally inappropriate if edited and inserted anywhere in the biblical record: "These are written that you may believe . . . and that by believing you may have life in his name" (John 20:31).

I conclude, therefore, that both Testaments confirm that the One who was mighty to create, the One who speaks in righteousness, the One who judges all—was, is, and forever shall be the One who is "mighty to save."

Notes

[1]This may also be designated the Abrahamic Covenant, but since its provisions were extended to Isaac and Jacob, the label "patriarch" is employed. See Genesis 13:14-17; 15:5-18; 26:3-5; 28:13-15.

[2]See chapter 6 of this book.

[3]For the first points of the profile, see Watts, *Teaching*, 324.

[4]See Romans 9—11.

[5]See the Introduction of this book.

[6]Note its use in Ugaritic (*bšr*) and Akkadian (*bussuru*), KB, 1:156. The Akkadian noun *bussurtu(m)* ("report, embassy") is also identified with this root; see Kasper Klaus Riemschneider, *An Akkadian Grammar*, 3rd ed., part 2, ed. Thomas A. Caldwell, John N. Oswalt and John F. X. Sheehan (Milwaukee: Marquette University Press, 1977), 6.

[7]See 1 Samuel 4:17.

[8]See Psalm 14:1-3; 53:1-3.

[9]See also Isaiah 26:19; Daniel 12:2; Hosea 13:14.

[10]John H. Hayes and Frederick C. Prussner, *Old Testament Theology: Its History and Development* (Atlanta: John Knox Press, 1985), 267. For example, see Walter C. Kaiser, Jr., *Toward an Old Testament Theology*, 1st paperback ed. (Grand Rapids: Zondervan Publishing House, 1991), 20-40.

[11]Hayes and Prussner, *Old Testament Theology*, 252.

[12]Ibid., 179-84.

[13]Ibid., 233-39.

[14]Ibid., 252-53.

[15]Ibid., 248-49.

[16]Ibid., 183.

[17]Ibid., 241.

[18]Ibid., 260.

[19]Kaiser, *Old Testament Theology*, 20-22.

[20]See ibid., 20-40.

[21]See chapter 3 of this book.

[22]Fluctuations in the object of the "promise" in Kaiser's outline (*Old Testament Theology*, 52-54) strongly suggest that promise is an intermediate consideration. McComiskey proposed that three "administrative" covenants (the covenant of circumcision, the Mosaic covenant, and the new covenant) are central in the "redemptive history." See Thomas Edward McComiskey, *The Covenants of Promise* (Grand Rapids: Baker Book House, 1985), 145. In the development of his thesis, though, he found it appropriate to minimize the covenant of circumcision.

[23]In other words, Messiah's life, death, burial, resurrection, ascension, and parousia.